the **go red**

FOR WOMEN

# cookbook

# the go red

## FOR WOMEN

## cookbook

cook your way to
a heart-healthy weight
and good nutrition

**CLARKSON POTTER/PUBLISHERS**
NEW YORK

# acknowledgments

**AMERICAN HEART ASSOCIATION CONSUMER PUBLICATIONS**

**Director**: Linda S. Ball

**Managing Editor**: Deborah A. Renza

**Senior Editor**: Robin P. Loveman

**Assistant Managing Editor**: Roberta W. Sullivan

**RECIPE DEVELOPERS**

Ellen Boeke

Nancy S. Hughes

Carol Ritchie

Diane Welland, R.D.

Francine Wolfe Schwartz

**NUTRITION ANALYST**

Tammi Hancock, R.D.

Your contributions to the American Heart Association support research
that helps make publications like this possible. For more information, call
1-800-AHA-USA1 (1-800-242-8721) or contact us online at www.heart.org.

© 2013, American Heart Association. Also known as the Heart Fund. Go Red and Go Red
For Women are trademarks of AHA. The Red Dress design is a trademark of U.S. DHHS.
National Wear Red Day® is a registered trademark of HHS and AHA.

Library of Congress Cataloging-in-Publication Data
Go Red For Women cookbook / American Heart Association. – First edition.
     pages cm
  Includes indexes.
  ISBN 978-0-385-34621-4 – ISBN 978-0-385-34622-1 (ebook)
1. Heart—Diseases—Diet therapy—Recipes. 2. Low-fat diet—Recipes.
3. Low-cholesterol diet—Recipes. 4. Salt-free diet—Recipes.
5. Heart diseases in women—United States—Prevention. I. American Heart Association.
  RC684.D5G59 2013
  641.5'6311—dc23

                    2013013591

ISBN 978-0-385-34621-4
eISBN 978-0-385-34622-1

Printed in the United States of America
Design by Ashley Tucker
Jacket front photograph by Valentin Casarsa/Getty Images
Jacket back photographs by Ben Fink

10  9  8  7  6  5  4  3  2  1

First Edition

# contents

# foreword
## by Jennie Garth

For over a decade, women have been working individually and together as part of the Go Red For Women® movement—the world's largest women's network to end heart disease. I am proud to say that I am a Go Red woman. I stand united with all the other women who have joined together to fight for healthier lives. I am living proof that preventing heart disease is possible.

Go Red has empowered more than 1.5 million women for the past 10 years, encouraging all women to take charge of their health and reduce their risk of heart disease. Now it's time for you to speak out and demand change for yourself and those you love. Each of us can use the power of our voices to spread the word among our friends, families, and loved ones that heart disease is the No. 1 killer of women. Working together as a united force, women have the influence to save lives. But we can't just talk the talk; we need to walk the walk. We need to take action in our lives for those things in our control—maintaining a healthy weight, knowing our numbers and personal risks, quitting smoking, exercising regularly, and eating healthy.

As a mom, I owe my three daughters the best head start I can give them when it comes to living a healthy lifestyle, and I know that eating nutritiously and being physically active are great ways to achieve that. As my family's health advocate, I try to be a positive role model for my kids, and I encourage you to be the same for yours. I not only teach my kids how to be healthy but also show them how to do it: We cook wholesome meals together as a family; I offer opportunities for my girls to try new foods; I limit sugary and salty snacks and convenience foods; and I make fruit readily available throughout the day. I also make sure my kids stay active with sports or play together as a family. It's important to me to make my entire family's heart health our No. 1 priority.

Consider your heart health as a non-negotiable part of your life. We all need to make smart choices on how to be good to our bodies and our hearts. We can do this by making healthy decisions every day about what we eat and how we move our bodies. It is important to keep our focus on living a heart-healthy lifestyle, and *The Go Red For Women® Cookbook* will help in your continued efforts!

# go red for women

For more than 10 years, the American Heart Association's Go Red For Women campaign has educated women about heart disease. It challenges women to know their personal risk for heart disease and use the tools it provides to take action to reduce that risk. Women who have joined this national movement have made incredible improvements in their heart health and are more likely to make healthy choices. From our research, we know that:

- More than one-third of Go Red women have lost weight.
- More than 50 percent of Go Red women have increased the amount of exercise they get.
- Six out of 10 Go Red women have improved their diets.
- More than 40 percent of Go Red women have had their cholesterol levels checked.
- One-third of Go Red women have talked with their health care professionals about developing heart-health plans.

## ways you can Go Red

You have the power to help yourself live a long, heart-healthy life. Here are some ways you can take action:

- Eat a healthy diet (pages 8–12).
- Share your commitment to being healthy with your family (pages 13–14).
- Host a healthy gathering with friends (pages 15–16).
- Live a healthy lifestyle (page 261).
- Know your risk factors for heart disease and stroke (page 262).
- Learn the warning signs of heart attack and stroke (page 263).
- Wear red on National Wear Red Day®—the first Friday in February each year.
- Watch our videos and short film "Just a *Little* Heart Attack" on YouTube.com/user/OfficialGoRed4Women.
- Join us on Facebook at facebook.com/GoRedForWomen.
- Follow us on Twitter @GoRedForWomen.
- Visit us at GoRedForWomen.org or GoRedCorazon.org.
- Call us at 1-888-MY-HEART.

# shop smart and eat well for better health

To be sure you include enough nutrient-rich foods in your daily eating plan and limit foods that are low in health benefits, keep the following guidelines in mind for an overall healthy diet.

## choose more nutrient-rich foods

Include a wide variety of **VEGETABLES AND FRUITS**, especially those that are deeply colored, such as broccoli, blueberries, and beets—they have the highest concentrations of nutrients. Choose fruits or vegetables that represent each color in the rainbow to ensure you get variety. When you're buying frozen or canned vegetables and fruits, shop for those that are not processed with salt or added sugars.

Eat high-fiber **WHOLE GRAINS** rather than refined grain products as often as possible. Serve whole-grain breads, pastas, cereals, and side dishes for the benefits of fiber and other important nutrients. Try to be sure at least half the grains you eat are whole grains. Shop for brown rice, bulgur, quinoa, barley, amaranth, and farro, as well as whole-grain breads, pastas, cereals, and crackers. Check that a whole grain is listed first in the ingredients. Compare nutrition facts labels for sodium amounts.

Include **FAT-FREE, 1%, AND LOW-FAT DAIRY** products daily and limit full-fat dairy products. If you use whole milk now, gradually transition to 2% fat milk, then to 1%, and finally to fat-free as your taste buds adjust. Shop for fat-free, 1%, and low-fat dairy products, such as milk, cheeses, and yogurt. Compare nutrition facts labels for sodium amounts.

Eat **FISH**, especially fish high in omega-3 fatty acids, such as salmon, tuna, and trout. Seafood is a good source of protein and is low in saturated fat. (Children, pregnant women, and those concerned about mercury should avoid fish with the potentially highest mercury contamination and consult credible online sources for the safest varieties. Remember, however, that for most people, the benefits of eating fish far outweigh the risk.) Shop for fresh fish when possible, but also look for canned very low sodium albacore tuna packed in water and canned boneless, skinless salmon as healthy alternatives.

Choose **LEAN POULTRY AND MEAT**. For poultry, eat white meat most often and discard the skin and all visible fat. Lean cuts of beef and pork are also heart-healthy if you discard all visible fat before cooking them. Shop for white-meat poultry and lean beef, such as sirloin and extra-lean ground beef, and pork, such as tenderloin and loin chops.

Add **LEGUMES, NUTS, AND SEEDS** to your diet. Legumes are a great source of fiber and meatless protein. Nuts and seeds are rich in monounsaturated fats, which may help keep blood cholesterol levels low when these fats are part of a diet that also is low in saturated fat and cholesterol. Include legumes, such as dried beans, peas, lentils, and peanuts, on your shopping list. Look for unsalted nuts and seeds for snacks or to add to salads or homemade whole-grain breads or muffins.

Include **HEALTHY FATS AND OILS** in your eating plan. Vegetable oils provide heart-healthy unsaturated fats. Shop for canola, corn, olive, safflower, soybean, and sunflower oils. Use these oils along with nonstick cooking sprays and light tub margarine as healthier choices. Avoid buying stick margarine, butter, and shortening.

## eat less of nutrient-poor foods

Cut back on **SODIUM**. Be mindful that most of the sodium you eat comes from packaged and processed foods, including restaurant meals. Even many popular condiments, such as ketchup, mustard, and barbecue sauce, are full of sodium (and added sugars). Compare the food labels of similar products to find the ones with less sodium; choose low-sodium or no-salt-added products, and be cautious of typically high-sodium foods such as soups and sandwiches when you dine out. When cooking, use little or no salt.

Limit **ADDED SUGAR**. Keep your intake of sugar-sweetened beverages to no more than 450 calories, or 36 ounces per week. (If you need fewer than 2,000 calories per day, avoid these beverages altogether.) Also, avoid sugary foods that are low in nutrients but high in calories. Buy them as occasional treats rather than including them as staples in your shopping cart.

Cut back on foods high in **SATURATED FAT, TRANS FAT, AND DIETARY CHOLESTEROL**. A diet high in these fats increases your risk of heart disease. Saturated fat is found primarily in foods from animals, such as meats, poultry, and full-fat dairy products, or in tropical oils, most commonly coconut, palm, and palm kernel. Trans fat is present in many manufactured foods that include partially hydrogenated oil. Cut back on trans fat by carefully reading labels when choosing snack products, cakes, cookies, pastries, pies, muffins, and fried foods. Common high-cholesterol foods include whole milk, full-fat cheese, egg yolks, and shellfish, so eat these foods sparingly.

## look for the heart-check mark

With so many products available on store shelves and all the marketing hype and health claims on packaging vying for your attention, making wise food decisions in the grocery store can be a challenge. Even when you see a front-of-package icon or wording that signals a health claim, you should still evaluate the information in the nutrition facts panel and the ingredient list before you make your selection. However, when you see a product with the American Heart Association's red-and-white Heart-Check Mark on the package, you can be sure that the product meets the certification program's limits for total fat, saturated fat, trans fat, cholesterol, and sodium. It also must include a minimum level of one of six beneficial nutrients.

## read the nutrition facts labels

To know what's really in the foods you buy, make it a habit to check the nutrition facts panel on the packaging. Be sure to compare among products to help you make the best choice.

1. **SERVING SIZE** is the basis for determining the number of calories, amount of each nutrient, and % Daily Values of a food. If you eat double the serving size listed, then you must double the number of calories and amounts of all the other nutrients shown.

2. If you want to manage your weight, **CALORIES** is an important section to note. The key is to balance how many calories you eat with how many calories your body needs. A calculator on the American Heart Association website, heart.org, can help you determine your personal calorie needs.

3. Look for low numbers for **SATURATED FAT, TRANS FAT,**

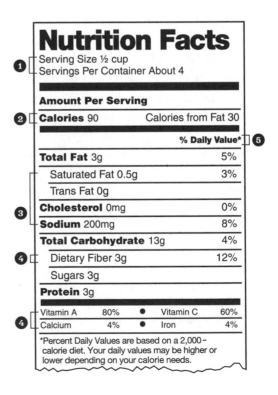

**CHOLESTEROL**, and **SODIUM**. Remember to check the serving size and calculate them accordingly.

4. Look for high numbers for **FIBER**, **VITAMIN A**, **VITAMIN C**, **CALCIUM**, and **IRON** to help you get 100 percent of the healthy nutrients you need each day.

5. The **% DAILY VALUE** section shows you the percentages of nutrients in a single serving based on a 2,000-calorie diet. For healthy nutrients, a higher number is best, but the lower the better for nutrients that should be limited—5 percent or less is low; 20 percent or more is high. When it comes to sodium, make sure that you read the milligrams (mg) of sodium and skip the % Daily Value, which is based on 2,400 mg. The American Heart Association recommends less than 1,500 mg of sodium a day for all Americans.

## meal planning

Creating your own meal plans gives you control over what you eat. Three major factors of a heart-smart eating plan are: (1) finding the right balance of foods to provide your body with adequate nutrition, (2) maintaining the right calorie count to meet your body's needs, and (3) limiting your intake of unhealthy nutrients. Use the following two sample meal plans as guides to create your own based on your preferences and calorie needs.

### 1,600 Calories

**BREAKFAST**
- 1 serving *Spanish-Style Potato Tortilla* (page 233)
- ½ 6-inch whole-grain pita pocket
- ½ cup grapes
- ½ cup fat-free milk

**MIDMORNING SNACK**
- 1 serving *Cherry-Nut Trail Mix* (page 32)
- 3 cups air-popped popcorn

**LUNCH**
- 1 serving *Hot-and-Sour Vegetable Soup* (page 37)
- 1 serving *Quinoa and Asian Pear Salad* (page 58)

**MIDAFTERNOON SNACK**
- 1 medium apple
- 3 whole-grain crispbreads
- 1½ ounces low-fat Swiss cheese

**DINNER**
- 1 serving *Plank-Grilled Tuna Steaks* (page 80)
- 8 grilled medium asparagus spears
- 2 slices grilled pineapple
- ¾ cup cooked brown rice
- 1 serving *Frozen Yogurt with Caramelized Banana and Orange Sauce* (page 258)

To create your own 1,600-calorie daily eating plan, aim for the following: *Each Day*—three to four servings of vegetables, four servings of fruits, six servings of grains (at least half should be whole grains), two to three servings of dairy, no more than one serving of lean meats and poultry, and two servings of healthy fats and oils. *Each Week*—at least two servings of fish (preferably those high in omega-3s) and three servings of nuts, seeds, and legumes.

## 2,000 Calories

### BREAKFAST

1 *Cherry-and-Peach Parfait* (page 236)

1 cup fat-free milk

1 whole-grain English muffin with 1 teaspoon light tub margarine

### MIDMORNING SNACK

2 servings *Tzatziki* (page 20)

4 whole-grain pita wedges, toasted

6 baby carrots

3 cups air-popped popcorn

### LUNCH

1 serving *Tuscan Tuna Salad* (page 82) in ½ 6-inch whole-grain pita pocket with 1 large dark green lettuce leaf

1 ounce baked potato chips (lowest sodium available)

1 medium orange

### MIDAFTERNOON SNACK

1 serving *Roasted Chickpea "Nuts"* (page 25)

¼ cup dried apricot halves

6 ounces fat-free plain Greek yogurt

### DINNER

3 ounces broiled or grilled flank steak

1 serving *Spring Asparagus and Strawberry Salad* (page 48)

½ cup steamed broccoli with fresh lemon juice and 1 tablespoon toasted sesame seeds

1 cup cooked bulgur

1 serving *Almond-Mango Mousse* (page 255)

To create your own 2,000-calorie daily eating plan, aim for the following: *Each Day*—four to five servings each of vegetables and fruits, six to eight servings of grains (at least half should be whole grains), two to three servings of dairy, up to two servings of lean meats and poultry, and two to three servings of healthy fats and oils. *Each Week*—at least two servings of fish (preferably those high in omega-3s) and four to five servings of nuts, seeds, and legumes.

When planning your *daily* eating plan for any calorie level, keep your intake of saturated fats to less than 7 percent and trans fat to less than 1 percent of your total calories; aim for less than 300 milligrams of dietary cholesterol; keep your consumption of sodium to less than 1,500 milligrams; and consume no more than 100 calories of added sugars if you are a woman and 150 if you are a man.

# go red with your family

Often, women Go Red not only for themselves but also for their families. Women want to be healthy for those who need them, especially their children, and want their kids to adopt healthy habits, too. It's important to create and maintain a healthy lifestyle together.

## eat more home cooking

The cornerstone of a healthy lifestyle is eating well, and what we feed ourselves and others is a decision we make several times a day. Making healthy food choices in the midst of busy schedules is not always easy, but the recipes in this book can help you. We've created several recipes that are ideal for breakfasts on the go, lunchbox fare, and after-school snacks. Look for lists of these on pages 264 and 265. Tips throughout the book offer ideas, including how to make recipes portable for school or after-school activities and adapting recipes to make them more appealing to kids.

**Breakfast on the Go** Food challenges can strike with the first meal of the day! When many of us are rushing to get the kids out of bed, dressed, and ready for school, along with getting ready for work ourselves, it can be an easy decision to either skip breakfast or eat a store-bought muffin or other convenience breakfast food, which is likely to be high in added sugars, fats, and sodium. Several of our breakfast recipes can be put in a to-go cup or thermos, or wrapped in wax paper, so they're easy to take on the bus or in the car. Try these healthy choices in the morning: Baked Oatmeal "Pie" (page 232), Banana-Nut Bread (page 226), or Honeyed Berry-Kiwi Cereal Parfaits (page 235).

**Lunchbox Ideas** Kids can consume as much as half their daily calories while at school, so it's important that their midday foods are nutritious. Many convenience-meal products are designed to be easily packed in a lunchbox and include packaged snacks, treats, or desserts. It's easy to be tempted by these processed foods. However, healthier alternatives that you make at home can be inexpensive and are easy to pack with insulated food jars and lunch bags and reusable ice packs. Today's thermoses have double-walled insulation that can keep cold food chilled and hot food hot for several hours, allowing for many portable lunch possibilities, including homemade soups and chilis. Send your kids off to school with homemade lunches, such as: Pumpkin-Apple Soup (page 43),

Italian Vegetable Soup with Mini Meatballs (page 140), or Beef and Hominy Chili (page 148). For sides, snacks, and treats, here are just a few suggestions: Crunchy Apple-Carrot Slaw (page 53), Applesauce Cake (page 244), and Strawberry-Melon Salsa (page 21) with baked tortilla chips.

**After-School Snacks** Snacks can be an easy way to get more healthy foods, such as fruits and nuts, into your kids' diet. Replace the packaged snacks with our kid-friendly recipes, including Autumn Apple "Fries" with Creamy Cranberry Dip (page 33), Frozen Chocolate-Covered Banana Pops (page 34), and Orange-Yogurt Dream Pops (page 259). If you're on the run to soccer practice, for example, you can quickly whip up some Chocolate–Peanut Butter Smoothies (page 242), put one serving in a thermos, and bring it with you on the road. Create a batch of Cherry-Nut Trail Mix (page 32) on a Sunday, divide it into airtight snack bags, and you have a healthy, portable snack to keep on hand for that time when hunger strikes between school and after-school activities.

## adopt an active lifestyle

Another way for you and your family to be healthy is to move more. Getting regular physical activity can help prevent or control high blood pressure, high blood cholesterol, and diabetes. Regular exercise is also a very important part of maintaining a healthy weight for you and your kids. Adults should aim each week for at least 150 minutes (2 hours and 30 minutes) of moderate-intensity activity or 75 minutes (1 hour and 15 minutes) of vigorous-intensity activity, or a combination. During moderate-intensity exercise, you should be able to talk but not sing. Vigorous-intensity activities should make you breathe rapidly and substantially increase your heart rate; you should be able to say only a few words without having to catch your breath.

Kids, too, need to get regular physical activity for their own good heart health. The recommendation for children is a total of 60 minutes a day of moderate-to-vigorous exercise. This can be accomplished through participation in organized sports, as well as through active play, such as running around the schoolyard at recess or jumping rope or shooting hoops with friends.

As a family, plan fun physical activities, such as bike riding on designated paths in your area, hiking in local parks on weekend mornings, or walking the dog together around the neighborhood after dinner. As a parent, you are your children's most important role model. If you eat healthfully and exercise, your kids will have a good example to follow for lifelong, heart-healthy living.

# host a go red gathering

Women uniting for a cause can be powerful. Together, we can learn, teach, and share. One way to do this is to plan an informal get-together whose purpose is to focus on women's heart health. Think about the women in your life—your friends, family, neighbors, and coworkers. What if you invited a few of them over for a Girls' Night In or Sunday brunch? Or perhaps you could incorporate going red into a group you're already part of, such as a book club, worship group, or Bunco group. Consider dedicating your get-together in February (American Heart Month) to celebrating women's heart health.

## cooking for the gathering

Planning the food and cooking for your guests needn't be intimidating or overwhelming. You can choose to make as many or as few dishes as you want—there is no right or wrong way to host a Go Red gathering! You can also decide to share the experience with your guests. You can invite them to cook with you or you could ask each guest to make a recipe from this cookbook and bring the dish to the gathering.

**Decide on the menu.** Are you planning a Saturday night get-together or a Sunday brunch? Either way, there are plenty of recipes throughout this book that will complement your gathering. For a party, you'll find plenty of choices of appetizers, drinks, and desserts, such as Italian Meatball Sliders (page 26), Sangría-Style Punch (page 239), and Chocolate and Red Wine Mini Cupcakes (page 245); and for brunch, you'll find an assortment of recipes that will complete the occasion, including Fruit Salad with Cranberry-Ginger Dressing (page 54), Hot Blueberry-Pomegranate Cider (page 243), and Cherry Phyllo Turnovers (page 248). On page 264, you'll find a list of recipes we recommend for a Go Red party or Go Red brunch from which you can pick and choose to suit your preferences.

**Look for the Go Red tips.** On many of the recipe pages throughout, you'll find ideas that will help you enhance or tweak a recipe for your Go Red get-together.

# going red at the gathering

With food and drink in hand, here are some ways you can continue to create a Go Red experience with your guests.

**Share stories.** As a group, discuss why it's important to each of you to be healthy. Share ideas and tips with one another about how to live a healthy lifestyle.

**Set goals.** Hand out index cards that say *I pledge to* _____. Ask your guests to think of an action they are willing to commit to in order to become healthier. Perhaps it's a commitment to get a physical exam. Maybe it's a commitment to walk around the neighborhood for 30 minutes a day. Have each woman write down her commitment and how she is going to accomplish it, then have her sign and date the card. Have each guest read her pledge and discuss any support she might need from others. Encourage your guests to place their pledges somewhere they can see them each day, such as on a mirror.

**Start your own support group.** Together, discuss how you can continue to support one another. You might suggest creating or joining a walking club, starting a cooking club, or taking fitness classes together. People are more apt to follow through with a physical activity if they know others are counting on them.

**Create personalized party cookbooks.** Provide each of your guests with a small, blank notebook or photo album or ask each guest to bring one for herself to create "My Go Red Cookbook." Provide or ask guests to bring craft supplies, such as ribbon, stickers, beads, glitter, and gems, so each guest can decorate her own personalized cookbook. Provide copies of the recipes you serve at your gathering for your guests to put into their cookbooks.

**Wear red.** Ask your guests to wear red dresses or workout gear or their favorite red piece of clothing or accessory. Clear some space in your home for guests to model their looks. As the party host, act as the announcer for the fashion show. Ask guests to strike a pose and share with the audience why they want to Go Red.

**Create vision boards.** Provide or ask your guests to bring craft supplies, including red poster board, large red photo frames, magazines, construction paper, markers, and scissors, to create their own personalized Go Red vision board. Encourage them to choose pictures and words that inspire them to be healthy.

**Take photos.** Be sure to visually document your get-together—including the food—and post the pictures on your social media sites to encourage others to Go Red.

# recipes

. . . . . . . . . . . . . . . . . . . . . . . . . . . . . . . . . . . . . . . . . . . . . . . . . . . . . . . . . . . . . . . . . . . . . . . . . . . . . . . . . . . . . . . . . . . . . . . . . . . . . . . . . . . . . . .

Each recipe in the book includes a nutritional analysis so you can decide how that dish fits with your dietary needs. These guidelines will give you some details on how the analyses were calculated.

• Each analysis is for a single serving; garnishes or optional ingredients are not included unless noted.

• Because of the many variables involved, the nutrient values provided should be considered approximate. When figuring portions, remember that the serving sizes are also approximate.

• When ingredient options are listed, the first one is analyzed. When a range of amounts is given, the average is analyzed.

• Values other than fats are rounded to the nearest whole number. Fat values are rounded to the nearest half gram. Because of the rounding, values for saturated, trans, monounsaturated, and polyunsaturated fats may not add up to the amount shown for total fat value.

• All the recipes are analyzed using unsalted or low-sodium ingredients whenever possible. In some cases, we call for unprocessed foods or no-salt-added and low-sodium products, then add table salt sparingly for flavor. We specify canola, corn, and olive oils in these recipes, but you can also use other heart-healthy unsaturated oils, such as safflower, soybean, and sunflower.

• Meats are analyzed as lean, with all visible fat discarded. Values for ground beef are based on lean meat that is 95 percent fat free.

• When meat, poultry, or seafood is marinated and the marinade is discarded, the analysis includes all of the sodium from the marinade but none of the other nutrients from it.

• If alcohol is used in a cooked dish, we estimate that most of the alcohol calories evaporate as the food cooks.

• Because product labeling in the marketplace can vary and change quickly, we use the generic terms "fat-free" and "low-fat" throughout to avoid confusion.

• We use the abbreviations "g" for gram and "mg" for milligram.

# starters
## and snacks

Four sources of onion flavor team up to create a robust dip reminiscent of the traditional onion soup party dip, but with much less sodium. Serve with red bell peppers and other raw vegetables, such as radishes, grape tomatoes, and broccoli and cauliflower florets.

# creamy onion dip

| serves 8 | 2 tablespoons per serving |

2 tablespoons dehydrated minced onion

2 tablespoons water

½ cup fat-free sour cream

¼ cup fat-free plain yogurt

2 tablespoons grated sweet onion, such as Vidalia, Maui, or Oso Sweet

2 tablespoons shredded carrot

2 tablespoons light mayonnaise

1 medium green onion, chopped

1 tablespoon salt-free onion-and-herb seasoning blend

½ teaspoon sugar

¼ to ½ teaspoon red hot-pepper sauce

⅛ teaspoon garlic powder

⅛ teaspoon salt

1. In a small bowl, stir together the dehydrated onion and water. Let stand for 5 minutes.

2. Meanwhile, in a medium bowl, stir together the remaining ingredients. Stir in the rehydrated onion. Let stand for 10 minutes. Serve at room temperature or cover and refrigerate for up to two days. The dip will thicken during the refrigeration time.

**cook's tip on green onions:** Green onions are usually sold by the bunch, but most recipes call for less than that. Leftovers can be sliced and then frozen in an airtight container or resealable plastic freezer bag. Use them in stir-fries, soups, or stews.

**cook's tip on dehydrated minced onion:** Dehydrated minced onion can be found in the spice aisle of the grocery store.

**per serving**

calories 35
total fat 1.0 g
  saturated fat 0.0 g
  trans fat 0.0 g
  polyunsaturated fat 0.5 g
  monounsaturated fat 0.0 g
cholesterol 4 mg

sodium 91 mg
carbohydrates 5 g
  fiber 0 g
  sugars 3 g
protein 2 g

dietary exchanges
½ starch

This Greek dip pairs perfectly with your favorite crudités or toasted whole-grain Pita Wedges (see page 22), but it also makes a deliciously different sandwich spread or a delectable sauce for grilled or roasted fish, poultry, or meat. You can omit either the dillweed or the mint, but it's better with both.

# tzatziki

| serves 10 | 2 tablespoons per serving |

8 ounces fat-free plain Greek yogurt

½ cup grated English, or hothouse, cucumber, drained and patted dry

2 tablespoons grated onion (sweet, such as Vidalia, Maui, or Oso Sweet, preferred)

1 tablespoon chopped fresh dillweed

1 tablespoon fresh lemon juice

2 teaspoons chopped fresh mint

2 teaspoons honey

2 large garlic cloves, minced

1 teaspoon olive oil (extra virgin preferred)

½ teaspoon dried oregano, crumbled

⅛ teaspoon salt

In a medium bowl, stir together all the ingredients. Serve immediately or cover and refrigerate for up to 24 hours.

**cook's tip:** Lightly spray a measuring spoon with cooking spray to keep honey from sticking to it.

**Go Red party tip:** For an elegant presentation, serve this dip in halved roasted red potatoes. Roast 10 potatoes, halve them, scoop out some of the flesh, and fill each half with about a tablespoon of the dip.

## per serving

calories 23
total fat 0.5 g
   saturated fat 0.0 g
   trans fat 0.0 g
   polyunsaturated fat 0.0 g
   monounsaturated fat 0.5 g
cholesterol 0 mg

sodium 38 mg
carbohydrates 3 g
   fiber 0 g
   sugars 2 g
protein 2 g
dietary exchanges
Free

Paired with no-salt-added baked tortilla chips as a snack or appetizer, or spooned atop grilled chicken breasts for dinner, this salsa is perfect summertime fare. Whether served at room temperature or chilled, this refreshing accompaniment is simply satisfying and versatile.

# strawberry-melon salsa

**serves 4** | ½ cup per serving

1 cup diced watermelon

1 cup diced hulled strawberries

2½ tablespoons chopped fresh mint

1 teaspoon grated lime zest

2 tablespoons fresh lime juice

1 tablespoon honey

### per serving

| | |
|---|---|
| calories 45 | sodium 3 mg |
| total fat 0.0 g | carbohydrates 11 g |
| saturated fat 0.0 g | fiber 1 g |
| trans fat 0.0 g | sugars 9 g |
| polyunsaturated fat 0.0 g | protein 1 g |
| monounsaturated fat 0.0 g | |
| cholesterol 0 mg | dietary exchanges |
| | 1 fruit |

In a small bowl, stir together all the ingredients. Serve immediately or cover and refrigerate for up to two days.

**Go Red brunch tip:** Serve this salsa with wedges of Spanish-Style Potato Tortilla (page 233) or as a topping for fat-free plain or vanilla yogurt. You also can serve this salsa on homemade sugar-cinnamon baked pita chips, using the recipe for Pita Wedges on page 22. Prepare as directed, but after spraying with cooking spray, sprinkle the wedges with a mixture of 2 teaspoons sugar, 2 teaspoons firmly packed light brown sugar, and ½ teaspoon ground cinnamon. Bake as directed.

Lots of roasted garlic and fresh rosemary flavor this healthful hummus-inspired spread. For a different approach, try it with baby carrots and celery sticks as dippers.

# tuscan white bean and roasted garlic spread with pita wedges

**serves 8** | 3 tablespoons spread and 4 pita wedges per serving

1 large garlic bulb, unpeeled

2 6-inch whole-grain pita pockets, each separated into top and bottom rounds

Cooking spray

1 15.5-ounce can no-salt-added cannellini or navy beans, liquid reserved, beans rinsed and drained

1 tablespoon olive oil and 1 teaspoon olive oil (extra virgin preferred), divided use

¾ to 1 teaspoon minced fresh rosemary

¼ teaspoon salt

Pepper to taste

1. Preheat the oven to 375°F.

2. Put the garlic bulb on a square of aluminum foil large enough to loosely enclose the garlic. Pull the edges of the foil to the center. Fold together to seal tightly.

3. Roast the garlic for 40 minutes, or until the garlic cloves are soft and golden brown. Remove from the oven and let cool for 30 minutes, or until easy to handle.

4. Separate the garlic into cloves. Squeeze the cloves into a medium bowl, discarding the skins. Using the back of a fork, mash the garlic.

5. Increase the oven temperature to 400°F. Lightly spray the top of each pita round with cooking spray. Stack half the pita rounds on a work surface. Cut the stack into eighths (32 wedges total). Repeat. Arrange in a single layer on a baking sheet.

**per serving**

| | |
|---|---|
| calories 108 | sodium 170 mg |
| total fat 3.0 g | carbohydrates 17 g |
| saturated fat 0.5 g | fiber 3 g |
| trans fat 0.0 g | sugars 1 g |
| polyunsaturated fat 0.5 g | protein 4 g |
| monounsaturated fat 1.5 g | dietary exchanges |
| cholesterol 0 mg | 1 starch, ½ fat |

6. Bake for 6 to 8 minutes, or until crisp and golden. Transfer the baking sheet to a cooling rack and let the pita wedges cool completely, about 20 minutes.

7. Stir the beans, 1 tablespoon oil, the rosemary, salt, and pepper into the garlic. Using the back of a spoon or fork, mash the beans, leaving some whole. (The mixture should be slightly thick and creamy with some lumps.) Stir in some of the reserved bean liquid if the mixture is too dry. Transfer to a serving bowl.

8. Drizzle the remaining 1 teaspoon oil over the spread. Serve with the pita wedges.

**Go Red party tip:** To give this spread a hint of red, sprinkle it with a bit of paprika and serve it with strips of red bell pepper.

For a luxurious, no-forks-needed appetizer, stuff juicy cherry tomatoes with a mouthwatering mixture of silky crab and avocado spiked with cilantro and sweet onion. Tuna is a tasty, budget-friendly substitute.

# crab-stuffed cherry tomatoes

### serves 8 | 2 tomatoes per serving

16 large cherry tomatoes

2 tablespoons minced sweet onion, such as Vidalia, Maui, or Oso Sweet

2 tablespoons finely chopped fresh cilantro and 16 fresh cilantro leaves, divided use

1½ tablespoons light mayonnaise

1 tablespoon fresh lemon juice

¼ teaspoon salt

Pinch of pepper

3 ounces lump crabmeat, drained, cartilage discarded, and flaked, or very low sodium albacore tuna packed in water, drained and flaked

¼ cup finely diced avocado

1. Cut a ¼-inch slice from the top of each tomato. Using the small end of a melon baller or a measuring teaspoon, carefully scoop out and discard the seeds, leaving a ¼-inch rim. If the tomato won't stand upright, cut a very thin slice from the bottom. Set the tomatoes aside.

2. In a medium bowl, stir together the onion, chopped cilantro, mayonnaise, lemon juice, salt, and pepper. Gently fold in the crabmeat and avocado. Spoon the crabmeat mixture into the tomatoes. Top each tomato with a cilantro leaf. Serve immediately or cover and refrigerate for up to 4 hours.

**per serving**

calories 33
total fat 1.5 g
   saturated fat 0.0 g
   trans fat 0.0 g
   polyunsaturated fat 0.5 g
   monounsaturated fat 0.5 g
cholesterol 9 mg

sodium 140 mg
carbohydrates 3 g
   fiber 1 g
   sugars 1 g
protein 3 g

dietary exchanges
½ lean meat

Warm from the oven, roasted chickpeas are similar to the roasted nuts you just love to munch. Diversify your snack routine with these spicy, crunchy legumes. Or, sprinkle them on top of a mixed-greens salad instead of croutons.

# roasted chickpea "nuts"

**serves 4** | ¼ cup per serving

1   15.5-ounce can no-salt-added chickpeas, rinsed and drained

½   teaspoon ground cinnamon

½   teaspoon ground cumin

½   teaspoon ground ginger

¼   teaspoon pepper (freshly ground preferred)

⅛   teaspoon salt

⅛   teaspoon cayenne (optional)

1   tablespoon olive oil

**per serving**

calories 143
total fat 4.5 g
  saturated fat 0.5 g
  trans fat 0.0 g
  polyunsaturated fat 0.5 g
  monounsaturated fat 2.5 g
cholesterol 0 mg

sodium 99 mg
carbohydrates 20 g
  fiber 5 g
  sugars 1 g
protein 6 g

dietary exchanges
1½ starch, ½ fat

1. Preheat the oven to 450°F. Line a rimmed baking sheet with aluminum foil. Set aside.

2. Lay a triple thickness of paper towels on a plate. Spread the chickpeas on the paper towels. Gently roll the chickpeas around, blotting them lightly with a separate paper towel. Set aside to dry.

3. Meanwhile, in a small bowl, stir together the remaining ingredients except the oil.

4. In a medium bowl, stir together the chickpeas and oil. Sprinkle with the cinnamon mixture, stirring lightly to coat.

5. Arrange the chickpeas in a single layer on the baking sheet. Place the baking sheet on the top rack of the oven. Roast for 25 to 30 minutes, or until the chickpeas are browned and crunchy, stirring twice. Transfer the baking sheet to a cooling rack. Let the chickpeas cool on the baking sheet for 8 to 10 minutes. Serve warm.

You'll slide into home plate with this winning appetizer! The pine nuts add a rustic touch and a splash of milk is the secret to keeping these extra-lean meatballs moist. This mini sandwich paired with a dark green leafy salad also makes for an ideal light lunch. *(See photo insert.)*

# italian meatball sliders

**serves 12** | 1 slider per serving

1 teaspoon olive oil

¼ cup diced onion

1 medium garlic clove, minced

1 6-ounce can no-salt-added tomato paste

2 8-ounce cans no-salt-added tomato sauce

1 teaspoon dried basil, crumbled

1 teaspoon dried oregano, crumbled

¼ teaspoon crushed red pepper flakes

Cooking spray

*(continued)*

1. In a medium skillet, heat the oil over medium-high heat, swirling to coat the bottom. Cook ¼ cup onion for about 3 minutes, or until soft, stirring frequently. Stir in the garlic. Cook for 1 minute, stirring frequently. Stir in the tomato paste. Cook for 1 minute, stirring constantly and scraping the bottom of the skillet. Stir in the tomato sauce, basil, oregano, and red pepper flakes. Bring to a simmer. Reduce the heat and simmer, covered, for 30 minutes.

2. Meanwhile, preheat the broiler. Lightly spray the broiler pan and rack with cooking spray.

3. In a medium bowl, using your hands or a spoon, gently combine the meatball ingredients except the egg. Don't overwork the mixture or it will become too compact and the meatballs will be heavy. Gently work in the egg. Shape into twelve ½-inch balls (about 1½ teaspoons each). Transfer to the broiler rack.

4. Broil the meatballs about 4 inches from the heat for 10 to 15 minutes, or until the tops are browned. Turn over. Broil for 10 to 15 minutes, or until the meatballs are browned on the outside and no longer pink in the center. Drain on paper towels.

5. Stir the meatballs into the sauce.

6. Just before serving, split open the rolls and toast them. Place 1 basil leaf on the bottom half of each roll. Top with 1 meatball and 2 tablespoons of sauce. Put the tops of the rolls on the sliders.

cook's tip: If you can't find whole-wheat, lower-sodium slider or dinner rolls, you can use 4 whole-wheat hot dog buns. Cut the buns crosswise into thirds to create 12 slider rolls.

## meatballs

 1 **pound extra-lean ground beef**
 ¼ **cup panko (Japanese-style bread crumbs)**
 ¼ **cup diced onion**
 1 **tablespoon minced pine nuts**
 1 **tablespoon dried parsley, crumbled**
 1 **tablespoon fat-free milk**
 2 **medium garlic cloves, minced**
 ½ **teaspoon pepper**
 ¼ **teaspoon crushed red pepper flakes**
 1 **large egg, lightly beaten with a fork**

 12 **whole-wheat slider or dinner rolls (lowest sodium available)**
 12 **fresh basil leaves (optional)**

...........................................................

### per serving

| | |
|---|---|
| calories 188 | sodium 191 mg |
| total fat 5.0 g | carbohydrates 25 g |
|   saturated fat 1.5 g |   fiber 4 g |
|   trans fat 0.0 g |   sugars 7 g |
|   polyunsaturated fat 1.5 g | protein 13 g |
|   monounsaturated fat 1.5 g | |
| cholesterol 36 mg | dietary exchanges |
| | 1½ starch, |
| | 1 vegetable, |
| | 1 lean meat |

Borek are Turkish pastries with savory fillings. Our version combines potatoes, kale, red bell pepper, onion, and feta inside crisp, flaky phyllo dough for a healthy, hearty appetizer with Mediterranean flair.

# turkish kale and potato borek

**serves 12** : 1 pastry per serving

1 tablespoon olive oil and 1 tablespoon olive oil, divided use

½ medium onion, finely diced

2 tablespoons finely diced red bell pepper

2 medium garlic cloves, minced

4 cups tightly packed chopped kale, any large stems discarded

¼ cup water and 1½ tablespoons water, divided use

¼ teaspoon sweet paprika and ¼ teaspoon sweet paprika, divided use

¼ teaspoon pepper

8 ounces peeled potatoes, boiled and mashed

2 ounces low-fat feta cheese, crumbled

1 large egg white

1 tablespoon fat-free plain Greek yogurt

6 14 × 9-inch frozen phyllo sheets, thawed

**1.** Preheat the oven to 375°F.

**2.** In a medium saucepan, heat 1 tablespoon oil over medium-high heat, swirling to coat the bottom. Cook the onion, bell pepper, and garlic for 2 minutes, or until almost soft, stirring frequently.

**3.** Stir in the kale, ¼ cup water, ¼ teaspoon paprika, and the pepper. Reduce the heat and simmer, covered, for 10 minutes, or until the kale is tender. Remove from the heat.

**4.** Uncover and let cool for 15 minutes. When the mixture has cooled, stir in the potatoes, feta, and egg white.

**5.** In a small bowl, whisk together the yogurt and the remaining 1 tablespoon oil and 1½ tablespoons water.

**6.** Keeping the unused phyllo covered with a damp cloth or damp paper towels to prevent drying, place 1 sheet on a work surface. Using a pastry brush, lightly brush the phyllo with the yogurt mixture. Top with a second sheet. Lightly brush with the yogurt mixture. Using scissors or a sharp knife, cut the stack lengthwise into 4 strips. Place 2 tablespoons of the filling on one

**per serving**

calories 78
total fat 3.0 g
    saturated fat 0.5 g
    trans fat 0.0 g
    polyunsaturated fat 0.5 g
    monounsaturated fat 1.5 g
cholesterol 2 mg

sodium 101 mg
carbohydrates 10 g
    fiber 1 g
    sugars 1 g
protein 3 g

dietary exchanges
½ starch, ½ fat

of the strips, leaving 1 inch at the bottom. Fold a corner across the filling and continue folding, corner to corner (the way one would fold a flag). Tuck the excess dough under the triangle. Transfer to a nonstick baking sheet. Repeat with the remaining phyllo, yogurt mixture, and filling (some yogurt mixture should remain).

7. Brush the tops of the pastries with the remaining yogurt mixture. Sprinkle with the remaining 1/4 teaspoon paprika. Bake for 20 minutes, or until lightly browned.

**cook's tip:** Make an easy casserole instead of the individual pastries: lightly spray a 2½-quart casserole dish with cooking spray. Layer 3 phyllo sheets in the dish, brushing each with the yogurt mixture and folding over the ends. Spoon the filling over the phyllo. Top with the remaining 3 phyllo sheets, brushing each with the yogurt mixture. Sprinkle with the remaining ¼ teaspoon paprika. Bake for 30 minutes. Cut into 3 × 4½-inch pieces (1 piece per serving).

This Vietnamese-inspired appetizer, filled with crunchy raw vegetables and bite-size shrimp, is served with a sweet-hot chile sauce. For easy rolling, arrange all the ingredients in assembly-line fashion before beginning.

# vegetable-shrimp spring rolls with honey-jalapeño dipping sauce

**serves 4** : 1 spring roll and 2 tablespoons sauce per serving

## rolls

- 2 lemon slices, about ¼ inch thick
- 12 raw small shrimp, peeled, rinsed, and patted dry
- 4 8-inch rice paper rounds
- 1 cup loosely packed, thinly sliced romaine
- ½ cup matchstick-size zucchini strips or coarsely grated zucchini
- ¼ cup matchstick-size carrot strips or coarsely grated carrot
- 4 sprigs of fresh cilantro, about 4 inches long

*(continued)*

1. Fill a small saucepan halfway with water. Add the lemon slices. Bring to a boil, covered, over high heat. Add the shrimp. Re-cover the pan and remove from the heat. Let stand for 2 to 3 minutes, or until the shrimp are pink on the outside. Transfer to a colander. Rinse with cold water to cool. Set aside.

2. Meanwhile, lay a double thickness of damp paper towels on a work surface. Put a shallow dish of water nearby. Soak each sheet of rice paper in the water for 10 to 20 seconds, or until softened. Transfer the rice paper to the paper towels.

3. For each spring roll, arrange 3 shrimp crosswise just below the center of the rice paper, leaving a 1½-inch border around the edges. Then layer as follows: ¼ cup romaine, 2 tablespoons zucchini, 1 tablespoon carrot, and 1 sprig of cilantro.

Tightly fold up the bottom side of the rice paper to enclose the filling, gently pressing to seal. Fold in the left and right sides, gently pressing to seal. Roll tightly from the bottom up. Transfer the roll with the seam side down to a plate. Repeat with the remaining rice paper, shrimp, romaine, zucchini, carrot, and cilantro. Cover the finished rolls with damp paper towels and plastic wrap to keep them moist.

4. Serve immediately or cover and refrigerate for up to 8 hours. Just before serving, whisk together the sauce ingredients. Serve the sauce with the spring rolls.

**cook's tip on rice paper rounds:** Rice paper rounds are available in Asian specialty markets and in the Asian section of some grocery stores. Translucent and made from rice flour and tapioca flour, they are sometimes called spring roll wrappers.

**sauce**

- ⅓ **cup plain rice vinegar**
- 2 **tablespoons warm water**
- 2 **teaspoons chopped fresh cilantro**
- 1 **to 2 teaspoons minced fresh jalapeño (red preferred), seeds and ribs discarded, or to taste (see cook's tip on page 109)**
- 1½ **teaspoons honey**
- ½ **teaspoon soy sauce (lowest sodium available)**

..................................................

**per serving**

calories 78
total fat 0.5 g
   saturated fat 0.0 g
   trans fat 0.0 g
   polyunsaturated fat 0.0 g
   monounsaturated fat 0.0 g
cholesterol 49 mg

sodium 121 mg
carbohydrates 11 g
   fiber 1 g
   sugars 3 g
protein 7 g

dietary exchanges
½ starch, 1 lean meat

You'll get a zip of citrus flavor from freshly grated lemon zest in every bite of this trail mix. It's an easy combination of just a handful of ingredients that yields a crisp and crunchy snack you and your family can enjoy all week.

# cherry-nut trail mix

................................................................................................................

## serves 12     ⅓ cup per serving

_____

3 cups high-fiber cluster cereal

½ cup dried tart cherries

¼ cup chopped walnuts, dry-roasted if desired

1 ounce unsalted shelled pumpkin seeds, dry-roasted (about ¼ cup)

1 tablespoon grated lemon zest

1. In a large bowl, stir together all the ingredients until well blended.

2. Store any leftover mix in an airtight container at room temperature for up to one week.

**cook's tip on dry-roasting nuts or seeds in the oven:** To dry-roast a large amount of nuts or seeds at one time, place them in a shallow baking dish. Roast them at 350°F for 10 to 15 minutes, stirring occasionally. You can freeze them in an airtight container or resealable plastic freezer bag so they can be ready at a moment's notice. You don't even need to thaw them before using them.

..................................................................

### per serving

| | |
|---|---|
| calories 98 | sodium 25 mg |
| total fat 3.5 g | carbohydrates 14 g |
|   saturated fat 0.5 g |   fiber 3 g |
|   trans fat 0.0 g |   sugars 6 g |
|   polyunsaturated fat 2.0 g | protein 4 g |
|   monounsaturated fat 1.0 g | dietary exchanges |
| cholesterol 0 mg | 1 starch, ½ fat |

These faux fries are delicious either raw or baked. They're so tasty when dunked in the sweet cranberry-studded dip that you won't miss the fact they aren't actually fried! The baked ones are slightly soft in texture and best eaten with a fork.

# autumn apple "fries" with creamy cranberry dip

**serves 4** | ½ cup "fries" and 2 tablespoons dip per serving

## dip

¼ cup fat-free plain Greek yogurt

¼ cup whole-berry cranberry sauce

1 teaspoon honey

½ teaspoon grated orange zest

———

1 large apple (if not baking) or 2 large apples (if baking), such as Granny Smith, Envy, Jazz, Fuji, Honeycrisp, or Gala, peeled if desired, cut into 2½ × ¼-inch strips

1 teaspoon firmly packed light brown sugar

¼ to ½ teaspoon pumpkin pie spice

Butter-flavor cooking spray (if baking)

**1.** In a small bowl, whisk together the dip ingredients.

**2.** To serve the apple "fries" raw, arrange the apple strips in a single layer on a plate. Sprinkle the brown sugar and pumpkin pie spice over the apples (use more pumpkin pie spice for tart apples, such as Granny Smith). Serve with the dip.

**3.** To bake the "fries," preheat the oven to 350°F.

**4.** Lightly spray a rimmed baking sheet with cooking spray. Arrange the apple strips in a single layer on the baking sheet. Sprinkle the brown sugar and pumpkin pie spice over the apples (use more pumpkin pie spice for tart apples, such as Granny Smith). Lightly spray the top of the apples with cooking spray. Bake for 15 to 20 minutes, or until tender but not mushy. Serve with the dip.

**cook's tip on citrus zest:** Keep citrus zest on hand by zesting the entire fruit and saving some for another time. Divide the zest into 1-teaspoon piles. Tightly wrap each pile in a small square of plastic wrap, squeezing out all the air. Put the bundles in an airtight container or resealable plastic freezer bag and freeze for up to three months.

### per serving

| | |
|---|---|
| calories 75 | sodium 9 mg |
| total fat 0.0 g | carbohydrates 17 g |
| saturated fat 0.0 g | fiber 1 g |
| trans fat 0.0 g | sugars 14 g |
| polyunsaturated fat 0.0 g | protein 1 g |
| monounsaturated fat 0.0 g | dietary exchanges |
| cholesterol 0 mg | 1 fruit |

Frozen bananas lightly coated with crisp chocolate are a fun and delicious way to incorporate some fruit into your day. Roll them in chopped nuts for a bit of crunch and added protein.

# frozen chocolate-covered banana pops

**serves 8** | ½ banana per serving

4 medium bananas, halved crosswise

½ cup firmly packed light or dark brown sugar

½ cup unsweetened Dutch-process cocoa powder

1 tablespoon cornstarch

1 tablespoon instant coffee granules (optional)

½ teaspoon ground cinnamon (optional)

½ cup fat-free milk

1 tablespoon canola or corn oil

1 teaspoon vanilla extract

½ cup finely chopped almonds

**per serving**

calories 186
total fat 5.5 g
   saturated fat 0.5 g
   trans fat 0.0 g
   polyunsaturated fat 1.0 g
   monounsaturated fat 3.0 g
cholesterol 0 mg

sodium 11 mg
carbohydrates 33 g
   fiber 3 g
   sugars 22 g
protein 4 g

dietary exchanges
1 fruit, 1 other carbohydrate, 1 fat

**cook's tip:** If you would like to make these ahead of time, freeze the coated bananas on the baking sheet for 1 hour, then store them in an airtight container for up to one week.

1. Line a small rimmed baking sheet with wax paper.

2. Using 8 wooden ice-pop sticks, firmly push a stick about halfway into the cut end of each banana half. Arrange the bananas in a single layer on the baking sheet. Freeze for at least 1 hour or overnight.

3. In a medium saucepan, stir together the brown sugar, cocoa, cornstarch, coffee granules, and cinnamon. Gradually whisk in the milk and oil until smooth. Cook over medium heat for 4 to 5 minutes, or until bubbly and thickened, stirring constantly. Remove from the heat. Stir in the vanilla.

4. Spread the almonds on a flat plate. Remove the baking sheet from the freezer. Set the baking sheet, pan, and plate in a row, assembly-line fashion.

5. Working quickly, dip the bananas into the chocolate mixture, turning to coat and letting the excess drip off. Roll the bananas in the almonds to lightly coat. Return the bananas to the baking sheet. Serve immediately.

# light soups and salads

This filling soup is brimming with fresh vegetables. It makes a great lunch when paired with a salad or sandwich, such as Dilled Chicken and Feta Stuffed Pitas (page 110) or Warm Barley, Mushroom, and Spinach Salad (page 55). *(See photo insert.)*

# fresh garden soup

**serves 6** · ¾ cup per serving

1 medium onion, diced

½ cup diced red or green bell pepper

2 tablespoons water

1 medium garlic clove, minced

1 pound carrots, grated

1 medium zucchini or yellow summer squash, grated

¾ cup frozen green peas, thawed

¾ cup fresh corn kernels or frozen whole-kernel corn, thawed if frozen

2 cups fat-free, low-sodium vegetable broth

1½ teaspoons fresh lemon juice

½ teaspoon dried basil, crumbled

1 sprig of fresh thyme, leaves removed and crushed

Pinch of cayenne

½ to 1 teaspoon salt-free all-purpose seasoning blend

Pepper to taste (freshly ground preferred)

2 tablespoons minced fresh parsley

1. In a large skillet over medium-high heat, stir together the onion, bell pepper, water, and garlic. Cook, covered, for 5 minutes, or until the vegetables are tender. Stir in the carrots, zucchini, peas, and corn. Cook for 5 to 10 minutes, or until the carrots are tender.

2. Stir in the broth, lemon juice, basil, thyme, and cayenne. Bring to a boil. Remove from the heat.

3. Stir in the seasoning blend and pepper. Just before serving, sprinkle with the parsley.

**lunchbox tip:** Pack some low-fat cheese and unsalted whole-grain crackers along with a thermos of this soup to keep your child fueled all afternoon. For added protein, add some leftover cooked chicken to the soup.

## per serving

calories 80
total fat 0.5 g
   saturated fat 0.0 g
   trans fat 0.0 g
   polyunsaturated fat 0.0 g
   monounsaturated fat 0.0 g
cholesterol 0 mg

sodium 86 mg
carbohydrates 17 g
   fiber 4 g
   sugars 8 g
protein 3 g

dietary exchanges
½ starch, 2 vegetable

This soup is chock-full of an array of veggies. It pairs perfectly with Asian entrées such as Chinese Flank Steak (page 137) or Chinese Chicken Stir-Fry (page 107).

# hot-and-sour vegetable soup

| serves 6 | 1 cup per serving |
|----------|-------------------|

1 teaspoon canola or corn oil

1 cup sliced button mushrooms

1 small zucchini, shredded

1 small yellow summer squash, shredded

1 medium carrot, shredded

1 teaspoon minced peeled gingerroot

2 cups fat-free, low-sodium chicken broth

2 cups fat-free, low-sodium beef broth

½ 8-ounce can sliced bamboo shoots, drained

3 tablespoons plain rice vinegar or white vinegar

1 tablespoon soy sauce (lowest sodium available)

2 teaspoons sugar

1 teaspoon toasted sesame oil

½ teaspoon pepper (white preferred)

3 tablespoons cornstarch

⅓ cup water

2 large egg whites, lightly beaten

1. In a large saucepan, heat the canola oil over medium-high heat, swirling to coat the bottom. Cook the mushrooms for 4 to 5 minutes, or until light golden brown and soft, stirring occasionally.

2. Stir in the zucchini, summer squash, carrot, and gingerroot. Cook for 1 to 2 minutes, or until the vegetables are tender-crisp, stirring occasionally.

3. Stir in both broths, the bamboo shoots, vinegar, soy sauce, sugar, sesame oil, and pepper. Bring to a simmer, stirring occasionally. Reduce the heat and simmer for 5 minutes, or until the vegetables are tender, stirring occasionally.

4. Put the cornstarch in a small bowl. Add the water, stirring to dissolve. Stir into the soup.

5. Increase the heat to medium high. Cook for 1 to 2 minutes, or until the soup is slightly thickened, stirring occasionally. Slowly drizzle in the egg whites. Cook for 8 to 10 seconds without stirring, then stir gently. Cook for about 30 seconds, or until the egg white strands look slightly thicker and more opaque and begin to feather. They should resemble very short bits of thin string when lifted with a spoon. Serve the soup immediately.

## per serving

| | |
|---|---|
| calories 65 | sodium 156 mg |
| total fat 1.5 g | carbohydrates 9 g |
|   saturated fat 0.0 g |   fiber 1 g |
|   trans fat 0.0 g |   sugars 4 g |
|   polyunsaturated fat 0.5 g | protein 4 g |
|   monounsaturated fat 1.0 g | dietary exchanges |
| cholesterol 0 mg | ½ starch, 1 vegetable |

Some recipes for beet soup use a chicken-stock base, some include meat, and many offer a variety of vegetables. With its vibrant color and sweet, earthy taste, this meatless version is especially delightful with Polish Pierogi (page 194) or Pork Schnitzel with Sweet-and-Sour Red Cabbage (page 156).

# borscht

**serves 8** : 1 cup per serving

6 cups water and 4 cups water, divided use

1 pound beets, stems trimmed to about 2 inches

2 cups fat-free, low-sodium vegetable broth

2 cups shredded green cabbage

1 medium onion, chopped

½ teaspoon sugar

¼ teaspoon salt

⅛ teaspoon pepper

1 tablespoon red wine vinegar

¼ cup fat-free sour cream

## per serving

calories 45
total fat 0.0 g
  saturated fat 0.0 g
  trans fat 0.0 g
  polyunsaturated fat 0.0 g
  monounsaturated fat 0.0 g
cholesterol 1 mg

sodium 136 mg
carbohydrates 10 g
  fiber 2 g
  sugars 6 g
protein 2 g

dietary exchanges
2 vegetable

1. In a large saucepan, bring 6 cups water to a boil over high heat. Add the beets. Reduce the heat and simmer for 35 to 40 minutes, or until tender (easily pierced with the point of a knife). Drain the beets. Set aside until cool enough to handle.

2. Meanwhile, in a medium saucepan, bring the broth, cabbage, onion, sugar, salt, pepper, and the remaining 4 cups water to a simmer over medium-high heat. Reduce the heat to low and cook for 30 minutes, stirring occasionally.

3. When the beets have cooled, peel them and discard the stems. Using a box grater or a food processor fitted with a shredding blade, grate or shred the beets.

4. Stir the beets and vinegar into the cabbage mixture. Increase the heat to medium and cook for 5 minutes. Ladle into bowls. Or, cover and refrigerate to serve cold. Top each serving with the sour cream.

**cook's tip on beets:** Peel beets under running water to prevent the beet juice from staining your hands.

The next time you're craving the classic comfort of tomato soup, kick the flavor up a notch with smoky chipotle pepper and a squeeze of tart lime. This quick soup is an ideal partner for a simple spinach salad or Cool Lettuce-Wrap Tacos (page 186).

# chipotle tomato soup

| serves 4 | 1 cup per serving |
| --- | --- |

2  **cups grape tomatoes, quartered**

2  **cups water**

4  **ounces diced pimiento, drained**

1  **tablespoon minced chipotle pepper canned in adobo sauce**

2  **teaspoons adobo sauce (from chipotle peppers canned in adobo sauce)**

2  **packets (2 teaspoons) salt-free instant vegetable bouillon**

¼  **cup chopped fresh cilantro**

2  **teaspoons olive oil (extra virgin preferred)**

⅛  **teaspoon salt**

1  **medium lime, cut into 4 wedges**

**1.** In a large saucepan, stir together the tomatoes, water, pimiento, chipotle pepper, adobo sauce, and bouillon. Bring to a boil over high heat. Reduce the heat and simmer, covered, for 15 minutes, or until the tomatoes are very tender, stirring occasionally. Remove from the heat.

**2.** Stir in the cilantro, oil, and salt. Serve with the lime wedges.

**lunchbox tip:** To make this soup kid-friendly, reduce or omit the chipotle pepper.

**per serving**

calories 65
total fat 3.0 g
  saturated fat 0.5 g
  trans fat 0.0 g
  polyunsaturated fat 0.5 g
  monounsaturated fat 1.5 g
cholesterol 0 mg

sodium 177 mg
carbohydrates 9 g
  fiber 2 g
  sugars 5 g
protein 1 g

dietary exchanges
2 vegetable, ½ fat

Richly browned onions and fresh thyme give this rustic soup a deep, hearty flavor, while the yellow squash keeps it light enough for summertime. It makes a great starter early or late in the season, when there's a chill in the evening air.

# summer squash soup

**serves 4** | ¾ cup per serving

1 teaspoon olive oil, 1 teaspoon olive oil, and 1 teaspoon olive oil, divided use

1 cup diced onion

12 ounces yellow summer squash, quartered lengthwise into spears and thinly sliced crosswise

2 teaspoons fresh thyme

¾ teaspoon sugar

2 cups water

2 packets (2 teaspoons) salt-free instant chicken bouillon

½ teaspoon pepper (coarsely ground preferred)

⅛ teaspoon salt

½ cup fat-free sour cream

1. In a large saucepan, heat 1 teaspoon oil over medium-high heat, swirling to coat the bottom. Cook the onion for 5 minutes, or until the edges begin to brown, stirring occasionally.

2. Reduce the heat to medium. Stir in 1 teaspoon oil. Stir in the squash, thyme, and sugar. Cook for 4 minutes, or until the squash is tender-crisp, stirring frequently.

3. Stir in the water and bouillon. Increase the heat to high and bring to a boil. Reduce the heat and simmer, covered, for 10 minutes, or until the onion is very soft. Remove from the heat.

4. Stir in the pepper, salt, and the final 1 teaspoon oil. Let the soup stand for 5 minutes so the flavors blend. Ladle the soup into bowls. Top with the sour cream.

**cook's tip:** When recipes call for letting dishes stand a certain amount of time, it's important not to skip this step. The standing time allows the flavors to mellow and blend without overcooking the ingredients.

**per serving**

| | |
|---|---|
| calories 99 | sodium 105 mg |
| total fat 3.5 g | carbohydrates 14 g |
|   saturated fat 0.5 g |   fiber 2 g |
|   trans fat 0.0 g |   sugars 6 g |
|   polyunsaturated fat 0.5 g | protein 4 g |
|   monounsaturated fat 2.5 g | dietary exchanges |
| cholesterol 5 mg | ½ starch, 1 vegetable, ½ fat |

This light, Italian-inspired soup teams fresh carrots and spinach with shredded chicken in a broth seasoned with onion, garlic, and Italian parsley. It goes well with salads such as Lemony Shrimp and Feta Salad (page 86) or Tuscan Tuna Salad (page 82).

# chicken and spinach soup

**serves 6** ┊ ¾ cup per serving

- 1 **teaspoon olive oil and 1 teaspoon olive oil, divided use**
- 1 **small onion, chopped**
- ½ **cup chopped fresh Italian (flat-leaf) parsley**
- 2 **large garlic cloves, minced**
- 1 **medium carrot, thinly sliced crosswise**
- 6 **cups fat-free, low-sodium chicken broth**
- 8 **ounces boneless, skinless chicken breasts or chicken tenders, all visible fat discarded, flattened to ¼-inch thickness**
- 1 **cup chopped spinach**
- 1 **tablespoon dried oregano, crumbled**

**per serving**

calories 83
total fat 2.5 g
  saturated fat 0.5 g
  trans fat 0.0 g
  polyunsaturated fat 0.5 g
  monounsaturated fat 1.5 g
cholesterol 24 mg

sodium 120 mg
carbohydrates 4 g
  fiber 1 g
  sugars 1 g
protein 11 g

dietary exchanges
1 vegetable, 1½ lean meat

1. In a medium saucepan, heat 1 teaspoon oil over medium-low heat, swirling to coat the bottom. Cook the onion, parsley, and garlic for 5 minutes, or until the onion is soft, stirring frequently. Stir in the carrot. Cook for 2 to 3 minutes, stirring occasionally. Stir in the broth. Reduce the heat and simmer, covered, for 1 hour, stirring occasionally.

2. Meanwhile, in a medium skillet, heat the remaining 1 teaspoon oil over medium-high heat, swirling to coat the bottom. Cook the chicken for 4 minutes. Turn over. Cook for 2 to 4 minutes, or until no longer pink in the center. Transfer to a plate and let cool. Shred into bite-size pieces.

3. Stir the chicken, spinach, and oregano into the broth. Reduce the heat to medium. Cook for 10 minutes, or until just beginning to simmer, stirring occasionally.

**cook's tip:** If you prefer a thicker soup, follow the directions until the chicken is cooked. Strain out the cooked onion, parsley, garlic, and carrot. In a food processor or blender (vent the blender lid), process the onion mixture until smooth. Stir the mixture back into the broth. Stir in the spinach, oregano, and chicken. Continue cooking as directed.

Potatoes and leeks are the foundation for this rich, creamy soup. Butternut squash lends a sweet flavor and deepens the soup's golden color. Serve it with an autumnal salad, such as Spinach Salad with Apples and Caramelized Radishes (page 47), for a complete meal.

# golden leek-and-potato soup

**serves 8** | 1 cup per serving

1 tablespoon canola or corn oil

2 medium leeks, sliced

4 cups fat-free, low-sodium vegetable broth

4 cups cubed peeled yellow potatoes (½-inch cubes)

3 cups cubed peeled butternut squash (½-inch cubes)

12 ounces fat-free evaporated milk

½ teaspoon pepper

½ cup finely shredded low-fat Swiss cheese

¼ cup chopped fresh chives

**per serving**

calories 164
total fat 2.5 g
   saturated fat 0.5 g
   trans fat 0.0 g
   polyunsaturated fat 0.5 g
   monounsaturated fat 1.0 g
cholesterol 4 mg

sodium 96 mg
carbohydrates 29 g
   fiber 3 g
   sugars 8 g
protein 9 g

dietary exchanges
1½ starch, ½ fat-free milk

1. In a large Dutch oven, heat the oil over medium heat, swirling to coat the bottom. Cook the leeks for 5 to 6 minutes, or until tender, stirring frequently. Stir in the broth, potatoes, and squash. Increase the heat to high and bring to a boil. Reduce the heat and simmer, covered, for 12 to 15 minutes, or until the vegetables are tender.

2. In a food processor or blender (vent the blender lid), process the soup in batches until smooth. Carefully return the soup to the pot. Stir in the evaporated milk and pepper.

3. If needed, warm the soup over medium-low heat until heated through. Don't let it boil. Ladle the soup into bowls. Sprinkle with the Swiss cheese and chives.

**cook's tip:** To avoid having the steam and pressure from the hot soup pop the top off the blender, don't fill it more than halfway. Start blending on the lowest speed and gradually increase the speed until the soup is smooth.

An apple adds a touch of sweetness to this rich, velvety pumpkin soup redolent with warm spices. Paired with a salad, such as Warm Barley, Mushroom, and Spinach Salad (page 55), it makes a fabulous fall meal.

# pumpkin-apple soup

**serves 4** | ¾ cup per serving

1 teaspoon canola or corn oil

1½ cups diced onion

1 medium red apple, such as Jonathan or Gala, peeled and diced

¼ cup water and 1¼ cups water, divided use

½ 15-ounce can solid-pack pumpkin (not pie filling)

1½ tablespoons sugar

1 teaspoon pumpkin pie spice; or ½ teaspoon ground cinnamon, ¼ teaspoon ground nutmeg, and ¼ teaspoon ground ginger

⅛ teaspoon salt

¾ cup fat-free half-and-half

2 teaspoons light tub margarine

**per serving**

calories 128
total fat 2.5 g
  saturated fat 0.0 g
  trans fat 0.0 g
  polyunsaturated fat 0.5 g
  monounsaturated fat 1.0 g
cholesterol 0 mg

sodium 140 mg
carbohydrates 26 g
  fiber 4 g
  sugars 16 g
protein 5 g

dietary exchanges
½ fruit, 1 vegetable, ½ other carbohydrate, ½ fat

1. In a large saucepan, heat the oil over medium-high heat, swirling to coat the bottom. Cook the onion for 5 minutes, or until the edges begin to brown, stirring occasionally.

2. Stir in the apple and ¼ cup water. Cook for 2 minutes, or until the onion is soft, stirring occasionally. Set aside ¼ cup of the onion mixture.

3. Stir in the pumpkin, sugar, pumpkin pie spice, salt, and the remaining 1¼ cups water. Bring to a boil. Reduce the heat and simmer, covered, for 20 minutes, or until the onion is very soft.

4. In a food processor or blender (vent the blender lid), process the soup in batches until smooth. Carefully return the soup to the pan.

5. Bring the soup to a boil over high heat. Remove from the heat.

6. Stir in the half-and-half and margarine. Ladle the soup into bowls. Top with the reserved onion mixture.

**lunchbox tip:** Send along apple slices for some extra fruit and a little low-fat cheese for more protein.

This soup packs a lot of flavor into each serving, and it can easily be made vegetarian by using vegetable broth instead of chicken broth. A last-minute sprinkle of hazelnuts and cranberries adds crunchiness and sweetness. *(See photo insert.)*

# asparagus and mushroom soup

**serves 8** | scant ¾ cup per serving

⅓ cup uncooked unseasoned brown and wild rice blend

1 teaspoon olive oil

1 medium carrot, diced

1 medium rib of celery, diced

½ medium onion, diced

6 cups fat-free, low-sodium chicken broth

2 medium dried bay leaves

1½ cups thinly sliced brown (cremini) mushrooms

⅓ cup whole-wheat orzo

1 teaspoon chopped fresh thyme or ¼ teaspoon dried thyme, crumbled

½ teaspoon dried marjoram, crumbled

¼ teaspoon pepper

6 to 8 medium asparagus spears, diced (1½ cups)

2 tablespoons plus 1 teaspoon finely chopped hazelnuts, dry-roasted

2 tablespoons plus 1 teaspoon chopped sweetened dried cranberries

1. Prepare the rice using the package directions, omitting the salt and margarine. Set aside.

2. About 15 minutes before the rice is done, in a large saucepan, heat the oil over medium-high heat, swirling to coat the bottom. Cook the carrot, celery, and onion for 3 to 5 minutes, or until the vegetables are soft and begin to release their juices.

3. Stir in the broth and bay leaves. Bring to a boil. Stir in the mushrooms, orzo, thyme, marjoram, and pepper. Reduce the heat and simmer, covered, for 10 minutes (no stirring needed).

4. Stir in the asparagus. Simmer, covered, for 5 to 7 minutes, or until the asparagus is tender.

5. Stir in the rice. Cook for 1 minute, or until heated through. Discard the bay leaves.

6. Ladle the soup into bowls. Sprinkle with the hazelnuts and cranberries.

**cook's tip:** If you can't find a brown and wild rice blend, you can make your own by combining 1 cup of brown rice with ¼ cup of wild rice.

**per serving**

| | |
|---|---|
| calories 107 | sodium 58 mg |
| total fat 2.5 g | carbohydrates 17 g |
|   saturated fat 0.5 g |   fiber 3 g |
|   trans fat 0.0 g |   sugars 4 g |
|   polyunsaturated fat 0.5 g | protein 5 g |
|   monounsaturated fat 1.5 g | dietary exchanges |
| cholesterol 0 mg | 1 starch |

Making soup just couldn't get any easier than this. All you have to do is purée the ingredients! Don't be afraid to add the whole jalapeño; it won't make the soup overly spicy. You can discard the ribs and seeds, if you prefer.

# cool avocado-cilantro soup

**serves 4** | ¾ cup per serving

1 medium avocado, halved

½ 15.5-ounce can no-salt-added navy beans, rinsed and drained

¾ cup fat-free milk

½ cup fat-free sour cream

½ cup chopped fresh cilantro and 1 tablespoon plus 1 teaspoon chopped fresh cilantro, divided use

2 tablespoons fresh lime juice

2 tablespoons fresh lemon juice

1 medium fresh jalapeño, stem discarded (see cook's tip on page 109)

1 medium garlic clove

⅛ teaspoon salt

1. In a food processor or blender, process all the ingredients except the remaining 1 tablespoon plus 1 teaspoon cilantro until smooth.

2. Serve the soup immediately or cover and refrigerate for up to 4 hours. Just before serving, garnish the soup with the remaining 1 tablespoon plus 1 teaspoon cilantro.

**per serving**

calories 179
total fat 7.5 g
   saturated fat 1.0 g
   trans fat 0.0 g
   polyunsaturated fat 1.0 g
   monounsaturated fat 5.0 g
cholesterol 6 mg

sodium 124 mg
carbohydrates 22 g
   fiber 6 g
   sugars 7 g
protein 8 g

dietary exchanges
1 starch, ½ fat-free milk, 1 fat

Nutrient-packed kale teams with a brightly flavored dressing, juicy grapefruit, and crunchy walnuts to create this winning salad. *(See photo insert.)*

# kale salad with citrus dressing

| serves 4 | 2 cups salad and 1½ tablespoons dressing per serving |
| --- | --- |

7 **cups coarsely chopped kale, any large stems discarded**

2 **medium carrots, shredded**

¼ **cup golden raisins**

2 **medium green onions, thinly sliced**

1 **medium grapefruit (red preferred), or 2 blood oranges, or 2 Cara Cara oranges**

2 **tablespoons plain rice vinegar**

2 **tablespoons agave nectar or honey**

1 **teaspoon olive oil (extra virgin preferred)**

¼ **teaspoon salt**

¼ **teaspoon pepper (freshly ground preferred)**

¼ **cup chopped walnuts, dry-roasted**

1. In a large bowl, toss together the kale, carrots, raisins, and green onions.

2. Put the grapefruit on a cutting board. Using a sharp knife, suprême the grapefruit by slicing off the top and bottom. Holding the knife blade horizontally, carefully cut downward, following the contour of the fruit, to remove the peel, the bitter white pith, and the outer membrane (a little of the flesh will be removed, too). Holding the grapefruit over a medium bowl to catch any juice, cut between the membrane and the flesh of each segment to release the segment from the membrane. Discard any seeds. Add the grapefruit segments to the salad, tossing gently.

3. Squeeze the membrane and any peel with flesh clinging to it into the medium bowl (you should get about 2 tablespoons of juice). Discard the membrane and peel.

4. Whisk the remaining ingredients except the walnuts into the grapefruit juice. Pour the dressing over the salad, tossing gently to coat. Sprinkle with the walnuts.

**cook's tip on grapefruit:** Grapefruit can interact with a number of medications, including many heart medicines. Be sure to check with your doctor or pharmacist if you take any medication, and use the oranges as an alternative ingredient if necessary.

## per serving

calories 218
total fat 7.0 g
  saturated fat 0.5 g
  trans fat 0.0 g
  polyunsaturated fat 4.0 g
  monounsaturated fat 1.5 g
cholesterol 0 mg

sodium 152 mg
carbohydrates 39 g
  fiber 6 g
  sugars 21 g
protein 6 g

**dietary exchanges**
1 fruit, 3 vegetable,
½ other carbohydrate,
1½ fat

Get your meal off to a great start with this salad. Roasting the radishes softens their bite and adds so much flavor that little dressing is needed.

# spinach salad with apples and caramelized radishes

| serves 4 | 2 cups salad and 1 tablespoon dressing per serving |

½ **pound radishes, quartered**

¼ **cup diced red onion**

1 **teaspoon olive oil and 2 teaspoons olive oil (extra virgin preferred), divided use**

1 **teaspoon honey**

½ **teaspoon fresh rosemary, finely chopped, or ⅛ teaspoon dried rosemary, crushed**

¹⁄₁₆ **teaspoon salt and ¹⁄₁₆ teaspoon salt, divided use**

1 **tablespoon plus ½ teaspoon cider vinegar**

2½ **teaspoons 100% apple juice**

1 **teaspoon Dijon mustard (lowest sodium available)**

¹⁄₁₆ **teaspoon pepper**

6 **cups baby spinach, chopped**

½ **large apple, chopped into 1-inch pieces**

½ **cup shredded carrot**

1. Preheat the oven to 425°F.

2. Place the radishes and onion in an 8-inch square glass baking dish. Drizzle with 1 teaspoon oil and the honey. Sprinkle with the rosemary and ¹⁄₁₆ teaspoon salt. Stir until well coated.

3. Roast for 30 minutes, or until the radishes are fork-tender, stirring once or twice. Transfer to a cooling rack and let cool for 5 to 10 minutes.

4. Meanwhile, in a small bowl, whisk together the vinegar, apple juice, mustard, pepper, and the remaining 2 teaspoons oil and ¹⁄₁₆ teaspoon salt.

5. Put the spinach on salad plates. Arrange the radish mixture, apple, and carrot on top. Spoon the dressing over all.

**cook's tip:** To save time, you can roast the radishes and onion the night before. When you're ready to assemble the salads, microwave the radish mixture on 100 percent power (high) for about 30 seconds, or until warm.

## per serving

calories 83
total fat 4.0 g
  saturated fat 0.5 g
  trans fat 0.0 g
  polyunsaturated fat 0.5 g
  monounsaturated fat 2.5 g
cholesterol 0 mg

sodium 167 mg
carbohydrates 12 g
  fiber 3 g
  sugars 7 g
protein 2 g

dietary exchanges
½ fruit, 1 vegetable,
1 fat

Contrasting flavors, textures, and colors make this salad a treat for the eyes and palate, as well as an inspired way to feature the "first fruits" of the spring garden. Baby spinach makes a tender bed for delicate asparagus, sweet strawberries, and juicy oranges bathed in a piquant vinaigrette.

# spring asparagus and strawberry salad

**serves 4** | ½ cup cup asparagus mixture and 1 cup spinach per serving

12 ounces thin asparagus spears, trimmed and cut into 2-inch pieces (about 3 cups of pieces)

1 cup sliced hulled strawberries

1 medium orange, peeled, quartered, and sliced crosswise

¼ cup thinly sliced green onions

2 tablespoons sherry vinegar, champagne vinegar, or white wine vinegar

1 tablespoon olive oil (extra virgin preferred)

1 small garlic clove, minced

¼ teaspoon pepper

⅛ teaspoon salt

4 cups loosely packed baby spinach

1. In a medium saucepan, steam the asparagus for 3 to 5 minutes, or until tender-crisp. Rinse under cold water. Drain well.

2. In a large bowl, stir together the asparagus, strawberries, orange, and green onions.

3. In a small bowl, whisk together the vinegar, oil, garlic, pepper, and salt. Pour the dressing over the asparagus mixture, tossing to coat. Arrange the spinach on salad plates. Spoon the asparagus mixture over the spinach.

**cook's tip on oranges:** When peeling an orange, carefully cut off all the bitter white pith for the most attractive presentation and sweetest taste.

**per serving**

calories 89
total fat 4.0 g
  saturated fat 0.5 g
  trans fat 0.0 g
  polyunsaturated fat 0.5 g
  monounsaturated fat 2.5 g
cholesterol 0 mg

sodium 101 mg
carbohydrates 13 g
  fiber 4 g
  sugars 7 g
protein 3 g

dietary exchanges
½ fruit, 1 vegetable, 1 fat

Nutty edamame meet crisp, sweet red bell peppers and mild water chestnuts in this quick-to-make Asian-inspired salad flavored with lime juice, ginger, and fresh herbs. Try it with Plank-Grilled Tuna Steaks (page 80) or Grilled Sweet Chile Pork Tenderloin (page 149).

# edamame and red bell pepper salad

**serves 4** | ½ cup per serving

1 cup shelled edamame, thawed if frozen, patted dry

1 small red bell pepper, diced

½ 8-ounce can sliced water chestnuts, drained and cut into thin strips

2 tablespoons chopped fresh cilantro

2 tablespoons chopped fresh basil

2 tablespoons fresh lime juice

1 tablespoon canola or corn oil

1 teaspoon minced peeled gingerroot

⅛ teaspoon salt

In a medium bowl, stir together all the ingredients. Serve immediately.

**per serving**

calories 98
total fat 5.5 g
   saturated fat 0.5 g
   trans fat 0.0 g
   polyunsaturated fat 1.5 g
   monounsaturated fat 3.0 g
cholesterol 0 mg

sodium 79 mg
carbohydrates 8 g
   fiber 3 g
   sugars 3 g
protein 5 g

dietary exchanges
½ starch, ½ lean meat, ½ fat

Tender green beans, rich walnuts, and sweet-tart tomatoes are combined with fragrant onion and garlic, then coated with a smooth vinaigrette in this summery salad. Try it with grilled entrées, such as Coffee-Rubbed Salmon with Horseradish Sauce (page 65) or Turkey and Bell Pepper Kebabs (page 113).

# green bean, tomato, and walnut salad

**serves 4** | **½ cup per serving**

8 ounces fresh green beans, trimmed and cut into 1½-inch pieces, or frozen cut green beans

1 teaspoon canola or corn oil and 1 teaspoon canola or corn oil, divided use

¼ cup chopped onion

¼ cup chopped walnuts

1 medium garlic clove, minced

1 large tomato, chopped

1 tablespoon red wine vinegar

1 teaspoon Dijon mustard (lowest sodium available)

⅛ teaspoon salt

⅛ teaspoon pepper

**per serving**

calories 101
total fat 7.5 g
   saturated fat 0.5 g
   trans fat 0.0 g
   polyunsaturated fat 4.0 g
   monounsaturated fat 2.0 g
cholesterol 0 mg

sodium 105 mg
carbohydrates 8 g
   fiber 3 g
   sugars 4 g
protein 3 g

dietary exchanges
2 vegetable, 1½ fat

1. Put the green beans in a medium saucepan. Add enough water to cover. Bring to a boil over high heat. Cook for 4 to 8 minutes, or just until tender-crisp. Transfer to a colander. Rinse with cold water to stop the cooking process. Spread on paper towels and pat dry. Set aside.

2. In a small skillet, heat 1 teaspoon oil over medium-high heat, swirling to coat the bottom. Reduce the heat to medium. Cook the onion and walnuts for 4 to 5 minutes, or until the onion is soft and the walnuts are toasted, stirring frequently.

3. Stir in the garlic. Cook for about 30 seconds, or until fragrant, stirring frequently and watching carefully so it doesn't burn.

4. Transfer the green beans, onion mixture, and tomato to a medium serving bowl.

5. In a small bowl, whisk together the vinegar, mustard, salt, pepper, and the remaining 1 teaspoon oil. Pour over the salad, tossing to coat. Serve at room temperature or cover and refrigerate for 30 minutes to serve chilled, stirring occasionally.

This simple salad combines juicy tomatoes with the crunch of cucumber, bell pepper, and sweet red onion, along with a touch of creamy cheese. It briefly marinates in a light but flavorful vinaigrette that lets the veggies shine.

# fresh tomato and cucumber salad

**serves 4** | **½ cup per serving**

### salad

- 1 **cup grape tomatoes, halved**
- ½ **cup chopped cucumber (English, or hothouse, preferred)**
- ¼ **cup chopped red bell pepper**
- ¼ **cup chopped red onion**
- ¼ **cup chopped fresh basil**
- ¼ **cup shredded low-fat 4-cheese Italian blend**

### dressing

- 2 **tablespoons plain rice vinegar**
- 1½ **teaspoons sugar**
- ½ **teaspoon olive oil (extra virgin preferred)**
- 1 **small garlic clove, minced**

1. In a medium bowl, stir together the salad ingredients.

2. In a small bowl, whisk together the dressing ingredients. Pour over the salad, tossing gently to coat. For peak flavor, cover and refrigerate for 30 minutes to 1 hour before serving.

**cook's tip:** If the Italian cheese blend isn't available, you can use fat-free mozzarella cheese. You'll miss out on a pleasant smoky flavor, however.

### per serving

| | |
|---|---|
| calories 54 | sodium 61 mg |
| total fat 2.0 g | carbohydrates 7 g |
| saturated fat 0.5 g | fiber 1 g |
| trans fat 0.0 g | sugars 4 g |
| polyunsaturated fat 0.0 g | protein 3 g |
| monounsaturated fat 0.5 g | dietary exchanges |
| cholesterol 3 mg | 1 vegetable, ½ fat |

This crisp coleslaw is the perfect cooling accompaniment to spicy Mexican or Southwestern food. Try it with Chicken and Black Bean Enchiladas (page 108) or Pork and Green Onion Tacos (page 159).

# cool jícama-cabbage slaw

| serves 8 | 1 cup per serving |

## slaw

- 6 cups thinly sliced green cabbage
- 2 cups shredded peeled jícama
- 2 medium carrots, shredded
- 1 medium red bell pepper, chopped
- ½ cup sliced green onions
- ½ cup chopped fresh cilantro

## dressing

- ¾ cup fat-free plain yogurt
- ¼ cup low-fat buttermilk
- 1 teaspoon grated lime zest
- 2 tablespoons fresh lime juice
- 1 small garlic clove, minced
- ½ teaspoon ground cumin
- ¼ teaspoon pepper
- ⅛ teaspoon salt

- ½ cup diced avocado
- 2 tablespoons unsalted shelled pumpkin seeds, dry-roasted

1. In a large bowl, stir together the slaw ingredients.

2. In a small bowl, whisk together the dressing ingredients. Pour over the cabbage mixture, tossing to coat. Cover and refrigerate for 4 hours, stirring occasionally.

3. Just before serving, top with the avocado and sprinkle with the pumpkin seeds.

**cook's tip on jícama:** Also known as a Mexican potato, the jícama has white flesh that's crisp, slightly starchy, and sweet—similar to the flesh of a water chestnut. Peel and discard the jícama's thin brown skin before using it.

## per serving

calories 85
total fat 2.5 g
   saturated fat 0.5 g
   trans fat 0.0 g
   polyunsaturated fat 0.5 g
   monounsaturated fat 1.5 g
cholesterol 1 mg

sodium 90 mg
carbohydrates 13 g
   fiber 5 g
   sugars 6 g
protein 4 g

dietary exchanges
2 vegetable, ½ fat

This slaw joins sweet apple and carrot strips with an orange-flavored vinaigrette. A bit of banana pepper adds just a hint of zesty heat. *(See photo insert.)*

# crunchy apple-carrot slaw

| serves 6 | ½ cup per serving |
|----------|-------------------|

### slaw

- 1 cup matchstick-size carrot strips
- 1 medium red apple, such as Gala or Fuji, cut into matchstick-size strips
- 1 medium fresh banana pepper, seeds and ribs discarded, halved lengthwise, and thinly sliced crosswise

### dressing

- 1 teaspoon grated orange zest
- 2 tablespoons fresh orange juice
- 2 tablespoons cider vinegar
- 1½ tablespoons sugar
- 1½ tablespoons canola or corn oil

1. In a medium bowl, stir together the slaw ingredients.

2. In a small bowl, whisk together the dressing ingredients until the sugar is dissolved. Pour over the carrot mixture, tossing to coat. Cover and refrigerate for at least 30 minutes, stirring occasionally.

**lunchbox tip:** This is a kid-friendly slaw, but if your kids prefer a milder version, use half a small diced red bell pepper instead of the banana pepper.

### per serving

calories 73
total fat 3.5 g
  saturated fat 0.5 g
  trans fat 0.0 g
  polyunsaturated fat 1.0 g
  monounsaturated fat 2.0 g
cholesterol 0 mg

sodium 16 mg
carbohydrates 10 g
  fiber 2 g
  sugars 8 g
protein 0 g

dietary exchanges
1 fruit, 1 fat

Poppy seeds add a bit of crunch to this sweet summertime salad that's perfect for outdoor dining. Serve it at your next backyard barbecue, along with a grilled entrée such as Turkey and Bell Pepper Kebabs (page 113) or Grilled Orange Tuna Steaks (page 79).

# fruit salad with cranberry-ginger dressing

| serves 6 | heaping ¾ cup fruit and 2 tablespoons dressing per serving |
|----------|-----------------------------------------------------------|

**dressing**

1 teaspoon cornstarch

¾ cup 100% cranberry juice

1 tablespoon sugar

1 teaspoon grated peeled gingerroot

½ teaspoon grated orange zest (optional)

½ teaspoon poppy seeds

**salad**

2 cups cubed watermelon

1 cup strawberries, hulled and quartered

½ cup halved seedless green grapes

½ cup blueberries

1. Put the cornstarch in a small saucepan. Add the cranberry juice, whisking to dissolve. Bring to a boil over medium-high heat. Boil for 1 minute. Pour into a shallow bowl and refrigerate until completely cooled, about 10 minutes. Whisk in the remaining dressing ingredients.

2. Arrange the salad ingredients on salad plates. Spoon the dressing over the fruit.

**Go Red brunch tip:** Use the leftover cranberry juice to make Sparkling Cranberry Spritzers (page 238) for your guests.

**per serving**

calories 65
total fat 0.5 g
    saturated fat 0.0 g
    trans fat 0.0 g
    polyunsaturated fat 0.0 g
    monounsaturated fat 0.0 g
cholesterol 0 mg

sodium 2 mg
carbohydrates 16 g
    fiber 1 g
    sugars 14 g
protein 1 g

dietary exchanges
1 fruit

This side salad combines chewy barley and mild mushrooms with baby spinach and a bright citrus-based dressing.

# warm barley, mushroom, and spinach salad

serves 4 | ¾ cup per serving

¾ cup uncooked quick-cooking barley

2 tablespoons fresh orange juice

1½ tablespoons fresh lemon juice

1 tablespoon olive oil and 1½ teaspoons olive oil (extra virgin preferred), divided use

¼ teaspoon salt

Pepper to taste

8 ounces button mushrooms, thinly sliced

2 medium garlic cloves, chopped

6 ounces baby spinach

**per serving**

calories 206
total fat 6.0 g
   saturated fat 1.0 g
   trans fat 0.0 g
   polyunsaturated fat 1.0 g
   monounsaturated fat 4.0 g
cholesterol 0 mg

sodium 186 mg
carbohydrates 34 g
   fiber 7 g
   sugars 3 g
protein 7 g

dietary exchanges
2 starch, 1 vegetable, 1 fat

1. Prepare the barley using the package directions, omitting the salt. Drain well in a colander. Let stand for 5 minutes.

2. Meanwhile, in a small bowl, whisk together both juices, 1 tablespoon oil, the salt, and pepper. Set aside.

3. In a large nonstick skillet, heat the remaining 1½ teaspoons oil over medium-high heat, swirling to coat the bottom. Cook the mushrooms for 5 minutes, stirring occasionally.

4. Stir in the garlic. Cook for 5 minutes, or until the mushrooms are browned, stirring frequently. Remove from the heat.

5. Add the spinach to the mushroom mixture, tossing to combine and slightly wilt the spinach. Immediately transfer to a large bowl.

6. Stir in the barley. Pour the dressing over the salad, tossing to coat. Let the salad stand for at least 10 minutes to allow the barley to absorb the dressing. Serve warm or at room temperature.

Fresh tomatoes and cucumbers pick up the heady flavor of fresh basil to partner perfectly with tender cannellini beans. The beans and bulgur make this a hearty salad. Just add chopped grilled chicken breasts to turn this into an entrée.

# lemon-bulgur salad

**serves 4** | **½ cup per serving**

### salad

- ½ cup uncooked instant, or fine-grain, bulgur
- ½ cup canned no-salt-added cannellini, navy, or Great Northern beans, rinsed and drained
- ¼ cup chopped tomato
- ¼ cup chopped peeled cucumber
- ¼ cup chopped fresh basil
- 2 tablespoons chopped sweet onion, such as Vidalia, Maui, or Oso Sweet

### dressing

- 1 tablespoon fresh lemon juice
- 1½ teaspoons water
- 1 medium garlic clove, minced
- ½ teaspoon Dijon mustard (lowest sodium available)
- ½ teaspoon olive oil (extra virgin preferred)
- ¼ teaspoon pepper

1. Prepare the bulgur using the package directions, omitting the salt. Transfer to a medium bowl. Fluff with a fork.

2. Stir in the remaining salad ingredients.

3. Meanwhile, in a small bowl, whisk together the dressing ingredients. Pour over the salad, tossing to coat. Cover and refrigerate for 1 hour, or until chilled.

### per serving

calories 99
total fat 1.0 g
   saturated fat 0.0 g
   trans fat 0.0 g
   polyunsaturated fat 0.0 g
   monounsaturated fat 0.5 g
cholesterol 0 mg

sodium 27 mg
carbohydrates 19 g
   fiber 5 g
   sugars 1 g
protein 4 g

dietary exchanges
1½ starch

Baby potatoes are more common in supermarkets and farmers' markets these days. This creamy salad highlights the tender morsels by leaving them whole, but you can cut them in half after cooking, if you prefer.

# tiny-potato salad

serves 6 | 1 cup per serving

1½ **pounds baby red or yellow potatoes, or larger red potatoes cut into 1-inch cubes**

⅓ **cup low-fat sour cream**

¼ **cup light mayonnaise**

1 **tablespoon cider vinegar**

1 **tablespoon finely chopped dill pickle**

1 **teaspoon sugar**

1 **small garlic clove, minced**

½ **teaspoon smoked paprika and ⅛ teaspoon smoked paprika, divided use**

½ **teaspoon dry mustard**

¼ **teaspoon pepper**

¾ **cup chopped red bell pepper**

¼ **cup sliced green onions**

¼ **cup slivered red onion**

2 **to 4 tablespoons fat-free milk (optional)**

1. Put the potatoes in a medium saucepan. Add enough water to cover. Bring to a boil. Boil for 8 to 10 minutes, or just until tender. Drain in a colander. Rinse with cold water to cool. Drain well.

2. Meanwhile, in a large bowl, stir together the sour cream, mayonnaise, vinegar, pickle, sugar, garlic, ½ teaspoon paprika, the mustard, and pepper. Add the potatoes, bell pepper, green onions, and red onion, tossing gently to coat.

3. Cover and refrigerate for 1 to 2 hours, or until chilled. If the salad seems dry, gently stir in the milk before serving. Sprinkle with the remaining ⅛ teaspoon paprika.

**per serving**

calories 137
total fat 4.5 g
  saturated fat 1.0 g
  trans fat 0.0 g
  polyunsaturated fat 2.0 g
  monounsaturated fat 1.0 g
cholesterol 9 mg

sodium 135 mg
carbohydrates 22 g
  fiber 3 g
  sugars 3 g
protein 3 g

dietary exchanges
1½ starch, ½ fat

Crisp Asian pear, snow peas, and red bell pepper contrast with fluffy quinoa in this pecan-studded salad. The simple dressing, with a touch of lemon and toasted sesame oil, makes this an ideal accompaniment for grilled fish or chicken.

# quinoa and asian pear salad

**serves 6** | 1 cup per serving

1 cup uncooked quinoa, rinsed and drained

4 ounces snow peas, trimmed

1 large Asian pear, peeled and chopped into ½-inch pieces

¼ cup red bell pepper, diced

¼ cup chopped pecans, dry-roasted

1 medium green onion, chopped (green part only)

1 teaspoon sesame seeds, dry-roasted

2 tablespoons fresh lemon juice

1 tablespoon olive oil (extra virgin preferred)

1 teaspoon toasted sesame oil

¼ teaspoon salt

¼ teaspoon pepper

1. Prepare the quinoa using the package directions, omitting the salt. Transfer to a medium bowl. Fluff with a fork. Let cool.

2. Meanwhile, fill a small saucepan halfway with water. Bring to a boil over high heat. Cook the snow peas for about 45 seconds, or until bright green and tender-crisp. Drain in a colander. Plunge into a bowl of cold water to stop the cooking process. Drain well in a colander. Cut the snow peas into ½-inch pieces.

3. Stir the snow peas, pear, bell pepper, pecans, green onion, and sesame seeds into the quinoa.

4. In a small bowl, whisk together the remaining ingredients. Stir into the quinoa mixture, tossing gently to coat. Let stand for 15 minutes so the flavors blend. Serve at room temperature or cover and refrigerate for 1 hour to serve chilled.

**cook's tip:** To prevent the Asian pear from browning, place the chopped pieces in cold water until you're ready to use them. If Asian pears aren't available, you can substitute a sweet eating apple, such as a Gala, or another crisp pear, such as a Bosc.

**per serving**

calories 198
total fat 8.5 g
  saturated fat 1.0 g
  trans fat 0.0 g
  polyunsaturated fat 2.5 g
  monounsaturated fat 4.5 g
cholesterol 0 mg

sodium 101 mg
carbohydrates 26 g
  fiber 5 g
  sugars 6 g
protein 5 g

dietary exchanges
1½ starch, 1 fat

# seafood

Roasted Barramundi Provençal 60

Catfish Tacos 61

Halibut Ragout 62

Halibut and Apple Kebabs 63

Ginger-Lime Halibut 64

Coffee-Rubbed Salmon
with Horseradish Sauce 65

Sautéed Salmon with Mango Salsa 66

Orange-Chipotle Salmon Stir-Fry 67

Salmon with Creamy
Lemon-Caper Sauce 68

Salmon-Corn Chowder 70

Creamed Spinach with Salmon 71

Thai Salmon Patties
with Sweet Cucumber Relish 72

Lime-Basil Tilapia 74

Blackened Tilapia Sandwiches
with Broccoli Slaw 75

Trout en Papillote with Dill-Dijon
Dipping Sauce 76

Trout with Herb Vinaigrette 77

Trout Piccata 78

Grilled Orange Tuna Steaks 79

Plank-Grilled Tuna Steaks 80

Honey-Mustard Tuna Steaks 81

Tuscan Tuna Salad 82

Tuna and Macaroni Skillet
Casserole 83

Italian-Style Mussels 84

Miso-Marinated Scallops
on Soba Noodles 85

Lemony Shrimp and Feta Salad 86

Spicy Shrimp and Grits 87

Shrimp and Fennel Linguine 88

Baja Shrimp Bowls 89

Roasting is a great healthy cooking method because it intensifies flavors without adding excess sodium or unhealthy fats. In this dish, the flavors of France's Provence region—fennel, leeks, garlic, artichokes, and tomatoes—are roasted with barramundi, a mild, meaty white fish.

# roasted barramundi provençal

**serves 4** : 3 ounces fish and 1 cup vegetables per serving

1 medium fennel bulb, cut into 1-inch squares

1 medium leek, cut into 1-inch squares

1 medium garlic clove, thinly sliced

1 teaspoon olive oil and 1 teaspoon olive oil, divided use

⅛ teaspoon salt and ⅛ teaspoon salt, divided use

⅛ teaspoon pepper and ⅛ teaspoon pepper, divided use

1 cup cherry tomatoes

1 cup frozen artichoke hearts, thawed, drained, and halved

1 teaspoon capers, drained and chopped if large

½ teaspoon dried thyme, crumbled, or 1½ teaspoons fresh thyme, finely chopped

12 ounces barramundi fillets, thawed if frozen, rinsed and patted dry

¼ cup dry white wine (regular or nonalcoholic)

1. Preheat the oven to 400°F.

2. In a large roasting pan, stir together the fennel, leek, garlic, and 1 teaspoon oil. Sprinkle with ⅛ teaspoon salt and ⅛ teaspoon pepper. Roast for 20 minutes.

3. Meanwhile, in a medium bowl, stir together the tomatoes, artichoke hearts, capers, thyme, and the remaining 1 teaspoon oil, ⅛ teaspoon salt, and ⅛ teaspoon pepper.

4. Remove the pan from the oven. Push the fennel mixture to one side of the pan. Arrange the fish in the center of the pan. Spoon the tomato mixture around the other three sides of the fish. Pour the wine over the fish.

5. Roast for 15 minutes, or until the fish flakes easily when tested with a fork.

**cook's tip:** If you can't find barramundi fillets in the freezer section of your grocery store, you can substitute mahimahi, grouper, or red snapper fillets.

## per serving

calories 161
total fat 3.5 g
   saturated fat 0.5 g
   trans fat 0.0 g
   polyunsaturated fat 1.0 g
   monounsaturated fat 2.0 g
cholesterol 35 mg

sodium 260 mg
carbohydrates 15 g
   fiber 6 g
   sugars 3 g
protein 20 g

**dietary exchanges**
3 vegetable, 2½ lean meat

Southern catfish goes south of the border when it gets nestled in a corn tortilla and topped with lettuce, tomato, cilantro, and a creamy cucumber-and-avocado dressing.

# catfish tacos

| serves 4 | 2 tacos per serving |
| --- | --- |

1 teaspoon chili powder

1 teaspoon ground cumin

1 teaspoon garlic powder

¼ teaspoon pepper

Cooking spray

1 large green bell pepper, thinly sliced

1 small onion, thinly sliced

½ medium avocado, diced

½ medium cucumber, peeled, seeded, grated, and patted until dry

¼ cup fat-free plain Greek yogurt

1 tablespoon fresh lime juice

⅛ teaspoon salt

4 catfish fillets (about 4 ounces each), rinsed and patted dry

8 6-inch corn tortillas

1 cup shredded romaine lettuce

¼ cup finely chopped fresh cilantro

1 small tomato, chopped

½ cup chipotle salsa (lowest sodium available)

1. In a small bowl, stir together the chili powder, cumin, garlic powder, and pepper.

2. Lightly spray a medium skillet with cooking spray. Heat over medium-high heat. Put the bell pepper and onion in the skillet. Sprinkle with half the chili powder mixture. Cook for 5 to 6 minutes, or until the bell pepper is tender-crisp and the onion is soft, stirring frequently. Transfer the vegetables to a bowl. Cover to keep warm. Wipe the skillet with paper towels.

3. In a separate small bowl, using a fork, mash the avocado. Stir in the cucumber, yogurt, lime juice, and salt. Set aside.

4. Sprinkle the remaining chili powder mixture over both sides of the fish. Using your fingertips, gently press the mixture so it adheres to the fish.

5. Lightly spray the same skillet with cooking spray. Heat over medium heat. Cook the fish for 4 minutes on each side, or until it flakes easily when tested with a fork. Remove from the heat. Cut each fillet in half.

6. Warm the tortillas. Place half a fillet in the center of each tortilla. Top with, in order, the bell pepper mixture, avocado mixture, lettuce, cilantro, tomato, and salsa.

**per serving**

| calories 278 | sodium 293 mg |
| --- | --- |
| total fat 8.5 g | carbohydrates 28 g |
|   saturated fat 1.5 g |   fiber 6 g |
|   trans fat 0.0 g |   sugars 7 g |
|   polyunsaturated fat 2.0 g | protein 24 g |
|   monounsaturated fat 4.0 g | **dietary exchanges** |
| cholesterol 66 mg | 1 starch, 2 vegetable, 3 lean meat |

seafood

A ragout, from the French verb meaning "to stimulate the appetite," is a thick, rich stew. Our version is lightened with fish and fresh vegetables, but it's no less hearty. Serve with a crisp mixed-greens salad and some crusty whole-grain bread to sop up the sauce.

# halibut ragout

**serves 8** : 1 cup per serving

2 tablespoons canola or corn oil

3 medium carrots, cut into matchstick-size strips

3 medium ribs of celery, sliced diagonally

½ cup chopped onion

¼ cup chopped green bell pepper

1 medium garlic clove, minced

2 14.5-ounce cans no-salt-added diced tomatoes, undrained

1 cup dry white wine (regular or nonalcoholic)

1 tablespoon minced fresh parsley and 2 tablespoons minced fresh parsley, divided use

¼ teaspoon dried thyme, crumbled

¼ teaspoon dried basil, crumbled

Pepper to taste (freshly ground preferred)

2 pounds halibut fillets, rinsed, patted dry, and cut into 1-inch pieces

1. In a large saucepan, heat the oil over medium-high heat, swirling to coat the bottom. Cook the carrots, celery, onion, bell pepper, and garlic for 3 to 4 minutes, or until the onion is soft, stirring occasionally.

2. Stir in the tomatoes with liquid, wine, 1 tablespoon parsley, the thyme, basil, and pepper. Reduce the heat and simmer, covered, for 20 minutes.

3. Stir in the fish. Simmer, covered, for 5 to 10 minutes, or until the fish flakes easily when tested with a fork. Just before serving, sprinkle with the remaining 2 tablespoons parsley.

**cook's tip:** This dish reheats and freezes well, so store any leftovers in the freezer or ladle some into a thermos for a hot, hearty lunch at the office.

**per serving**

calories 198
total fat 5.0 g
  saturated fat 0.5 g
  trans fat 0.0 g
  polyunsaturated fat 1.5 g
  monounsaturated fat 3.0 g
cholesterol 56 mg

sodium 123 mg
carbohydrates 9 g
  fiber 2 g
  sugars 5 g
protein 22 g

dietary exchanges
2 vegetable, 3 lean meat

Sporting chunks of mild halibut, crunchy Granny Smith apple, and assertive red onion, all brushed with a citrus marinade before grilling, these healthful kebabs are a deliciously complex-flavored main dish. Every bite combines sweet, tart, tangy, and meaty flavors along with soft and crisp textures.

# halibut and apple kebabs

**serves 4** | **1 kebab per serving**

Cooking spray

2 **teaspoons chopped fresh thyme or** ¼ **teaspoon dried thyme, crumbled**

1 **teaspoon grated lime zest**

2 **tablespoons fresh lime juice**

1 **teaspoon grated lemon zest**

2 **teaspoons fresh lemon juice**

1 **teaspoon olive oil**

¼ **teaspoon pepper**

1 **pound halibut fillets, rinsed and patted dry, cut into 16 1-inch cubes**

1 **large Granny Smith apple, peeled, cut into 16 1-inch cubes**

½ **medium red onion, cut into 16 1-inch squares**

**per serving**

| | |
|---|---|
| calories 135 | sodium 78 mg |
| total fat 1.5 g | carbohydrates 8 g |
| saturated fat 0.5 g | fiber 1 g |
| trans fat 0.0 g | sugars 7 g |
| polyunsaturated fat 0.5 g | protein 21 g |
| monounsaturated fat 0.5 g | |
| cholesterol 56 mg | dietary exchanges |
| | ½ fruit, 3 lean meat |

**cook's tip:** A perforated grill sheet, which is usually flat like a cookie sheet with small holes that allow the heat and smoke to pass through, keeps the fish from falling through the grill rack.

1. Soak four 10- to 12-inch wooden skewers for at least 10 minutes in cold water to keep them from charring, or use metal skewers.

2. Lightly spray the grill rack or a broiler pan with cooking spray. Preheat the grill on medium high or preheat the broiler.

3. In a small bowl, stir together the thyme, lime zest, lime juice, lemon zest, lemon juice, oil, and pepper.

4. On each skewer, thread, in order, 1 halibut cube, 1 apple cube, and 1 onion square. Repeat this pattern three times on each skewer. Brush all sides of the kebabs with all the citrus mixture. It's preferable to grill the kebabs as soon as possible because the acidity of the citrus will begin to "cook" the fish (much like the citrus juices "cook" the fish in a ceviche). If desired, though, the kebabs can marinate for 30 minutes. Cover and refrigerate them.

5. Grill the kebabs, or broil them 6 inches from the heat, for 8 minutes, or until the fish flakes easily when tested with a fork and is still moist, turning every 2 minutes to cook on all sides.

This dish is quick, easy, and full of flavor from the aromatic green onion mixture that tops it. Serve the fish with instant brown rice or soba noodles and Snow Pea and Sesame Stir-Fry (page 220) for a healthful, Asian-themed meal that's ready in minutes.

# ginger-lime halibut

**serves 4** : 3 ounces fish and 1 tablespoon sauce per serving

¼ teaspoon pepper

⅛ teaspoon salt

4 halibut fillets (about 4 ounces each), rinsed and patted dry

2 teaspoons canola or corn oil and 1 teaspoon canola or corn oil, divided use

¼ cup thinly sliced green onions

1 tablespoon minced peeled gingerroot

1 medium garlic clove, minced

2 teaspoons grated lime zest

1 tablespoon fresh lime juice

1 tablespoon soy sauce (lowest sodium available)

⅛ teaspoon toasted sesame oil

**1.** Sprinkle the pepper and salt all over the fish.

**2.** In a large nonstick skillet, heat 2 teaspoons canola oil over medium-high heat, swirling to coat the bottom. Cook the fish for 2 minutes on each side, or until the fish is browned and flakes easily when tested with a fork. Transfer to a plate. Cover to keep warm.

**3.** In the same skillet, heat the remaining 1 teaspoon canola oil, swirling to coat the bottom. Cook the green onions, gingerroot, and garlic for 2 minutes, or until the green onions begin to wilt, stirring constantly. Remove from the heat.

**4.** Stir in the remaining ingredients. Spoon the sauce over the fish.

## per serving

calories 144
total fat 5.0 g
  saturated fat 0.5 g
  trans fat 0.0 g
  polyunsaturated fat 1.5 g
  monounsaturated fat 3.0 g
cholesterol 56 mg

sodium 250 mg
carbohydrates 2 g
  fiber 1 g
  sugars 1 g
protein 21 g

dietary exchanges
3 lean meat

A bold, spicy rub made with espresso powder plus a creamy horseradish sauce equals one sensational salmon dish. Serve it with grilled sweet potatoes and asparagus for an easy outdoor meal.

# coffee-rubbed salmon with horseradish sauce

**serves 4** | 3 ounces fish and 1 heaping tablespoon sauce per serving

Cooking spray

¼ cup fat-free sour cream

1 tablespoon chopped fresh parsley

2 teaspoons cider vinegar

1 teaspoon bottled white horseradish

1 teaspoon instant espresso powder

1 teaspoon ancho powder

½ teaspoon light brown sugar

¼ teaspoon dry mustard

¼ teaspoon ground cumin

4 salmon fillets with skin (about 5 ounces each), about ¾ inch thick, rinsed and patted dry

**1.** Lightly spray the grill rack with cooking spray. Preheat the grill on medium.

**2.** In a small bowl, whisk together the sour cream, parsley, vinegar, and horseradish. Set aside.

**3.** In a separate small bowl, stir together the remaining ingredients except the fish. Sprinkle the espresso mixture over the flesh side of the fish.

**4.** Grill the fish with the skin side down, covered, for 10 to 12 minutes, or to the desired doneness. Transfer to plates. Spoon the sauce over the fish.

**cook's tip:** You don't need to turn the fish when the skin is left on for grilling. When the fish is done, simply slide a spatula between the flesh and the skin and lift the fish off the grill, leaving the skin on the rack. The skin will dry and char in the remaining heat of the grill, making it easy to remove later.

## per serving

| | |
|---|---|
| calories 170 | sodium 115 mg |
| total fat 5.5 g | carbohydrates 4 g |
| saturated fat 1.0 g | fiber 0 g |
| trans fat 0.0 g | sugars 2 g |
| polyunsaturated fat 1.0 g | protein 25 g |
| monounsaturated fat 1.5 g | |
| cholesterol 56 mg | dietary exchanges |
| | 3 lean meat |

Vibrant sweet and spicy salsa perfectly complements savory stovetop salmon. The entire dish is ready in a flash. Serve it with Confetti Rice Pilaf (page 219) and your favorite green vegetable.

# sautéed salmon with mango salsa

| serves 4 | 3 ounces fish and ½ cup salsa per serving |
| --- | --- |

**salsa**

  2  **medium mangoes, diced**

  ½  **cup diced red onion**

  ¼  **cup finely chopped fresh cilantro**

  1  **serrano chile, seeds and ribs discarded, minced (see cook's tip on page 109)**

  1  **tablespoon fresh lime juice**

  ¼  **teaspoon salt**

    **Pepper to taste**

  4  **salmon fillets (about 4 ounces each), rinsed and patted dry**

  2  **teaspoons canola or corn oil**

1. In a small bowl, stir together the salsa ingredients. Cover and refrigerate until needed (can be made up to 2 hours in advance).

2. Sprinkle the salt and pepper over both sides of the fish.

3. In a large nonstick skillet, heat the oil over medium heat, swirling to coat the bottom. Cook the fish for 3 to 4 minutes on each side, or to the desired doneness. Serve topped with the salsa.

**per serving**

calories 279
total fat 8.0 g
  saturated fat 1.5 g
  trans fat 0.0 g
  polyunsaturated fat 1.5 g
  monounsaturated fat 3.5 g
cholesterol 53 mg

sodium 235 mg
carbohydrates 28 g
  fiber 3 g
  sugars 24 g
protein 25 g

dietary exchanges
2 fruit, 3 lean meat

This stir-fry, which can be served over brown basmati rice or another whole grain, gets its smoky heat from chipotle pepper and its sweetness from a bit of honey. The orange gives the black beans and broccoli a bright, zesty flavor.

# orange-chipotle salmon stir-fry

**serves 4**  |  **1½ cups per serving**

1 tablespoon canola or corn oil

8 ounces salmon fillets, rinsed and patted dry, cut into 1-inch pieces

4 cups broccoli florets, cut into 1-inch pieces

1 medium onion, thinly sliced

2 medium garlic cloves, minced

1 cup canned no-salt-added black beans, rinsed and drained

1 teaspoon grated orange zest

1 cup fresh orange juice

1 tablespoon minced chipotle pepper canned in adobo sauce

1 tablespoon honey

½ cup tightly packed fresh cilantro, coarsely chopped

**per serving**

calories 253
total fat 6.5 g
  saturated fat 1.0 g
  trans fat 0.0 g
  polyunsaturated fat 1.5 g
  monounsaturated fat 3.0 g
cholesterol 27 mg

sodium 127 mg
carbohydrates 31 g
  fiber 6 g
  sugars 16 g
protein 19 g

dietary exchanges
1 starch, ½ fruit, 2 vegetable, 2 lean meat

1. In a large skillet or wok, heat the oil over high heat, swirling to coat the bottom. Cook the fish for 3 minutes, or until the desired doneness, stirring constantly. Transfer to a plate. Cover to keep warm. Scrape the skillet to dislodge any browned bits. Wipe the skillet with paper towels.

2. In the same skillet, still over high heat, cook the broccoli, onion, and garlic for 3 minutes, stirring constantly. Cook, covered, for 2 minutes, stirring occasionally.

3. Stir in the beans, orange juice, chipotle pepper, and honey. Cook for 30 seconds, stirring constantly.

4. Return the fish to the skillet. Stir in the cilantro and orange zest. Cook for 2 minutes, stirring constantly, or until heated through.

**cook's tip on chipotle peppers:** Look in the Mexican food section of grocery stores for canned chipotle peppers (dried jalapeños that have a smoky flavor). You probably won't use an entire can for any single recipe, but the leftovers freeze nicely. Spread the peppers with sauce in a thin layer on a medium plate covered with cooking parchment or wax paper, then freeze them, uncovered, for about 2 hours, or just until firm. Transfer the peppers to an airtight container or a resealable plastic freezer bag and freeze.

seafood

The fish in this dish is oven-poached, so it remains moist and flavorful, and can be enjoyed hot or cold. Lemon and capers, both traditional salmon companions, are blended into a creamy yogurt sauce that adds a rich, elegant touch.

# salmon with creamy lemon-caper sauce

**serves 4** | 3 ounces fish and 2 tablespoons sauce per serving

**sauce**

½ cup fat-free plain Greek yogurt

1 tablespoon chopped capers, drained

1½ teaspoons grated lemon zest

1½ teaspoons fresh lemon juice

1½ teaspoons minced shallots

½ teaspoon minced parsley

⅛ teaspoon pepper (freshly ground preferred)

———

1 cup sauvignon blanc (regular or nonalcoholic) or fat-free, low-sodium vegetable broth

1 cup water

2 medium carrots, thinly sliced crosswise

1 medium onion, sliced

1 large rib of celery, thinly sliced crosswise

*(continued)*

1. In a small bowl, whisk together the sauce ingredients. Cover and refrigerate for 1 to 2 hours.

2. Preheat the oven to 400°F.

3. Meanwhile, in a medium saucepan, stir together the remaining ingredients except the fish. Bring to a boil over high heat. Remove from the heat.

4. Place the fish in an 11 × 7 × 2-inch glass baking dish, spacing the fillets about 2 inches apart. Pour the wine mixture over the fish.

**5.** Bake, tightly covered with aluminum foil, for 10 to 12 minutes, or to the desired doneness. Using the tines of a fork, carefully remove the foil away from you (to prevent steam burns). Using a slotted spatula, transfer the fish to plates.

**6.** Spoon the sauce over the fish.

cook's tip: Halibut or tuna may be substituted for the salmon with equally delicious results.

1 teaspoon peppercorns

1 teaspoon coriander seeds (optional)

2 sprigs of fresh thyme or ½ teaspoon dried thyme, crumbled

1 large garlic clove, thinly sliced

1 medium dried bay leaf (optional)

4 salmon fillets (about 4 ounces each), rinsed and patted dry

........................................................

### per serving

| | |
|---|---|
| calories 165 | sodium 161 mg |
| total fat 5.0 g | carbohydrates 2 g |
|    saturated fat 1.0 g |    fiber 0 g |
|    trans fat 0.0 g |    sugars 1 g |
|    polyunsaturated fat 1.0 g | protein 26 g |
|    monounsaturated fat 1.5 g | dietary exchanges |
| cholesterol 53 mg | 3½ lean meat |

This soup is full of salmon with its good-for-you omega-3s. Turkey bacon, fresh dillweed, and a full serving of corn enliven the flavor, while a few drops of hot-pepper sauce add a hint of heat. Round out the meal with a simple dark green leafy salad. *(See photo insert.)*

# salmon-corn chowder

| serves 4 | 1¼ cups per serving |
| --- | --- |

3 slices turkey bacon, chopped

2 medium onions, chopped

1 teaspoon olive oil

1 large garlic clove, minced

2 cups frozen whole-kernel corn

2 cups water

1 5-ounce vacuum-sealed pouch boneless, skinless pink salmon, flaked

¼ teaspoon pepper

½ cup fat-free milk

4 drops red hot-pepper sauce

¼ cup chopped fresh dillweed

**per serving**

calories 190
**total fat 4.5 g**
  saturated fat 1.5 g
  trans fat 0.0 g
  polyunsaturated fat 1.0 g
  monounsaturated fat 1.5 g
**cholesterol 23 mg**

sodium 343 mg
**carbohydrates 27 g**
  fiber 4 g
  sugars 9 g
**protein 13 g**

**dietary exchanges**
1½ starch,
1 vegetable, 1½ lean meat

1. In a large saucepan, cook the bacon over medium heat for 5 minutes, or until lightly browned, stirring occasionally.

2. Stir in the onions and oil. Cook for 5 minutes, or until the onions are soft, stirring occasionally.

3. Stir in the garlic. Cook for 30 seconds, or until fragrant.

4. Stir in the corn, water, salmon, and pepper. Increase the heat to medium high and bring to a boil. Reduce the heat and simmer for 10 minutes, or until the corn is tender, stirring occasionally.

5. Stir in the milk and hot-pepper sauce. Increase the heat to medium. Cook for 1 to 2 minutes, or just until hot, stirring occasionally. Don't let the soup boil or the milk will curdle. Stir in the dillweed.

A little leftover salmon stretches a long way in this satisfying dish. Try it with Honey-Orange Glazed Carrots (page 208) or a cup of Fresh Garden Soup (page 36).

# creamed spinach with salmon

**serves 4** | 1¼ cups per serving

1 cup uncooked instant brown rice

8 cups water

10 ounces spinach, stems discarded

2 tablespoons light tub margarine

2 tablespoons all-purpose flour

2 cups fat-free milk

¼ teaspoon pepper

⅛ teaspoon ground nutmeg

1 cup cooked fresh salmon, flaked (about 10 ounces before cooking)

## per serving

calories 270
total fat 6.5 g
  saturated fat 0.5 g
  trans fat 0.0 g
  polyunsaturated fat 1.5 g
  monounsaturated fat 2.5 g
cholesterol 36 mg

sodium 212 mg
carbohydrates 29 g
  fiber 3 g
  sugars 6 g
protein 23 g

dietary exchanges
1½ starch, ½ fat-free milk, 2 lean meat

1. Prepare the rice using the package directions, omitting the salt and margarine. Set aside.

2. In a large saucepan, bring the water to a boil over high heat. Reduce the heat to medium. Cook the spinach for 3 minutes, or until tender. Don't overcook. Drain well in a colander. Let cool slightly. Coarsely chop. Set aside.

3. Wipe the pan with paper towels. Reduce the heat to medium low. Put the margarine in the pan, swirling to melt it. Remove from the heat.

4. Whisk in the flour. Return to the heat. Cook for 30 seconds. Whisk in the milk, pepper, and nutmeg. Increase the heat to medium. Cook for 4 to 5 minutes, or until the mixture has thickened, whisking occasionally. Stir in the salmon and spinach. Cook for 2 minutes, or until the mixture is heated through. Serve over the rice.

**cook's tip on salmon:** If you don't have any leftover salmon, you can cook some quickly. In a large nonstick skillet, heat 1 teaspoon canola or corn oil over medium heat, swirling to coat the bottom. Cook the fish for 3 to 4 minutes on each side, or to the desired doneness.

seafood

Every bite of this seafood dish treats you to a little taste of Thailand—and much less sodium than is typically found in Thai entrées. Serve this with Marinated Asparagus (page 201) that you've made ahead of time or with Baby Bok Choy with Ginger and Garlic (page 202), which comes together very quickly.

# thai salmon patties with sweet cucumber relish

**serves 4** : 2 patties and 2 tablespoons relish per serving

## patties

- 1 5-ounce vacuum-sealed pouch boneless, skinless pink salmon, flaked
- 1/2 cup frozen brown rice, thawed
- 1/2 medium red bell pepper, finely chopped
- 4 medium green onions, finely chopped
- 2 large egg whites
- 1/3 cup chopped fresh cilantro
- 2 tablespoons white whole-wheat flour
- 2 tablespoons light mayonnaise
- 2 tablespoons fat-free milk
- 1 tablespoon grated peeled gingerroot
- 1/4 teaspoon salt
- 1 teaspoon canola or corn oil and 1 teaspoon canola or corn oil, divided use

*(continued)*

1. In a medium bowl, stir together the patty ingredients except the oil.

2. In a large nonstick skillet, heat 1 teaspoon oil over medium heat, swirling to coat the bottom. Spoon four 1/4-cup mounds of the salmon mixture into the skillet. Using the back of a fork or spoon, slightly flatten each mound to form a patty. Cook for 2 to 3 minutes on each side, or until golden

brown and cooked through, turning the patties gently so they don't break (a small spatula works well). Transfer to a large plate. Cover to keep warm. Repeat with the remaining 1 teaspoon oil and salmon mixture.

3. Meanwhile, in a small bowl, stir together the relish ingredients. Serve with the patties.

## relish

½ medium cucumber, peeled and finely chopped

2 tablespoons finely chopped green onions

2 tablespoons chopped fresh cilantro

1 tablespoon fresh lemon juice

1 teaspoon sugar

1 teaspoon grated peeled gingerroot

..................................................

### per serving

| | |
|---|---|
| calories 144 | sodium 355 mg |
| total fat 5.5 g | carbohydrates 13 g |
|   saturated fat 1.0 g |   fiber 2 g |
|   trans fat 0.0 g |   sugars 4 g |
|   polyunsaturated fat 2.5 g | protein 10 g |
|   monounsaturated fat 2.0 g | dietary exchanges |
| cholesterol 15 mg | ½ starch, 1 vegetable, 1 lean meat, ½ fat |

The double dose of citrus and basil in the marinade and the fresh bread-crumb coating brightens the mild flavor of tilapia. While the fish is marinating, prepare Broccoli with Caramelized Walnuts (page 203) or Green Bean, Tomato, and Walnut Salad (page 50).

# lime-basil tilapia

**serves 4**     3 ounces fish per serving

**fish**

1 teaspoon grated lime zest

1 tablespoon fresh lime juice

1 teaspoon dried basil, crumbled

¼ teaspoon salt

¼ teaspoon pepper

4 tilapia fillets (about 4 ounces each), rinsed and patted dry

Cooking spray

**coating**

2 slices whole-grain bread (lowest sodium available), torn into 2-inch pieces

¼ cup loosely packed fresh basil or 1 teaspoon dried basil, crumbled

¼ cup fresh parsley

2 teaspoons olive oil

1 teaspoon grated lime zest

1. In a shallow glass dish, whisk together 1 teaspoon lime zest, the lime juice, basil, salt, and pepper. Add the fish, turning to coat. Cover and refrigerate for up to 30 minutes, turning occasionally.

2. Meanwhile, preheat the oven to 400°F. Lightly spray a rimmed baking sheet with cooking spray.

3. In a food processor, process the coating ingredients until the mixture has the texture of soft, fine bread crumbs.

4. Drain the fish, discarding the marinade. Transfer the bread-crumb mixture to a shallow dish.

5. Dip the fish in the bread-crumb mixture, turning to coat. Transfer to the baking sheet. Lightly spray the top of the fish with cooking spray.

6. Bake for 10 to 12 minutes, or until the fish flakes easily when tested with a fork.

**per serving**

| | |
|---|---|
| calories 165 | sodium 261 mg |
| total fat 5.0 g | carbohydrates 6 g |
|   saturated fat 1.0 g |   fiber 1 g |
|   trans fat 0.0 g |   sugars 1 g |
|   polyunsaturated fat 1.0 g | protein 25 g |
|   monounsaturated fat 2.5 g | dietary exchanges |
| cholesterol 57 mg | ½ starch, 3 lean meat |

Spicy Cajun seasoning and high-heat cooking "blacken" mild tilapia fillets; they are complemented by a crunchy, cooling slaw in these easy-to-make and satisfying sandwiches. The slaw is also a tasty side dish, especially when served with a spicy main, such as Grilled Sweet Chile Pork Tenderloin (page 149).

# blackened tilapia sandwiches with broccoli slaw

| serves 4 | 1 sandwich per serving |

½ cup fat-free plain Greek yogurt

2 teaspoons fresh lime juice

½ teaspoon sugar

Dash of cayenne

2 cups broccoli slaw mix

2 tablespoons chopped fresh cilantro

1 teaspoon salt-free Creole or Cajun seasoning blend

4 tilapia fillets (about 4 ounces each), rinsed and patted dry

2 teaspoons olive oil

4 whole-grain round sandwich thins (lowest sodium available), toasted

**per serving**

calories 257
total fat 5.0 g
    saturated fat 1.0 g
    trans fat 0.0 g
    polyunsaturated fat 1.0 g
    monounsaturated fat 2.5 g
cholesterol 57 mg

sodium 250 mg
carbohydrates 26 g
    fiber 6 g
    sugars 5 g
protein 30 g

dietary exchanges
1½ starch, 3 lean meat

1. In a medium bowl, stir together the yogurt, lime juice, sugar, and cayenne. Stir in the broccoli slaw and cilantro, tossing to coat. Set aside. Stir occasionally.

2. Sprinkle the seasoning blend all over the fish. Using your fingertips, gently press the seasoning so it adheres to the fish.

3. In a large nonstick skillet, heat the oil over medium-high heat, swirling to coat the bottom. Cook the fish for 2 to 3 minutes on each side, or until it flakes easily when tested with a fork.

4. Place the fish on the bottoms of the sandwich thins. Spoon the slaw over the fish. Put the tops of the sandwich thins on the sandwiches. Serve immediately.

cook's tip: To make your own salt-free Creole or Cajun seasoning blend, stir together ½ teaspoon each of chili powder, ground cumin, onion powder, garlic powder, paprika, and pepper, and, if you wish, ⅛ teaspoon of cayenne. This makes just over 1 tablespoon of the blend; double or triple the amounts if you like, and keep the extra in a container with a shaker top to use in other seafood, poultry, meat, and vegetable dishes.

Trout fillets are topped with colorful veggies, then sealed in aluminum foil to lock in the natural juices and flavors while they bake. The hot packets are then served with a quick and creamy dipping sauce. This dish cooks in less than 15 minutes and is a breeze to clean up—a perfect recipe for a busy night.

# trout en papillote with dill-dijon dipping sauce

| serves 4 | 3 ounces fish, ½ cup vegetables, and 2 tablespoons sauce per serving |
|---|---|

4 **trout or tilapia fillets (about 4 ounces each), rinsed and patted dry**

¼ **teaspoon pepper (coarsely ground preferred)**

4 **ounces bite-size fresh or frozen broccoli florets, thawed if frozen**

½ **cup matchstick-size carrot strips**

1 **medium green onion, finely chopped**

¼ **teaspoon salt**

**sauce**

¼ **cup fat-free sour cream**

3 **to 4 tablespoons fat-free milk**

1½ **tablespoons light mayonnaise**

2 **teaspoons Dijon mustard (lowest sodium available)**

¾ **teaspoon dried dillweed, crumbled**

⅛ **teaspoon salt**

1. Preheat the oven to 425°F.

2. Cut eight 12-inch-square pieces of aluminum foil. Place the fish in the center of 4 of the foil squares. Sprinkle the pepper over the fish. Put the broccoli, carrot, and green onion on the fish. Sprinkle ¼ teaspoon salt over all. Place 1 of the remaining foil squares over the fish. Fold the edges of both foil pieces together several times to seal the packets securely. Repeat the process to make the remaining packets. Transfer to a large baking sheet.

3. Bake the packets for 12 minutes. Using the tines of a fork, carefully open a packet away from you (to prevent steam burns). If the fish flakes easily when tested with a fork, carefully open the remaining packets and serve. If the fish isn't cooked enough, reclose the open packet and continue baking all the packets for 1 to 2 minutes.

4. Meanwhile, in a small bowl, whisk together the sauce ingredients. Serve the fish and vegetables in the packets with the sauce on the side for dipping.

**per serving**

| | |
|---|---|
| calories 190 | sodium 393 mg |
| total fat 5.5 g | carbohydrates 8 g |
|   saturated fat 1.0 g |   fiber 2 g |
|   trans fat 0.0 g |   sugars 3 g |
|   polyunsaturated fat 2.5 g | protein 26 g |
|   monounsaturated fat 1.5 g | dietary exchanges |
| cholesterol 72 mg | 1 vegetable, 3 lean meat |

Cooking thin white fish fillets in very hot oil gives them a slight crispness around the edges. A simple vinegar reduction and a sprinkling of fresh parsley and chives contribute a sprightly tang to this fast-and-easy entrée.

# trout with herb vinaigrette

**serves 4** | 3 ounces fish per serving

4 trout or other thin mild white fish fillets (about 4 ounces each), rinsed and patted dry

¼ teaspoon pepper

⅛ teaspoon salt

1 tablespoon olive oil

¼ cup white balsamic vinegar or sherry vinegar

2 tablespoons sliced almonds, dry-roasted

1 tablespoon chopped fresh parsley

1 tablespoon chopped fresh chives

**per serving**

calories 188
**total fat 8.5 g**
  saturated fat 1.5 g
  trans fat 0.0 g
  polyunsaturated fat 2.0 g
  monounsaturated fat 4.5 g
cholesterol 67 mg

sodium 114 mg
carbohydrates 3 g
  fiber 0 g
  sugars 2 g
**protein 24 g**

dietary exchanges
3 lean meat

1. Sprinkle both sides of the fish with the pepper and salt.

2. In a large nonstick skillet, heat the oil over medium-high heat, swirling to coat the bottom. Cook the fish for 2 to 3 minutes on each side, or until it flakes easily when tested with a fork. Transfer to a serving platter. Cover to keep warm.

3. In the same skillet, still over medium-high heat, carefully pour in the vinegar (it may splatter a bit because the skillet is hot). Bring to a boil and boil for 1 to 2 minutes, or until reduced by half (to about 2 tablespoons). Spoon over the fish. Sprinkle the fish with the almonds, parsley, and chives.

**cook's tip on dry-roasting nuts on the stovetop:** Arrange the nuts in a single layer in a small skillet. Cook them over medium heat for 3 to 4 minutes, or until they're just fragrant, stirring frequently. Watch carefully so they don't burn. Remove them from the skillet immediately to stop the cooking process.

In this easy and elegant dish, mild trout gets an assertive coating of spices, then is quickly cooked with sweet shallots and tart capers. A squeeze of bright lemon completes the dish. Serve with whole-grain pasta or brown rice and your favorite green vegetable.

# trout piccata

**serves 4** | 3 ounces fish per serving

1 teaspoon paprika

1 teaspoon garlic powder

1 teaspoon dried dillweed, crumbled

¼ teaspoon pepper

4 trout fillets with skin (about 5 ounces each), rinsed and patted dry

2 teaspoons olive oil

2 medium shallots, thinly sliced

2 tablespoons capers, drained and chopped if large

1 medium lemon, cut into 4 wedges

1. In a small bowl, stir together the paprika, garlic powder, dillweed, and pepper. Sprinkle over the flesh side of the fish. Using your fingertips, gently press the mixture so it adheres to the fish.

2. In a large skillet, heat the oil over medium heat, swirling to coat the bottom. Cook the fish with the seasoned side down for 3 minutes, or until the bottom is golden brown. Turn over. Sprinkle the shallots and capers around the fish. Cook for 2 minutes, or until the fish flakes easily when tested with a fork, stirring the shallots and capers occasionally.

3. Transfer the fish to plates with the skin side down. Spoon the shallots and capers over the fish. Serve with the lemon wedges.

**per serving**

calories 169
total fat 6.5 g
   saturated fat 1.0 g
   trans fat 0.0 g
   polyunsaturated fat 1.5 g
   monounsaturated fat 3.0 g
cholesterol 67 mg

sodium 165 mg
carbohydrates 3 g
   fiber 1 g
   sugars 1 g
protein 24 g

dietary exchanges
3 lean meat

A marinade made with citrus juice and zest, smoky marsala, and sweet honey complements the mild flavor of fresh tuna. Serve with brown rice and grilled vegetables, or arrange slices of the cooked fish on crisp salad greens.

# grilled orange tuna steaks

| serves 4 | 3 ounces fish per serving |
| --- | --- |

## marinade

- 2 tablespoons grated orange zest
- ¼ cup fresh orange juice
- 3 tablespoons honey
- 2 tablespoons marsala, white wine (regular or nonalcoholic), or water
- 1 tablespoon teriyaki or soy sauce (lowest sodium available)
- 1 tablespoon olive oil
- 2 large garlic cloves, sliced
- ½ teaspoon spicy brown mustard (lowest sodium available)
- ½ teaspoon pepper (freshly ground preferred)

- 4 tuna steaks (about 4 ounces each), about 1 inch thick, rinsed and patted dry
- Cooking spray
- 1 teaspoon olive oil

1. In a shallow glass dish, whisk together the marinade ingredients. Add the fish, turning to coat. Cover and refrigerate for 45 minutes to 1 hour, turning occasionally.

2. Lightly spray the grill rack with cooking spray. Preheat the grill on high.

3. Meanwhile, drain the fish, discarding the marinade. Lightly brush the remaining 1 teaspoon oil all over the fish.

4. Grill the fish for 3 to 4 minutes on each side, or to the desired doneness.

cook's tip: To prevent fish from sticking to the grill, make sure the grill rack is very clean. Be patient and allow the fish to cook before turning it over. Keep the lid down as much as possible and turn the fish only once.

## per serving

calories 137
total fat 1.5 g
  saturated fat 0.5 g
  trans fat 0.0 g
  polyunsaturated fat 0.5 g
  monounsaturated fat 1.0 g
cholesterol 44 mg

sodium 161 mg
carbohydrates 1 g
  fiber 0 g
  sugars 1 g
protein 28 g

dietary exchanges
3 lean meat

Grilling fish on a cedar plank eliminates the need to turn it during cooking, and the wood imparts a sweet smokiness to the fish. A simple marinade made with minced fresh gingerroot and lime juice keeps the fish moist and at the peak of its flavor.

# plank-grilled tuna steaks

**serves 4** | 3 ounces fish per serving

2 tablespoons plain rice vinegar

1 tablespoon minced peeled gingerroot

1 tablespoon minced green onions

1 tablespoon chopped fresh cilantro

1 tablespoon fresh lime juice

2 teaspoons soy sauce (lowest sodium available)

1 teaspoon toasted sesame oil

1 medium garlic clove, minced

⅛ teaspoon crushed red pepper flakes (optional)

4 tuna steaks (about 4 ounces each), about 1 inch thick, rinsed and patted dry

**per serving**

calories 130
total fat 1.0 g
  saturated fat 0.5 g
  trans fat 0.0 g
  polyunsaturated fat 0.5 g
  monounsaturated fat 0.5 g
cholesterol 44 mg

sodium 116 mg
carbohydrates 0 g
  fiber 0 g
  sugars 0 g
protein 28 g

dietary exchanges
3 lean meat

1. Soak an untreated 14 × 6-inch cedar plank in water for at least 30 minutes.

2. Meanwhile, in a shallow glass dish, whisk together all the ingredients except the fish. Add the fish, turning to coat. Cover and refrigerate for 30 minutes, turning once halfway through.

3. Preheat the grill on medium high. Remove the cedar plank from the water. Pat dry with paper towels. Transfer to the grill rack. Heat the plank, covered, for 3 minutes.

4. Drain the fish, discarding the marinade. Turn the plank over. Place the fish on the plank.

5. Grill, covered, for 12 to 15 minutes, or until the fish is the desired doneness.

**cook's tip:** Cedar planks for grilling can be found with grilling supplies in supermarkets and hardware stores.

Brush a honey-based glaze on these tuna steaks, and they'll just start to caramelize as the fish finishes cooking, creating a shiny and richly hued presentation. Serve with your favorite green vegetable and a whole grain, such as Quinoa-Corn Toss (page 215) or Confetti Rice Pilaf (page 219).

# honey-mustard tuna steaks

**serves 4** 3 ounces fish and scant 1 tablespoon sauce per serving

3 tablespoons honey

2 tablespoons Dijon mustard (lowest sodium available)

1 tablespoon chopped fresh thyme

Dash of cayenne

4 tuna steaks (about 4 ounces each), about 1 inch thick, rinsed and patted dry

½ cup fat-free, low-sodium chicken broth

1 tablespoon white wine vinegar

1 tablespoon olive oil

1. In a small bowl, whisk together the honey, mustard, thyme, and cayenne. Brush 2 tablespoons of the mixture over both sides of the fish. Whisk the broth and vinegar into the remaining honey mixture. Set aside.

2. In a large nonstick skillet, heat the oil over medium-high heat, swirling to coat the bottom. Cook the fish for 4 to 5 minutes on each side, or until the desired doneness. Transfer to a serving platter. Cover to keep warm.

3. Pour the honey mixture into the skillet. Bring to a boil, still over medium-high heat. Boil for 4 to 5 minutes, or until the sauce is thickened and reduced by three-fourths (to about ⅓ cup), stirring occasionally. Spoon the sauce over the fish.

**per serving**

calories 215
total fat 4.5 g
  saturated fat 0.5 g
  trans fat 0.0 g
  polyunsaturated fat 0.5 g
  monounsaturated fat 2.5 g
cholesterol 44 mg

sodium 213 mg
carbohydrates 15 g
  fiber 0 g
  sugars 14 g
protein 29 g

dietary exchanges
1 other carbohydrate,
3 lean meat

seafood

When it's hot outside and you don't want to use your stove or oven, prepare this Italian tuna salad that's packed with protein.

# tuscan tuna salad

**serves 4** | **1 cup per serving**

## dressing

- ⅓ **cup fat-free sour cream**
- 3 **tablespoons plain rice vinegar**
- 1 **tablespoon sugar**
- 1 **teaspoon olive oil (extra virgin preferred)**
- ⅛ **teaspoon salt**

## salad

- 1 **15.5-ounce can no-salt-added cannellini beans, rinsed and drained**
- 1 **4.5-ounce can very low sodium albacore tuna, packed in water, drained and flaked**
- 1 **cup grape tomatoes, halved**
- 1 **medium rib of celery, chopped**
- ½ **medium red or yellow bell pepper, chopped**
- ½ **cup chopped red onion**
- 3 **tablespoons chopped green onions (green part only) or chives**
- 1½ **teaspoons dried oregano, crumbled**
- ¼ **teaspoon pepper**

1. In a small bowl, whisk together the dressing ingredients.

2. In a medium bowl, stir together the salad ingredients. Gently stir in the dressing. Refrigerate for 15 minutes so the flavors blend.

**Go Red brunch tip:** To make an attractive presentation, spoon this salad onto red leaf lettuce in the center of a serving platter. Arrange whole-wheat crackers, whole-grain crispbreads, or red bell pepper chunks around the edge of the platter.

### per serving

calories 190
total fat 3.0 g
   saturated fat 0.0 g
   trans fat 0.0 g
   polyunsaturated fat 0.5 g
   monounsaturated fat 1.0 g
cholesterol 17 mg

sodium 159 mg
carbohydrates 28 g
   fiber 6 g
   sugars 9 g
protein 16 g

dietary exchanges
1½ starch, 1 vege-
table, 1½ lean meat

This update of a classic one-dish meal layers tuna, bell pepper, and mushrooms over elbow macaroni and fresh broccoli florets bathed in a creamy, cheesy sauce.

# tuna and macaroni skillet casserole

**serves 4** | 1¼ cups per serving

- 4 ounces dried whole-grain medium elbow macaroni
- 1 cup small broccoli florets
- ¼ cup fat-free milk and 1 cup fat-free milk, divided use
- 2 tablespoons all-purpose flour
- ⅛ teaspoon cayenne
- 1 teaspoon canola or corn oil
- 4 ounces button mushrooms, sliced
- ½ medium red bell pepper, chopped
- ¾ cup low-fat shredded sharp Cheddar cheese
- ¼ teaspoon salt
- 1 4.5-ounce can very low sodium albacore tuna, packed in water, drained and flaked
- 2 tablespoons chopped fresh parsley

### per serving

calories 241
total fat 4.5 g
  saturated fat 1.0 g
  trans fat 0.0 g
  polyunsaturated fat 0.5 g
  monounsaturated fat 1.5 g
cholesterol 20 mg

sodium 337 mg
carbohydrates 31 g
  fiber 4 g
  sugars 7 g
protein 22 g

dietary exchanges
2 starch, 2½ lean meat

1. Prepare the pasta using the package directions, omitting the salt. During the last 3 minutes of cooking time, stir in the broccoli. Drain well in a colander. Set aside.

2. In a small bowl, whisk together ¼ cup milk, the flour, and cayenne.

3. Meanwhile, in a large nonstick skillet, heat the oil over medium-high heat, swirling to coat the bottom. Cook the mushrooms and bell pepper for 4 minutes, or until soft, stirring frequently. Transfer to a plate. Set aside.

4. Reduce the heat to medium. Pour the remaining 1 cup milk into the skillet. Cook for 30 seconds, or until heated through, stirring frequently.

5. Whisk the flour mixture into the milk in the skillet. Cook for 3 minutes, or until thickened, whisking frequently. Remove from the heat.

6. Stir the pasta mixture, Cheddar, and salt into the milk mixture. Sprinkle the tuna on top, then sprinkle with the mushroom mixture and parsley. Return to the heat. Cook, covered, still over medium heat, for 3 to 4 minutes, or until heated through (no stirring needed).

Fresh mussels steamed in a well-seasoned, tomato-based broth are an Italian favorite. Serve these with a green salad and some crusty whole-grain bread to soak up every tasty drop.

# italian-style mussels

| serves 4 | 6 mussels and ½ cup broth per serving |
|---|---|

1 teaspoon olive oil

6 medium garlic cloves, thinly sliced

1 14.5-ounce can no-salt-added diced tomatoes, undrained

½ cup dry white wine (regular or nonalcoholic) or fat-free, low-sodium chicken broth

½ cup fat-free, low-sodium chicken broth

1 teaspoon dried oregano, crumbled

¼ teaspoon pepper (freshly ground preferred)

⅛ teaspoon salt

24 fresh debearded and rinsed medium mussels (1½ to 2 pounds of mussels in shells)

1. In a large saucepan, heat the oil over medium-low heat, swirling to coat the bottom. Cook the garlic for 1 minute, or until light golden brown, stirring occasionally and watching carefully so the garlic doesn't burn.

2. Stir in the tomatoes with liquid, wine, broth, oregano, pepper, and salt. Increase the heat to medium-high and bring to a simmer. Reduce the heat and simmer, covered, for 10 minutes, stirring occasionally.

3. Increase the heat to medium. Add the mussels. Cook, covered, for 3 to 5 minutes, or until the mussels have opened. Discard any unopened mussels.

4. Spoon the mussels into shallow bowls. Spoon the tomato mixture around the mussels.

**per serving**

calories 136
total fat 3.5 g
  saturated fat 0.5 g
  trans fat 0.0 g
  polyunsaturated fat 0.5 g
  monounsaturated fat 1.5 g
cholesterol 27 mg

sodium 368 mg
carbohydrates 10 g
  fiber 1 g
  sugars 3 g
protein 13 g

dietary exchanges
1 vegetable, 2 lean meat

**cook's tip on mussels:** Purchase mussels within a day of cooking them. Take them out of any store packaging and refrigerate them in a bowl covered with a damp towel. When you're ready to cook them, rinse them in a colander with cold water. If any uncooked mussels are open, tap them on the counter. Discard any that don't close tightly.

This seafood main dish has five-star flavor. It's elegant, stylish, and very quick to prepare. What's not to love? Serve it with steamed sugar snap peas or Baby Bok Choy with Ginger and Garlic (page 202).

# miso-marinated scallops on soba noodles

**serves 4** | 2 ounces scallops and ½ cup noodles per serving

2 teaspoons white miso paste (shiro miso)

2 teaspoons mirin or dry sherry

2 teaspoons plain rice vinegar

1 teaspoon grated peeled gingerroot

1 medium garlic clove, minced

12 ounces sea scallops, rinsed and patted dry

4 ounces dried soba noodles

½ cup diagonally sliced green onions

1 teaspoon toasted sesame oil

1 teaspoon canola or corn oil

**per serving**

calories 185
total fat 3.0 g
  saturated fat 0.5 g
  trans fat 0.0 g
  polyunsaturated fat 1.0 g
  monounsaturated fat 1.5 g
cholesterol 20 mg

sodium 482 mg
carbohydrates 26 g
  fiber 2 g
  sugars 2 g
protein 15 g

dietary exchanges
2 starch, 2 lean meat

1. In a shallow glass dish, whisk together the miso, mirin, vinegar, gingerroot, and garlic. Add the scallops, turning to coat. Cover and refrigerate for up to 30 minutes, turning occasionally.

2. Prepare the noodles using the package directions, omitting the salt. Drain well in a colander. Transfer to a medium bowl. Stir in the green onions and sesame oil. Cover to keep warm.

3. In a large skillet, heat the canola oil over medium-high heat, swirling to coat the bottom. Cook the scallops for 6 to 8 minutes, or until golden brown on both sides and opaque in the center, turning once halfway through. Don't overcook or the scallops will be dry and rubbery.

4. Transfer the noodle mixture to a serving platter. Arrange the scallops on the noodle mixture.

**cook's tip on soba noodles:** Soba noodles are made from buckwheat flour, which comes from the buckwheat plant and is naturally gluten-free. Some brands add wheat, so check the labels if you are sensitive to gluten.

With its vibrant hues, this salad looks as sunny and fresh as it tastes.

# lemony shrimp and feta salad

| serves 4 | 2 ounces shrimp, heaping 2 cups salad, and 2 tablespoons dressing per serving |

3 cups water

½ medium lemon, thinly sliced

1 medium garlic clove, halved, and 1 medium garlic clove, minced, divided use

4 whole peppercorns

10 ounces raw medium shrimp, peeled, rinsed, and patted dry

½ teaspoon cornstarch

⅓ cup fat-free, low-sodium chicken broth

2 tablespoons fresh lemon juice

1 tablespoon chopped fresh oregano

1 tablespoon white wine vinegar

4 ounces romaine or mixed salad greens, torn into bite-size pieces

3 ounces spinach, torn into bite-size pieces

½ medium cucumber, thinly sliced

½ medium red bell pepper, thinly sliced

1 medium tomato, cut into 12 wedges

¼ small red onion, thinly sliced

2 tablespoons crumbled fat-free feta cheese

1. In a medium saucepan over medium heat, bring the water, lemon slices, halved garlic, and peppercorns just to a simmer, covered. Add the shrimp. Cook, uncovered, for 2 to 3 minutes, or just until the shrimp are pink on the outside. Drain well in a colander, discarding the lemon, garlic, and peppercorns. Arrange the shrimp in a single layer on a large plate. Refrigerate for 10 to 15 minutes, or until cooled.

2. Meanwhile, put the cornstarch in a small saucepan. Add the broth, whisking to dissolve. Cook over medium-high heat for 2 minutes, or until boiling and thickened, whisking constantly. Pour into a small bowl. Let cool at room temperature for 5 to 10 minutes.

3. Whisk the lemon juice, oregano, vinegar, and minced garlic into the broth mixture. Set aside.

4. Arrange the remaining ingredients except the feta cheese on plates. Top each salad with the shrimp. Drizzle with the dressing. Sprinkle with the feta cheese.

**per serving**

calories 87
total fat 1.0 g
    saturated fat 0.0 g
    trans fat 0.0 g
    polyunsaturated fat 0.0 g
    monounsaturated fat 0.0 g
cholesterol 89 mg

sodium 261 mg
carbohydrates 7 g
    fiber 2 g
    sugars 3 g
protein 13 g

dietary exchanges
1 vegetable, 2 lean meat

This quintessential Southern dish cooks up in minutes, making it an easy dinner for a busy night. A zesty blend of chili powder and spices flavors both the juicy shrimp and the creamy grits, which are also spiked with the heat of jalapeño. (*See photo insert.*)

# spicy shrimp and grits

| serves 4 | 2 ounces shrimp and ½ cup grits per serving |
|---|---|

¼ teaspoon chili powder

¼ teaspoon ground cumin

¼ teaspoon onion powder

¼ teaspoon garlic powder

¼ teaspoon pepper

⅛ teaspoon cayenne

10 ounces raw medium shrimp, peeled, rinsed, and patted dry

2 teaspoons canola or corn oil

4 cups fat-free, low-sodium chicken broth

2 tablespoons diced red bell pepper

1 medium fresh jalapeño, seeds and ribs discarded, diced (see cook's tip on page 109)

1 cup uncooked quick-cooking grits

¼ cup shredded or grated Parmesan cheese

2 tablespoons chopped fresh parsley

¼ teaspoon paprika (optional)

1. In a small bowl, stir together the chili powder, cumin, onion powder, garlic powder, pepper, and cayenne.

2. Put the shrimp in a medium bowl. Drizzle the oil over the shrimp, stirring gently to coat. Sprinkle 1⅛ teaspoons of the chili powder mixture over the shrimp. Stir gently to combine. Set aside.

3. In a medium saucepan, stir together the broth, bell pepper, jalapeño, and the remaining ¼ teaspoon chili powder mixture. Bring to a simmer over medium-high heat, stirring occasionally. Stir in the grits. Cook for 1 to 2 minutes, or until thickened, stirring constantly. Stir in the Parmesan. Remove from the heat.

4. Meanwhile, heat a large nonstick skillet over medium-high heat. Arrange the shrimp in a single layer in the skillet. Cook for 2 to 3 minutes, or until no longer pink and beginning to brown. Turn over. Cook for 2 minutes, or until the shrimp are beginning to brown on the outside and are opaque in the center.

5. Spoon the grits into shallow bowls. Top with the shrimp. Sprinkle with the parsley and paprika.

**per serving**

| | |
|---|---|
| calories 252 | sodium 309 mg |
| total fat 5.0 g | carbohydrates 33 g |
| saturated fat 1.0 g | fiber 1 g |
| trans fat 0.0 g | sugars 1 g |
| polyunsaturated fat 1.0 g | protein 17 g |
| monounsaturated fat 2.0 g | |
| cholesterol 93 mg | dietary exchanges |
| | 2 starch, 2 lean meat |

seafood

87

This one-dish meal lets every ingredient shine, from the tender shrimp to the juicy tomatoes and delicate, slightly sweet fennel and peas. Red pepper flakes add a bit of heat, while a last-minute squeeze of lemon provides just the right touch of tartness.

# shrimp and fennel linguine

**serves 4** | 1¾ cups per serving

1 tablespoon olive oil

1 medium fennel bulb, cut into thin wedges

1 medium shallot, thinly sliced

2 medium garlic cloves, minced

3 medium tomatoes, seeded and chopped

1 teaspoon sugar

¼ teaspoon crushed red pepper flakes

⅛ teaspoon salt

8 ounces dried whole-grain linguine

12 ounces raw medium shrimp, peeled, rinsed, and patted dry

1½ cups frozen green peas

¼ cup shredded or grated Parmesan cheese

1 medium lemon, cut into 4 wedges

1. In a large nonstick skillet, heat the oil over medium heat, swirling to coat the bottom. Cook the fennel, shallot, and garlic for 5 to 6 minutes, or until the fennel is tender-crisp, stirring occasionally. Stir in the tomatoes, sugar, red pepper flakes, and salt. Cook for 4 to 5 minutes, or until the tomatoes are tender, stirring occasionally. Transfer to a serving bowl.

2. Meanwhile, prepare the pasta using the package directions, omitting the salt. About 1 minute before the pasta is done, stir in the shrimp and peas. Cook for 2 to 3 minutes, or until the shrimp are pink on the outside. Drain well in a colander.

3. Stir the pasta mixture into the fennel mixture. Sprinkle with the Parmesan. Serve with the lemon wedges.

**cook's tip on fennel:** Fennel has a mild, aniselike flavor that mellows during cooking. To prepare a fennel bulb, trim off the core at the bottom and the fernlike fronds and stems at the top. Use a vegetable peeler to remove a thin layer of the bulb, if desired. Halve the bulb and discard the core. Slice the halves as directed.

**per serving**

| | |
|---|---|
| calories 399 | sodium 438 mg |
| total fat 7.5 g | carbohydrates 60 g |
|   saturated fat 1.5 g |   fiber 11 g |
|   trans fat 0.0 g |   sugars 9 g |
|   polyunsaturated fat 1.0 g | protein 25 g |
|   monounsaturated fat 3.5 g | dietary exchanges |
| cholesterol 111 mg | 3½ starch, 2 vegetable, 2 lean meat |

Lime, honey, and chipotle powder add Mexican flair to delicate shrimp, hearty black beans, and nutty brown rice in this flavorful dish, which is just as good cold as it is hot.

# baja shrimp bowls

**serves 4**  |  1½ cups per serving

1/3 cup fresh lime juice

2½ tablespoons olive oil

1 tablespoon honey

4 medium garlic cloves, minced

3/4 teaspoon chipotle powder or 1 teaspoon chopped chipotle pepper canned in adobo sauce

10 ounces raw medium shrimp, peeled, rinsed, and patted dry

1 scant cup uncooked brown rice

Cooking spray

1 large red onion, coarsely chopped

1 15.5-ounce can no-salt-added black beans, rinsed and drained

1/3 cup fresh cilantro, chopped

1/4 teaspoon salt

1 medium lime, cut into 4 wedges

**per serving**

| | |
|---|---|
| calories 426 | sodium 323 mg |
| total fat 10.5 g | carbohydrates 63 g |
|   saturated fat 1.5 g |   fiber 8 g |
|   trans fat 0.0 g |   sugars 10 g |
|   polyunsaturated fat 1.5 g | **protein 20 g** |
|   monounsaturated fat 6.5 g | |
| **cholesterol 89 mg** | **dietary exchanges** |
| | 4 starch, 1 vegetable, 2 lean meat |

1. In a shallow glass dish, whisk together the lime juice, oil, honey, garlic, and chipotle powder. Add the shrimp, turning to coat. Cover and refrigerate for 45 minutes, turning occasionally.

2. Meanwhile, prepare the rice using the package directions, omitting the salt and margarine. Set aside.

3. Drain the shrimp and pat dry, reserving the marinade.

4. In a small saucepan, bring the marinade to a boil over high heat. Boil for 3 to 4 minutes, or until reduced by half (to about 1/4 cup).

5. Meanwhile, lightly spray a large skillet with cooking spray. Heat over medium-high heat. Cook the onion for about 3 minutes, or until soft, stirring frequently. Move the onion to the edge of the skillet. Stir in the shrimp. Cook for 3 minutes, or until pink on the outside.

6. Stir in the beans and rice. Reduce the heat to low. Cook for 2 minutes, or until hot, stirring constantly. Stir in the marinade, cilantro, and salt. Serve with the lime wedges.

seafood

# poultry

Tandoori chicken is usually prepared in an Indian tandoor, or clay oven, which can reach temperatures around 900°F. Our version makes this dish more accessible by calling for you to broil the chicken but keep the traditional marinade.

# tandoori-spiced chicken

**serves 4** | **3 ounces chicken per serving**

4 skinless chicken breast halves with bone (about 6 ounces each), all visible fat discarded

¾ cup fat-free plain yogurt

1 tablespoon fresh lemon juice

2 teaspoons garam masala

2 medium garlic cloves, minced

1 teaspoon grated peeled gingerroot

¼ teaspoon turmeric

2 to 3 drops of red food coloring (optional)

1 tablespoon plus 1 teaspoon chopped fresh cilantro (optional)

**per serving**

calories 164
total fat 3.5 g
   saturated fat 1.0 g
   trans fat 0.0 g
   polyunsaturated fat 0.5 g
   monounsaturated fat 1.0 g
cholesterol 87 mg

sodium 170 mg
carbohydrates 1 g
   fiber 0 g
   sugars 1 g
protein 30 g

dietary exchanges
4 lean meat

1. Using a sharp knife, make two slits in each chicken breast.

2. In a large glass bowl, whisk together the remaining ingredients except the cilantro. Add the chicken, turning to coat. Using your fingertips, massage the yogurt mixture into the chicken. Cover and refrigerate for at least 8 hours or overnight.

3. When the chicken is marinated, preheat the broiler. Line a rimmed baking sheet with aluminum foil.

4. Drain the chicken, discarding the marinade. Place on the baking sheet with the rib side up. Broil the chicken about 4 inches from the heat for 10 to 12 minutes on each side, or until the chicken is no longer pink in the center.

5. Just before serving, sprinkle with the cilantro.

**cook's tip:** Red food coloring replaces the ground annatto seed (also called achiote seed) in tandoori paste that gives tandoori chicken its signature color. If you prefer to use the seed, look for it in the ethnic section of your grocery store or online.

**cook's tip on garam masala:** Garam masala is a seasoning mixture you can find in most supermarkets or Indian grocery stores. Although it's more cost-effective to buy it already mixed, if you can't find it or prefer to make your own, stir together ½ teaspoon ground cumin, ½ teaspoon turmeric, ½ teaspoon ground cardamom, ½ teaspoon ground coriander, ¼ teaspoon ground cinnamon, ¼ teaspoon ground cloves, ⅛ teaspoon ground nutmeg, and ⅛ teaspoon cayenne.

poultry

This steaming bowl of soup is vibrant, with its kicky flavors from lemongrass and red pepper flakes, and its vivid colors from the veggies.

# thai lemongrass chicken soup

**serves 4** | 1¼ cups per serving

1 stalk lemongrass, 1 teaspoon lemongrass paste, 1 teaspoon ground dried lemongrass, or 1 teaspoon grated lemon zest

4 cups fat-free, low-sodium chicken broth

¼ cup lite coconut milk

2 tablespoons cornstarch

1 teaspoon toasted sesame oil

8 ounces boneless, skinless chicken breasts, all visible fat discarded, cut into thin strips

½ cup diced red bell pepper

1 teaspoon grated peeled gingerroot

2 medium garlic cloves, minced

¼ teaspoon crushed red pepper flakes

1 cup chopped broccoli florets and stems

1 medium carrot, shredded

1 cup sugar snap peas, halved lengthwise

¼ cup loosely packed fresh cilantro

1 medium lime, cut into 4 wedges

**per serving**

calories 142
total fat 3.5 g
   saturated fat 1.0 g
   trans fat 0.0 g
   polyunsaturated fat 1.0 g
   monounsaturated fat 1.0 g
cholesterol 36 mg

sodium 154 mg
carbohydrates 11 g
   fiber 2 g
   sugars 3 g
protein 16 g

dietary exchanges
½ starch, 1 vegetable, 2 lean meat

1. Trim about 6 inches off the slender green end of the lemongrass stalk and discard. Remove the outer layer of leaves from the root of the stalk. Halve the stalk lengthwise. (Lemongrass stalks are slightly tough, so be careful as you slice.) Place the lemongrass in a large saucepan. Pour in the broth. Bring to a simmer over medium-high heat. Reduce the heat and simmer, covered, for 5 minutes, or until the lemongrass flavor infuses the broth. Discard the lemongrass stalk.

2. In a small bowl, whisk together the coconut milk, cornstarch, and sesame oil. Stir the mixture into the broth. Increase the heat to medium and cook, partially covered, for 1 minute, or until thickened, stirring occasionally.

3. Stir in the chicken, bell pepper, gingerroot, garlic, and red pepper flakes. Cook, partially covered, for 4 to 5 minutes, or until the chicken is no longer pink in the center, stirring occasionally.

4. Stir in the broccoli and carrot. Cook, partially covered, for 2 to 3 minutes, or until the broccoli is tender-crisp. Gently stir in the sugar snap peas. Cook for 30 seconds.

5. Ladle the soup into bowls. Sprinkle with the cilantro. Serve with the lime wedges.

Packed with flavorful ingredients, this salad looks and tastes good enough to be served at a restaurant, but it's adapted for guilt-free enjoyment at home.

# mexican chicken salad

| serves 4 | 1 cup chicken salad and 1 cup salad greens per serving |
| --- | --- |

Cooking spray

4 boneless, skinless chicken breast halves (about 4 ounces each), all visible fat discarded, halved lengthwise

1 cup frozen whole-kernel corn

1 cup canned no-salt-added black beans, rinsed and drained

1/3 cup chopped red onion

1/4 cup shredded fat-free Cheddar cheese

1/2 cup loosely packed chopped cilantro

1/4 cup fat-free plain yogurt

1/4 cup light mayonnaise

1 tablespoon chipotle peppers canned in adobo sauce

1 tablespoon fresh lime juice

4 cups mixed salad greens

1/4 cup crushed baked tortilla chips

1. Preheat the oven to 425°F.

2. Lightly spray 2 baking sheets with cooking spray. Put the chicken on 1 baking sheet. Spread the corn in a single layer on the other.

3. Bake both for 16 minutes, or until the chicken is no longer pink in the center and the corn is roasted and slightly crunchy, turning the chicken over and stirring the corn once halfway through.

4. Let the chicken cool slightly, about 2 minutes, or until easy to handle. Cut into bite-size pieces.

5. In a large bowl, gently toss the chicken, corn, beans, onion, and Cheddar.

6. In a food processor or blender, process the cilantro, yogurt, mayonnaise, chipotle pepper, and lime juice until well blended. Pour over the chicken mixture, tossing gently to combine.

7. Put the salad greens on plates. Spoon the chicken mixture over the greens. Sprinkle with the tortilla chips.

**Go Red party tip:** To serve this dish party-style, spoon the chicken salad into a chip-and-dip or serving bowl instead of over greens. Also, rather than using the baked tortilla chips as a garnish, serve them with the chicken salad.

## per serving

calories 314
total fat 7.0 g
  saturated fat 1.0 g
  trans fat 0.0 g
  polyunsaturated fat 3.5 g
  monounsaturated fat 2.0 g
cholesterol 79 mg

sodium 436 mg
carbohydrates 29 g
  fiber 5 g
  sugars 6 g
protein 34 g

dietary exchanges
2 starch, 4 lean meat

The combination of bright green spinach, rich red tomatoes, and shiny black olives makes this pasta salad pop with color as well as taste. Tangy blue cheese adds creamy richness and a pungent punch.

# pasta salad with chicken

**serves 4** | **1½ cups per serving**

4 ounces dried whole-grain rotini

1½ cups cubed cooked skinless chicken breasts, cooked without salt, all visible fat discarded

9 ounces frozen artichoke hearts, thawed and coarsely chopped

1 cup grape tomatoes, halved

1 cup baby spinach

⅓ cup finely chopped red onion

1 2.25-ounce can sliced black olives, drained

3 tablespoons red wine vinegar

1 tablespoon olive oil (extra virgin preferred)

½ teaspoon dried rosemary, crushed

¼ cup crumbled low-fat blue cheese

1. Prepare the pasta using the package directions, omitting the salt. Transfer to a colander. Rinse with cold water to stop the cooking process and cool the pasta quickly.

2. Meanwhile, in a large bowl, stir together the remaining ingredients except the blue cheese.

3. Stir in the pasta. Gently fold in the blue cheese.

**cook's tip:** It's so convenient to cook extra chicken breasts to keep in the freezer for those hectic nights, but if you don't have any available for this dish, discard all the visible fat from 10 ounces of skinless, boneless chicken breasts, then cut the chicken into bite-size pieces. Lightly spray a small skillet with cooking spray. Heat over medium-high heat. Cook the chicken for 3 to 4 minutes, or until no longer pink in the center, stirring constantly.

**lunchbox tip:** If the blue cheese is too strong for your kids, substitute a more kid-friendly cheese, such as low-fat Cheddar, Parmesan, or mozzarella.

## per serving

calories 310
total fat 9.5 g
  saturated fat 2.5 g
  trans fat 0.0 g
  polyunsaturated fat 1.5 g
  monounsaturated fat 5.0 g
cholesterol 48 mg

sodium 299 mg
carbohydrates 32 g
  fiber 9 g
  sugars 4 g
protein 24 g

dietary exchanges
1½ starch,
2 vegetable, 2½ lean meat

This deeply flavored soup is a great way to use leftover chicken. Poblano peppers add a mild heat and cumin contributes smokiness, while toppings of low-fat cheese and fat-free sour cream give the dish extra richness.

# chicken and poblano soup

**serves 4** | 1½ cups per serving

2 teaspoons canola or corn oil

1 cup chopped onion

2 poblano peppers, seeds and ribs discarded, diced (see cook's tip on page 109)

2 medium garlic cloves, minced

1 teaspoon ground cumin

4 cups fat-free, low-sodium chicken broth

1 14.5-ounce can no-salt-added diced tomatoes, undrained

¼ teaspoon salt

¼ teaspoon pepper

1 15.5-ounce can no-salt-added pinto beans, rinsed and drained

12 ounces cooked skinless chicken breasts, cooked without salt, all visible fat discarded, shredded

¼ cup shredded low-fat Monterey Jack or Cheddar cheese

¼ cup fat-free sour cream

1. In a large saucepan, heat the oil over medium heat, swirling to coat the bottom. Cook the onion and poblanos for 5 minutes, or until softened, stirring frequently.

2. Stir in the garlic and cumin. Cook for 2 minutes, stirring occasionally.

3. Stir in the broth, tomatoes with liquid, salt, and pepper. Bring to a boil, still over medium heat. Reduce the heat and simmer for 20 minutes.

4. Stir in the beans and chicken. Cook for 5 minutes, or until heated through.

5. Sprinkle each serving with the Monterey Jack. Top with the sour cream.

**per serving**

calories 358
total fat 7.5 g
   saturated fat 2.0 g
   trans fat 0.0 g
   polyunsaturated fat 1.5 g
   monounsaturated fat 3.0 g
cholesterol 79 mg

sodium 344 mg
carbohydrates 30 g
   fiber 6 g
   sugars 10 g
protein 39 g

dietary exchanges
1½ starch,
2 vegetable,
4 lean meat

Inspired by the sweet-and-sour dishes of Germany, this entrée features succulent chicken, cabbage, carrots, apples, and raisins gently braised to perfection in a warmly spiced sauce. Celery seeds add a slight tanginess.

# braised chicken with cabbage, carrots, and apples

**serves 4** : 3 ounces chicken and 1½ cups vegetables per serving

1¼ cups unsweetened apple cider or 100% apple juice

¼ cup dry white wine (regular or nonalcoholic)

2 tablespoons cider vinegar

1 tablespoon Dijon mustard (lowest sodium available)

1 teaspoon celery seeds

⅛ teaspoon pumpkin pie spice

1 teaspoon olive oil and 1 teaspoon olive oil, divided use

1 pound boneless, skinless chicken breasts, all visible fat discarded, cut into ½-inch pieces

¼ teaspoon salt

¼ teaspoon pepper

1 medium onion, thinly sliced

10 ounces savoy cabbage, shredded

1 large carrot, thinly sliced crosswise

2 medium garlic cloves, minced

*(continued)*

1. Preheat the oven to 325°F.

2. In a medium bowl, whisk together the cider, wine, vinegar, mustard, celery seeds, and pumpkin pie spice. Set aside.

3. In a large ovenproof skillet with a tight-fitting lid and straight sides, heat 1 teaspoon oil over medium-high heat, swirling to coat the bottom. Put the chicken in the skillet. Sprinkle the salt and pepper over the chicken. Cook the chicken for 1 minute on each side, or until lightly browned. (The chicken won't be done at this point.) Transfer to a plate.

4. In the same skillet, still over medium-high heat, heat the remaining 1 teaspoon oil, swirling to coat the bottom. Cook the onion for about 3 minutes, or until soft. Stir in ½ cup of the cider mixture, scraping to dislodge any browned bits. Stir in the cabbage, carrot, and garlic. Cook for

10 minutes, or until the liquid is evaporated and the vegetables begin to brown (add more of the cider mixture if they brown too quickly), stirring occasionally.

5. Stir in the remaining cider mixture, scraping to dislodge any browned bits. Reduce the heat and simmer, tightly covered, for 15 minutes.

6. Stir in the chicken, apple, raisins, and sage. Bake, covered, for 45 minutes.

**cook's tip:** You don't want too much steam to escape from the skillet during simmering or the finished dish will be dry. If your skillet does not have a tight-fitting lid, wrap aluminum foil around the skillet and lid to form a tight seal.

**cook's tip on savoy cabbage:** Savoy cabbage is tenderer than regular green cabbage and has a milder flavor. If you can't find it, you can substitute napa cabbage.

1 large sweet apple, such as Gala or Fuji, peeled and chopped

¼ cup raisins

1 tablespoon chopped fresh sage or 1 teaspoon dried rubbed sage

............................................................

**per serving**

calories 304
total fat 6.0 g
    saturated fat 1.0 g
    trans fat 0.0 g
    polyunsaturated fat 1.0 g
    monounsaturated fat 2.5 g
cholesterol 73 mg

sodium 394 mg
carbohydrates 35 g
    fiber 6 g
    sugars 24 g
protein 27 g

dietary exchanges
1½ fruit, 2 vegetable, 3 lean meat

Your whole family will love this simply delicious oven-baked chicken any night of the week. To add some color and crunch to your meal, try Roasted Radishes (page 216), which cook at the same temperature and are done within minutes of the chicken.

# chicken oreganata

**serves 4** | 3 ounces chicken per serving

Cooking spray

4 boneless, skinless chicken breast halves (about 4 ounces each), all visible fat discarded, flattened to ¼-inch thickness

2 teaspoons grated lemon zest

1 tablespoon fresh lemon juice

½ cup whole-wheat panko (Japanese-style bread crumbs)

2 tablespoons olive oil (extra virgin preferred)

½ teaspoon onion powder

½ teaspoon dried oregano, crumbled

¼ teaspoon garlic powder

¼ teaspoon salt and ⅛ teaspoon salt, divided use

1. Preheat the oven to 425°F. Lightly spray a 13 × 9 × 2-inch baking dish with cooking spray.

2. Arrange the chicken in a single layer in the baking dish. Sprinkle with the lemon juice.

3. In a small bowl, stir together the lemon zest, panko, oil, onion powder, oregano, garlic powder, and ¼ teaspoon salt. Spoon the mixture over the chicken.

4. Bake for 18 minutes, or until the chicken is no longer pink in the center and the crust begins to brown. Sprinkle with the remaining ⅛ teaspoon salt.

**lunchbox tip:** This crunchy chicken is just as good the next day, when the lemony flavor and seasonings have permeated the meat. Send it off in a lunchbox with either Cool Jícama-Cabbage Slaw (page 52) or Crunchy Apple-Carrot Slaw (page 53).

**per serving**

calories 228
total fat 10.0 g
  saturated fat 1.5 g
  trans fat 0.0 g
  polyunsaturated fat 1.0 g
  monounsaturated fat 6.0 g
cholesterol 73 mg

sodium 362 mg
carbohydrates 8 g
  fiber 1 g
  sugars 0 g
protein 26 g

dietary exchanges
½ starch, 3 lean meat

the go red for women cookbook

Creamy avocado and sweet mango combine with crunchy red bell pepper and fresh cilantro in this easy, cooling salsa that's the perfect foil for spicy grilled chicken. Because the chicken is boldly flavored, it's best to offset the heat with simple sides such as brown rice and Cool Jícama-Cabbage Slaw (page 52).

# jerk chicken with mango-avocado salsa

**serves 4** | 3 ounces chicken and ½ cup salsa per serving

Cooking spray

1 medium mango, chopped

1 medium avocado, chopped

½ cup finely chopped red bell pepper

2 tablespoons chopped fresh cilantro

2 tablespoons fresh lime juice

2 teaspoons salt-free jerk seasoning blend

4 boneless, skinless chicken breast halves (about 4 ounces each), all visible fat discarded

### per serving

calories 268
total fat 10.5 g
  saturated fat 2.0 g
  trans fat 0.0 g
  polyunsaturated fat 1.5 g
  monounsaturated fat 6.0 g
cholesterol 73 mg

sodium 137 mg
carbohydrates 19 g
  fiber 5 g
  sugars 13 g
protein 26 g

dietary exchanges
1½ fruit, 3 lean meat

1. Lightly spray the grill rack with cooking spray. Preheat the grill on medium.

2. In a medium bowl, stir together the mango, avocado, bell pepper, cilantro, and lime juice. Set aside.

3. Sprinkle the seasoning blend over both sides of the chicken. Using your fingertips, gently press the seasoning so it adheres to the chicken. Lightly spray both sides of the chicken with cooking spray. Grill, covered, for 4 to 5 minutes on each side, or until the chicken is no longer pink in the center. Serve the salsa with the chicken.

**cook's tip:** If you can't readily find salt-free jerk seasoning blend, sometimes called Jamaican jerk seasoning, or want only a small amount of it, make your own. In a small bowl, stir together 1 teaspoon ground cumin, ½ teaspoon ground allspice, and ½ teaspoon ground cinnamon, plus black pepper and/or cayenne to taste.

A crisp cucumber relish spiked with red onion and ginger pairs perfectly with chicken marinated in the familiar Asian flavors of soy sauce and rice vinegar.

# chicken and cucumber relish

**serves 4** | 3 ounces chicken and ¼ cup relish per serving

2 tablespoons soy sauce (lowest sodium available)

1½ teaspoons plain rice vinegar

1½ teaspoons canola or corn oil

4 boneless, skinless chicken breast halves (about 4 ounces each), all visible fat discarded, flattened to ¼-inch thickness

### relish

½ medium cucumber, peeled if desired, seeded, and diced

2 tablespoons finely chopped red onion

2 teaspoons minced peeled gingerroot

2 teaspoons fresh lemon juice

1½ teaspoons sugar

1½ teaspoons plain rice vinegar

⅛ teaspoon salt

————

Cooking spray

¼ teaspoon pepper (coarsely ground preferred)

1. In a shallow glass dish, whisk together the soy sauce, 1½ teaspoons vinegar, and the oil. Add the chicken, turning to coat. Cover and refrigerate for 30 minutes, turning occasionally.

2. Meanwhile, in a small bowl, stir together the relish ingredients. Set aside.

3. Lightly spray the grill rack with cooking spray. Preheat the grill on medium high or use a grill pan.

4. Drain the chicken, discarding the marinade. Grill the chicken for 4 minutes on each side, or until no longer pink in the center. Transfer to plates. Sprinkle with the pepper. Serve with the relish.

### per serving

calories 147
total fat 3.0 g
  saturated fat 0.5 g
  trans fat 0.0 g
  polyunsaturated fat 0.5 g
  monounsaturated fat 1.0 g
cholesterol 73 mg

sodium 400 mg
carbohydrates 4 g
  fiber 0 g
  sugars 3 g
protein 25 g

dietary exchanges
½ other carbohydrate,
3 lean meat

The spices in this beautiful dish are a powerful blend of sweet and savory, reminiscent of Indian flavor combinations. Add your favorite steamed vegetable to complete the meal.

# apricot-plum chicken

| serves 4 | 3 ounces chicken, ⅓ cup sauce, and ½ cup couscous per serving |
|---|---|

½ teaspoon curry powder

½ teaspoon ground ginger

¼ teaspoon ground cinnamon

¼ teaspoon ground cumin

⅛ teaspoon salt

⅛ teaspoon cayenne

4 boneless, skinless chicken breast halves (about 4 ounces each), all visible fat discarded

1 8-ounce can no-salt-added tomato sauce

8 dried apricot halves, chopped

8 dried pitted plums, chopped (orange essence preferred)

¼ cup fresh orange juice

2 teaspoons honey

1 teaspoon olive oil

1 cup uncooked whole-wheat couscous

¼ cup sliced green onions

2 tablespoons chopped fresh parsley

1. In a small bowl, stir together the curry powder, ginger, cinnamon, cumin, salt, and cayenne. Sprinkle over both sides of the chicken. Using your fingertips, gently press the mixture so it adheres to the chicken.

2. In a medium bowl, stir together the tomato sauce, apricots, plums, orange juice, and honey. Set aside.

3. In a large nonstick skillet, heat the oil over medium-high heat, swirling to coat the bottom. Cook the chicken for 2 to 3 minutes on each side, or until browned. Carefully stir in the tomato sauce mixture. Reduce the heat and simmer, covered, for 10 to 15 minutes, or until the chicken is no longer pink in the center.

4. Meanwhile, prepare the couscous using the package directions, omitting the salt. Fluff with a fork. Transfer the couscous to a serving platter.

5. Place the chicken on the couscous. Spoon the sauce over all. Sprinkle with the green onions and parsley.

**per serving**

calories 393
total fat 5.0 g
  saturated fat 1.0 g
  trans fat 0.0 g
  polyunsaturated fat 0.5 g
  monounsaturated fat 1.5 g
cholesterol 73 mg

sodium 218 mg
carbohydrates 59 g
  fiber 7 g
  sugars 16 g
protein 32 g

dietary exchanges
2½ starch, 1 fruit,
1 vegetable, 3 lean
meat

Easy to make, this interesting dish has the sweet island taste of pineapple with a sour tang suggestive of Philippine adobo seasoning, distinguished by its use of vinegar, soy, and garlic. The chicken marinates and cooks in the same skillet, making cleanup a breeze. Serve hot or cold with vegetables and a whole grain, such as quinoa or bulgur.

# philippine-style chicken

**serves 4** | 3 ounces chicken per serving

## marinade

⅓ cup white wine vinegar

⅓ cup 100% pineapple juice

2 tablespoons soy sauce (lowest sodium available)

1 medium garlic clove, minced

⅛ teaspoon pepper

———

4 boneless, skinless chicken breast halves (about 4 ounces each), all visible fat discarded

1. In a large skillet, whisk together the marinade ingredients. Put the chicken in the skillet. Refrigerate, covered, for 30 minutes, turning once halfway through.

2. Remove the skillet from the refrigerator. Heat over medium-high heat, or until the marinade comes to a boil, stirring frequently. Reduce the heat and simmer, covered, for 20 minutes, or until the chicken is no longer pink in the center, turning once halfway through.

**lunchbox tip:** This chicken is just as good served cold, so it's a great way to send your child off to school with a healthy lunch. Add some baby carrots, edamame, or sugar snap peas, along with apple slices or grapes.

## per serving

calories 153
total fat 3.0 g
   saturated fat 0.5 g
   trans fat 0.0 g
   polyunsaturated fat 0.5 g
   monounsaturated fat 1.0 g
cholesterol 73 mg

sodium 328 mg
carbohydrates 5 g
   fiber 0 g
   sugars 3 g
protein 25 g

dietary exchanges
½ other carbohydrate,
3 lean meat

In typical Creole fashion, this dish features tomatoes, onion, celery, and garlic. The accompanying brown rice is perfect to soak up the sauce.

# chicken creole

| serves 4 | 1 cup chicken mixture and ½ cup rice per serving |

1 cup uncooked instant brown rice

Cooking spray

1 teaspoon canola or corn oil

½ cup thinly sliced onion

1 cup thinly sliced mushrooms

½ cup chopped celery

1 tablespoon minced garlic

1½ teaspoons chopped fresh oregano or ½ teaspoon dried oregano, crumbled

1½ teaspoons chopped fresh basil or ½ teaspoon dried basil, crumbled

1 cup sliced green bell pepper

1 cup diced peeled tomatoes

¼ cup dry white wine (regular or nonalcoholic)

1 tablespoon fresh lemon juice

¼ teaspoon crushed red pepper flakes

¼ teaspoon pepper, or to taste

1 pound boneless, skinless chicken breasts, all visible fat discarded, cut into ½-inch cubes

1 tablespoon finely chopped fresh parsley

1. Prepare the rice using the package directions, omitting the salt and margarine. Set aside. Cover to keep warm.

2. Meanwhile, lightly spray a large skillet with cooking spray. Pour in the oil, swirling to coat the bottom. Heat over medium-high heat. Cook the onion for 2 to 3 minutes, or until soft. Stir in the mushrooms. Cook for 3 to 4 minutes, or until the liquid evaporates. Stir in the celery, garlic, oregano, and basil. Cook for 1 minute. Stir in the bell pepper. Cook for 2 minutes. Stir in the tomatoes. Cook for 5 minutes, stirring occasionally. Stir in the wine, lemon juice, and red pepper flakes. Remove from the heat.

3. Lightly spray a separate large skillet with cooking spray. Heat over high heat. Sprinkle the pepper over the chicken. Cook for 5 to 6 minutes, or until lightly browned, stirring occasionally. (The chicken won't be done at this point.)

4. Gently stir in the onion mixture. Reduce the heat and simmer for 5 to 10 minutes, or until the sauce is heated through and the chicken is no longer pink in the center. Just before serving, sprinkle with the parsley.

## per serving

calories 262
total fat 5.0 g
  saturated fat 1.0 g
  trans fat 0.0 g
  polyunsaturated fat 1.0 g
  monounsaturated fat 2.0 g
cholesterol 73 mg

sodium 153 mg
carbohydrates 24 g
  fiber 3 g
  sugars 3 g
protein 28 g

dietary exchanges
1 starch, 1 vegetable, 3 lean meat

poultry

Southerners turn chicken or turkey hash into a great meal by adding corn cakes, which are pancakes made with corn bread batter—quick, easy, and delicious. Add a simple vegetable, such as okra or collard greens, for color and to complete your meal.

# down south chicken hash and corn cakes

| serves 4 | 1½ cups hash and 1 corn cake per serving |
|---|---|

## hash

- 1 teaspoon canola or corn oil
- 1 medium onion, minced
- 8 ounces button mushrooms, thinly sliced
- 1½ pounds potatoes, peeled, diced, and cooked
- 12 ounces boneless, skinless chicken breasts, all visible fat discarded, cut into ½-inch cubes
- 1 teaspoon dried thyme, crumbled
- ½ to 1 teaspoon pepper
- 1 cup fat-free, low-sodium chicken broth
- 1 tablespoon all-purpose flour
- 2 medium tomatoes, peeled, seeded, and finely chopped

*(continued)*

1. Preheat the oven to 200°F.

2. In a Dutch oven or large saucepan, heat 1 teaspoon oil over medium-high heat, swirling to coat the bottom. Cook the onion for 1 minute, stirring occasionally.

3. Increase the heat to high. Stir in the mushrooms. Cook for 3 to 4 minutes, or until the mushrooms are slightly browned, stirring occasionally.

4. Reduce the heat to medium. Stir in the potatoes. Cook for 4 to 5 minutes, stirring occasionally.

5. Stir in the chicken, thyme, and ½ to 1 teaspoon pepper. Cook for 5 minutes, or until the chicken is no longer pink in the center, stirring occasionally.

6. In a small bowl, whisk together the broth and 1 tablespoon flour until smooth. Stir into the chicken mixture. Increase the heat to high and bring to a boil. Boil for 2 to 3 minutes, or until the gravy thickens and barely coats the hash ingredients.

7. Stir in the tomatoes. Spoon the hash into an ovenproof casserole dish. Cover and put in the oven to keep warm.

8. In a small bowl, stir together the cornmeal, baking powder, baking soda, salt, and the remaining 2 tablespoons flour and 1/8 teaspoon pepper.

9. In a medium bowl, whisk together the buttermilk and egg whites. Whisk in the remaining 1 tablespoon oil. Add the cornmeal mixture, blending with a few swift strokes.

10. Lightly spray a large griddle with cooking spray. Heat over medium-high heat until drops of water sizzle on the surface. Working quickly (because the batter will begin to "rise"), and using 1/4 cup for each corn cake, pour the batter onto the griddle. (You may need to make more than one batch, depending on the size of your griddle.) Cook for 2 to 3 minutes, or until bubbles form on the tops and the bottoms are lightly browned. Turn over. Cook for about 2 minutes, or until the other sides are lightly browned. If the corn cakes seem to be browning too quickly, reduce the heat. Transfer the cakes to an ovenproof dish. Put in the oven to keep warm while you cook any remaining batter.

11. Just before serving, sprinkle the hash with the parsley. Serve the corn cakes on the side.

## corn cakes

1 cup cornmeal

2 tablespoons all-purpose flour

1 teaspoon baking powder

1/2 teaspoon baking soda

1/8 teaspoon salt

1/8 teaspoon pepper

1 cup low-fat buttermilk

2 large egg whites

1 tablespoon canola or corn oil

Cooking spray

––––––––––

1/2 cup minced fresh parsley

...................................................

### per serving

calories 488
total fat 8.5 g
   saturated fat 1.5 g
   trans fat 0.0 g
   polyunsaturated fat 2.0 g
   monounsaturated fat 4.0 g
cholesterol 57 mg

sodium 558 mg
carbohydrates 74 g
   fiber 9 g
   sugars 10 g
protein 32 g

dietary exchanges
4½ starch,
1 vegetable, 3 lean meat

Orange sweet potato, red bell pepper, and deep green kale make a beautiful and nourishing soul-food stew. Enjoy this dish with fresh-baked Whole-Wheat Corn Muffins (page 228).

# chicken, sweet potato, and kale stew

**serves 4** | 1½ cups per serving

1 tablespoon olive oil

1 pound boneless, skinless chicken breasts, all visible fat discarded, cut into ¾-inch pieces

½ cup chopped onion

1 medium garlic clove, minced

3 cups fat-free, low-sodium chicken broth

1 large sweet potato, peeled and cut into ½-inch cubes

1 medium red bell pepper, chopped

3 cups loosely packed, coarsely chopped kale, any large stems discarded

1 teaspoon chopped fresh thyme or ¼ teaspoon dried thyme, crumbled

1. In a large saucepan, heat the oil over medium-high heat, swirling to coat the bottom. Cook the chicken for 5 minutes, stirring occasionally. Stir in the onion and garlic. Cook for 4 to 5 minutes, or until the onion is soft, stirring occasionally.

2. Stir in the broth, sweet potato, and bell pepper. Bring to a boil. Reduce the heat and simmer, covered, for 10 minutes. Stir in the kale and thyme. Simmer, partially covered, for 8 to 10 minutes, or until the chicken is no longer pink in the center and the vegetables are tender, stirring occasionally.

**cook's tip:** If you prefer your stew thick rather than soupy, reduce the amount of chicken broth to 1½ to 2 cups.

**per serving**

calories 284
total fat 7.0 g
   saturated fat 1.0 g
   trans fat 0.0 g
   polyunsaturated fat 1.0 g
   monounsaturated fat 3.5 g
cholesterol 73 mg

sodium 247 mg
carbohydrates 26 g
   fiber 5 g
   sugars 6 g
protein 29 g

dietary exchanges
1 starch, 2 vegetable, 3 lean meat

It takes just a few minutes to prepare your own delicious, healthful stir-fry. Our version combines juicy chicken with plenty of veggies. *(See photo insert.)*

# chinese chicken stir-fry

| serves 6 | 1 cup chicken mixture and ½ cup rice per serving |
|---|---|

1½ cups uncooked instant brown rice

3 tablespoons cornstarch

1⅓ cups fat-free, low-sodium chicken broth

3 tablespoons dry sherry or fresh orange juice

2 tablespoons soy sauce (lowest sodium available)

1 tablespoon plain rice vinegar

2 teaspoons chili oil

1 tablespoon grated peeled gingerroot

3 medium garlic cloves, minced

1 pound boneless, skinless chicken breasts, all visible fat discarded, cut into 1-inch cubes

2 teaspoons toasted sesame oil

8 ounces mushrooms, sliced

1 cup diced red bell pepper

1 8-ounce can water chestnuts, drained

¾ cup sliced green onions

½ cup pecan halves, dry-roasted

¼ teaspoon crushed red pepper flakes

1. Prepare the rice using the package directions, omitting the salt and margarine. Set aside. Cover to keep warm.

2. Put the cornstarch in a medium bowl. Add the broth, sherry, soy sauce, and vinegar, whisking to dissolve. Set aside.

3. In a large skillet or wok, heat the chili oil over high heat, swirling to coat the bottom. Cook the gingerroot and garlic for 1 minute, stirring constantly. Reduce the heat to medium high. Stir in the chicken. Cook for 4 minutes, or until the chicken is lightly browned, stirring constantly. (The chicken won't be done at this point.) Transfer to a plate. Wipe the skillet with paper towels.

4. In the same skillet, still over medium-high heat, heat the sesame oil, swirling to coat the bottom. Cook the mushrooms, bell pepper, and water chestnuts for 5 to 7 minutes, stirring frequently.

5. Whisk the broth mixture. Stir it into the mushroom mixture. Stir in the chicken. Cook for 3 to 4 minutes, or until the chicken is no longer pink in the center.

6. Stir the green onions, pecans, and red pepper flakes into the chicken mixture. Cook for 2 minutes, stirring frequently. Serve over the rice.

**per serving**

| | |
|---|---|
| calories 317 | sodium 248 mg |
| total fat 12.0 g | carbohydrates 30 g |
|   saturated fat 1.5 g |   fiber 4 g |
|   trans fat 0.0 g |   sugars 4 g |
|   polyunsaturated fat 3.5 g | protein 21 g |
|   monounsaturated fat 5.5 g | |
| cholesterol 48 mg | dietary exchanges |
| | 1½ starch, 1 vegetable, 2½ lean meat, ½ fat |

Soft corn tortillas enclose a filling of shredded chicken and black beans simmered in a spicy tomato sauce, then are topped with freshly cooked salsa and a dusting of Mexican cheeses. This dish tastes even better reheated the next day.

# chicken and black bean enchiladas

**serves 6** : **2 enchiladas per serving**

3 **cups water**

12 **ounces boneless, skinless chicken tenders, all visible fat discarded**

2 **cups canned no-salt-added black beans, rinsed and drained**

1 **teaspoon ground cumin**

1 **teaspoon chipotle powder**

½ **teaspoon dried oregano, crumbled**

⅛ **teaspoon pepper**

1 **teaspoon canola or corn oil and 1 teaspoon canola or corn oil, divided use**

2 **medium garlic cloves, minced**

½ **cup no-salt-added tomato sauce and ½ cup no-salt-added tomato sauce, divided use**

2 **tablespoons finely chopped fresh cilantro and 1 cup tightly packed fresh cilantro, coarsely chopped, divided use**

¾ **cup diced red onion**

*(continued)*

1. In a medium skillet, bring the water to a boil over high heat. Add the chicken and additional water, if needed, to cover the chicken. Reduce the heat and simmer for 6 minutes. (The chicken won't be done at this point.) Turn off the heat. Let the chicken stand in the water for at least 2 minutes, or until no longer pink in the center and slightly cool. Transfer the chicken to a medium bowl. Reserve the cooking liquid.

2. Using two forks, shred the chicken. Stir in the beans, cumin, chipotle powder, oregano, and pepper.

3. In a large skillet, heat 1 teaspoon oil over medium-high heat, swirling to coat the bottom. Cook the garlic for 30 seconds, stirring constantly. Stir in the chicken mixture. Cook for 30 seconds. Stir in 1 cup of the reserved cooking liquid and ½ cup tomato sauce. Simmer, partially covered, for 5 to 6 minutes so the flavors blend. Stir in 2 tablespoons cilantro. Remove from the heat. Set aside to cool.

**4.** Preheat the oven to 375°F.

**5.** In a stockpot or large Dutch oven, heat the remaining 1 teaspoon oil over medium heat, swirling to coat the bottom. Cook the onion and jalapeño for about 3 minutes, or until they begin to soften, stirring occasionally. Stir in the tomatoes and the remaining 1/2 cup tomato sauce. Simmer for 5 to 7 minutes, or until the tomatoes release their liquid and begin to break down. Stir in the lime juice and the remaining 1 cup cilantro.

**6.** Spread 1 cup of sauce in a glass baking dish large enough to hold the enchiladas. Place the tortillas on a work surface. Spoon the chicken mixture down the center of each tortilla. Roll up jelly-roll style and place with the seam side down in the pan. Top with the remaining sauce. Sprinkle with the Mexican blend cheese.

**7.** Bake, covered, for 25 minutes. Uncover and bake for 5 to 10 minutes, or until the enchiladas are hot and the sauce is bubbly.

**cook's tip on handling hot chiles:** Hot chiles contain oils that can burn your skin, lips, and eyes. Wear plastic gloves or wash your hands thoroughly with warm, soapy water immediately after handling chiles.

1 **small fresh jalapeño, seeds and ribs discarded, finely chopped**

3 **medium tomatoes, diced**

1 **tablespoon fresh lime juice**

12 **6-inch corn tortillas**

1 **cup shredded low-fat 4-cheese Mexican blend**

................................................................

**per serving**

calories 304
**total fat 7.5 g**
    saturated fat 2.5 g
    trans fat 0.0 g
    polyunsaturated fat 1.0 g
    monounsaturated fat 2.5 g
**cholesterol 48 mg**

sodium 277 mg
**carbohydrates 35 g**
    fiber 7 g
    sugars 7 g
**protein 25 g**

**dietary exchanges**
2 starch, 1 vegetable, 3 lean meat

These warm pita pockets are packed with spring greens and onion tossed with a creamy garlic and feta dressing, then topped with peppery chicken strips and fresh dill. Add a salad or cup of soup, such as Summer Squash Soup (page 40), for a complete meal.

# dilled chicken and feta stuffed pitas

**serves 4** | **1 stuffed pita half per serving**

1½ teaspoons salt-free steak grilling blend

6 boneless, skinless chicken tenders (about ¾ pound), all visible fat discarded, halved lengthwise into strips

1 teaspoon canola or corn oil

1 tablespoon chopped fresh dillweed

2 6-inch whole-grain pita pockets, halved crosswise

⅓ cup low-fat buttermilk

1 tablespoon light mayonnaise

2 medium garlic cloves, minced

2 cups tightly packed mixed spring greens

½ cup diced onion

1½ ounces crumbled low-fat feta cheese

½ cup grape tomatoes, quartered

1. Sprinkle the grilling blend over both sides of the chicken. Using your fingertips, gently press the mixture so it adheres to the chicken.

2. In a large nonstick skillet, heat the oil over medium heat, swirling to coat the bottom. Cook the chicken for 6 minutes, or until no longer pink in the center, turning occasionally. Transfer to a medium plate. Set aside to cool slightly. Sprinkle the chicken with the dillweed.

3. Meanwhile, warm the pita pockets using the package directions.

4. In a large bowl, whisk together the buttermilk, mayonnaise, and garlic. Add the greens and onion, tossing gently until well coated. Add the feta, tossing gently.

5. Fill each pita half with the greens mixture. Sprinkle with the tomatoes. Top with the chicken.

**per serving**

calories 244
total fat 6.5 g
    saturated fat 1.5 g
    trans fat 0.0 g
    polyunsaturated fat 2.0 g
    monounsaturated fat 2.0 g
cholesterol 60 mg

sodium 464 mg
carbohydrates 23 g
    fiber 3 g
    sugars 3 g
protein 25 g

dietary exchanges
1 starch, 1 vegetable, 3 lean meat

The seasoned panko coats the tender chicken in crispness, while fresh mint and lemon zest perk up the cool, creamy dipping sauce. *(See photo insert.)*

# crunchy chicken fingers with yogurt sauce

| serves 4 | 3 ounces chicken and 2 tablespoons sauce per serving |

½ cup fat-free plain Greek yogurt

2 large egg whites

¾ cup whole-wheat panko (Japanese-style bread crumbs)

1 teaspoon paprika

½ teaspoon garlic powder

½ teaspoon dried oregano, crumbled

8 boneless, skinless chicken tenders (about 1 pound), all visible fat discarded

2 tablespoons canola or corn oil

¼ teaspoon salt

**sauce**

⅓ cup fat-free plain Greek yogurt

¼ cup finely chopped fresh mint

2 tablespoons fat-free milk

1 teaspoon grated lemon zest

⅛ teaspoon salt

⅛ teaspoon coarsely ground pepper

1. In a medium bowl, whisk together ½ cup yogurt and the egg whites. In a medium shallow dish, stir together the panko, paprika, garlic powder, and oregano. Put the bowl, dish, and a large plate in a row, assembly-line fashion. Dip the chicken in the yogurt mixture, then in the panko mixture, turning to coat at each step and gently shaking off any excess. Using your fingertips, gently press the coating so it adheres to the chicken. Transfer to the plate, arranging the pieces in a single layer.

2. In a large skillet, heat the oil over medium-high heat, swirling to coat the bottom. Put the chicken in the skillet. Reduce the heat to medium. Cook for 6 minutes on each side, or until no longer pink in the center. Transfer to a serving dish. Sprinkle with ¼ teaspoon salt.

3. Meanwhile, whisk together the sauce ingredients. Serve as a dip with the chicken.

**lunchbox tip:** These chicken fingers pair well with Crunchy Apple-Carrot Slaw (page 53).

**per serving**

calories 287
total fat 10.5 g
    saturated fat 1.0 g
    trans fat 0.0 g
    polyunsaturated fat 2.5 g
    monounsaturated fat 5.5 g
cholesterol 73 mg

sodium 419 mg
carbohydrates 14 g
    fiber 2 g
    sugars 3 g
protein 33 g
**dietary exchanges**
1 starch, 4 lean meat

Any meat that has been sautéed and then stewed qualifies as a fricassee. The key to a good one is the fresh herbs. If you're not a fan of thyme, try tarragon or marjoram instead. Served over brown rice or whole-grain no-yolk noodles, this is comfort food with a French accent.

# chicken fricassee

| serves 4 | 3 ounces chicken, ⅓ cup vegetables, and ¼ cup sauce per serving |
|---|---|

1 tablespoon olive oil

4 boneless, skinless chicken thighs (about 4 ounces each), all visible fat discarded

2 medium carrots, sliced

½ cup frozen pearl onions

½ cup fat-free, low-sodium chicken broth

½ cup dry white wine (regular or nonalcoholic) or 100% apple juice

2 medium garlic cloves, sliced

1 medium dried bay leaf

2 tablespoons all-purpose flour

¼ cup fat-free milk

¼ cup chopped fresh parsley

1 tablespoon chopped fresh thyme

1 teaspoon white wine vinegar

¼ teaspoon pepper

1. In a large nonstick skillet, heat the oil over medium-high heat, swirling to coat the bottom. Cook the chicken for 2 to 3 minutes on each side, or until browned.

2. Stir in the carrots, onions, broth, wine, garlic, and bay leaf. Bring to a boil, still over medium-high heat. Reduce the heat and simmer, covered, for 15 to 20 minutes, or until the chicken is no longer pink in the center, the carrots are tender, and the onions are soft. Discard the bay leaf.

3. Using a slotted spoon, transfer the chicken and vegetables to a serving dish. Cover to keep warm.

4. Put the flour in a small bowl. Add the milk, stirring to dissolve. Whisk the mixture into the liquid in the skillet. Cook for 1 minute, stirring constantly. Stir in the parsley, thyme, vinegar, and pepper. Spoon the sauce over the chicken and vegetables.

**per serving**

calories 237
total fat 6.5 g
   saturated fat 1.0 g
   trans fat 0.0 g
   polyunsaturated fat 1.0 g
   monounsaturated fat 3.5 g
cholesterol 73 mg

sodium 177 mg
carbohydrates 12 g
   fiber 1 g
   sugars 4 g
protein 26 g

dietary exchanges
2 vegetable, 3 lean meat

These kebabs use what is known as an "instant marinade." Because it is highly acidic and intensely seasoned, it needs only about 30 minutes to infuse the turkey with big flavor.

# turkey and bell pepper kebabs

| serves 4 | 1 kebab per serving |

½ cup fresh orange juice

3 tablespoons fresh lime juice

1 tablespoon canola or corn oil

1 tablespoon dark molasses

1 medium garlic clove, minced

1 teaspoon minced peeled gingerroot

⅛ teaspoon crushed red pepper flakes

1 1-pound turkey tenderloin, all visible fat discarded, cut into 16 1-inch cubes

1 large yellow, orange, or red bell pepper, cut into 16 1-inch squares

Cooking spray

1. In a shallow glass dish, whisk together the orange juice, lime juice, oil, molasses, garlic, gingerroot, and red pepper flakes. Add the turkey and bell pepper, turning to coat. Cover and refrigerate for 30 minutes, turning occasionally.

2. Meanwhile, soak four 12-inch wooden skewers for at least 10 minutes in cold water to keep them from charring, or use metal skewers.

3. Lightly spray the grill rack with cooking spray. Preheat the grill on medium.

4. Drain the turkey and bell pepper, discarding the marinade. Alternate the turkey cubes and bell pepper squares as you thread them onto the skewers.

5. Grill the kebabs, covered, for 5 to 6 minutes on each side, or until the turkey is no longer pink in the center.

**per serving**

calories 138
total fat 1.0 g
  saturated fat 0.5 g
  trans fat 0.0 g
  polyunsaturated fat 0.0 g
  monounsaturated fat 0.0 g
cholesterol 70 mg

sodium 57 mg
carbohydrates 3 g
  fiber 0 g
  sugars 1 g
protein 28 g

dietary exchanges
3 lean meat

This turkey breast is extra moist because it's cooked at a low temperature to prevent it from drying out. A fragrant rub of fresh lemon, garlic, and rosemary cooks right against the meat and mixes with the juices to create a light sauce. Whether it's for a crowd or a week's worth of sandwiches for you and your family, this is one recipe you'll rely on.

# rosemary-garlic roast turkey breast

**serves 14** : 3 ounces turkey per serving

Cooking spray

1 5½- to 6-pound turkey breast with bone and skin, thawed if frozen

1 tablespoon grated lemon zest

2 tablespoons fresh lemon juice

1 tablespoon olive oil

4 medium garlic cloves, minced

1 teaspoon dry mustard

1 teaspoon dried rosemary, crushed

¾ teaspoon pepper (coarsely ground preferred)

¼ teaspoon crushed red pepper flakes

¼ teaspoon salt and ¼ teaspoon salt, divided use

⅔ cup cold water

1. Preheat the oven to 325°F.

2. Lightly spray a large glass baking dish with cooking spray. Put the turkey in the baking dish.

3. In a small bowl, stir together the lemon zest, lemon juice, oil, garlic, mustard, rosemary, pepper, red pepper flakes, and ¼ teaspoon salt.

4. Using your fingers and keeping the skin attached, carefully lift the skin from the meat of the turkey so you can spread the lemon zest mixture between the skin and the meat. Cover as much area as possible, being careful not to tear the skin. Gently pull the skin back over the top and sides.

5. Roast the turkey for 1 hour 45 minutes to 2 hours, or until an instant-read thermometer inserted into the thickest part of the breast registers 170°F. Transfer the turkey to a cutting board. Let stand for 20 minutes for easier slicing and to let the turkey continue cooking (the internal

**per serving**

calories 127
total fat 1.5 g
  saturated fat 0.5 g
  trans fat 0.0 g
  polyunsaturated fat 0.5 g
  monounsaturated fat 1.0 g
cholesterol 71 mg

sodium 128 mg
carbohydrates 1 g
  fiber 0 g
  sugars 0 g
protein 26 g

dietary exchanges
3 lean meat

temperature will rise at least 5°F). Cover to keep warm. Discard the skin and any visible fat before slicing the turkey.

6. Meanwhile, add the water and the remaining $1/4$ teaspoon salt to the cooking juices in the baking dish, stirring until well blended. Pour the mixture into a quart-size resealable plastic bag. Seal the bag tightly. Place in the freezer for 15 minutes to allow the fat to rise to the top of the bag. Remove from the freezer.

7. Holding the bag over a small saucepan, use scissors to cut about $1/4$ inch off one corner of the bag. The cooking juices mixture will pour into the pan. Stop the flow before the fat begins to be released.

8. Just before serving, bring the au jus to a boil over medium-high heat. Remove from the heat. Drizzle over the turkey slices.

**cook's tip:** The cold water helps separate the fat from the au jus more quickly.

**cook's tip:** To hold the plastic bag in place while pouring in the cooking juices mixture, put the bag in a tall glass and fold the two sides of the top over the rim of the glass.

**lunchbox tip:** Create lunch roll-ups by rolling together thin slices of turkey and fat-free cheese, such as Swiss. Or, you can divide a light string cheese stick in half or thirds lengthwise and roll a slice of turkey around each piece.

If you crave the flavors of Thanksgiving year-round, this dish is the perfect solution. It pairs heart-healthy, quick-cooking turkey medallions with cinnamon-spiced and walnut-studded sweet potatoes for a festive one-skillet dinner that's delicious any time of year and easy enough for a weeknight. *(See photo insert.)*

# turkey medallions with sweet potato–walnut mash

| serves 4 | 3 ounces turkey, ¾ cup mash, and 1 tablespoon sauce per serving |
|---|---|

¼ teaspoon salt and ¼ teaspoon salt, divided use

¼ teaspoon pepper, ¼ teaspoon pepper, and pinch of pepper, divided use

1 1-pound turkey tenderloin, all visible fat discarded, cut crosswise into 8 medallions

2 teaspoons olive oil

2 medium sweet potatoes, peeled and thinly sliced

1 medium onion, thinly sliced

1 large Granny Smith apple, peeled and thickly sliced

¼ teaspoon ground cinnamon

⅔ cup unsweetened apple cider or 100% apple juice and ¼ cup unsweetened apple cider or 100% apple juice, divided use

¼ cup chopped walnuts, dry-roasted

*(continued)*

1. Sprinkle ¼ teaspoon salt and ¼ teaspoon pepper over both sides of the turkey.

2. In a large skillet, heat the oil over medium-high heat, swirling to coat the bottom. Cook the turkey for 2 minutes on each side, or until browned. (The turkey won't be done at this point.) Transfer to a large plate.

3. In the same skillet, stir together the sweet potatoes and onion. Reduce the heat to medium. Cook for 7 minutes, or until the onion is golden, stirring frequently.

4. Stir in the apple, cinnamon, and the remaining ¼ teaspoon salt and ¼ teaspoon pepper. Cook for 5 minutes, stirring frequently.

5. Place the turkey medallions among the sweet potato and apple slices. Pour in ⅔ cup cider. Bring to a boil, still over medium heat. Reduce the heat and simmer, covered, for 3 to 5 minutes, or until the turkey is no longer pink in the center and the sweet potatoes are tender. Remove from the heat. Transfer the turkey to a separate

large plate, leaving the sweet potato mixture in the skillet. Cover the turkey loosely to keep warm.

**6.** Using a potato masher, mash the sweet potato mixture. Stir in the walnuts. Transfer the sweet potato mixture to plates.

**7.** Quickly pour the remaining ¼ cup cider into the skillet, scraping to dislodge any browned bits. Stir in the mustard, green onions, and final pinch of pepper. Remove from the heat.

**8.** Serve the turkey on the sweet potato mixture. Drizzle the sauce over the turkey.

1 **tablespoon coarse-grain mustard (lowest sodium available)**

2 **tablespoons minced green onions (green part only)**

...................................................................

### per serving

| | |
|---|---|
| calories 338 | sodium 475 mg |
| total fat 8.0 g | carbohydrates 36 g |
|   saturated fat 1.0 g |   fiber 5 g |
|   trans fat 0.0 g |   sugars 17 g |
|   polyunsaturated fat 4.0 g | protein 31 g |
|   monounsaturated fat 2.5 g | |
| cholesterol 70 mg | **dietary exchanges** |
| | 1½ starch, 1 fruit, 3 lean meat |

Canned chipotle peppers—smoked dried jalapeños—are packed in a rich adobo sauce that gives this dish its bold, spicy flavor. A touch of sweet maple syrup softens the chile's assertiveness.

# spiced turkey cutlets with maple-chipotle sauce

**serves 4** : 3 ounces turkey and 1 tablespoon sauce per serving

½ teaspoon dried thyme, crumbled

¼ teaspoon ground nutmeg

¼ teaspoon ground cinnamon

⅛ teaspoon ground allspice

⅛ teaspoon salt

4 turkey breast cutlets (about 4 ounces each), about ½ inch thick, all visible fat discarded

½ cup fat-free, low-sodium chicken broth

2 tablespoons pure maple syrup

1 to 2 chipotle peppers canned in adobo sauce, chopped

2 teaspoons cider vinegar

1 tablespoon olive oil

2 tablespoons chopped fresh parsley

1. In a small bowl, stir together the thyme, nutmeg, cinnamon, allspice, and salt. Sprinkle over both sides of the turkey. Using your fingertips, gently press the mixture so it adheres to the turkey.

2. In a separate small bowl, stir together the broth, maple syrup, chipotle pepper, and vinegar. Set aside.

3. In a large nonstick skillet, heat the oil over medium-high heat, swirling to coat the bottom. Cook the turkey for 4 to 5 minutes on each side, or until no longer pink in the center. Transfer to plates. Cover to keep warm.

4. Pour the broth mixture into the skillet. Bring to a boil, still over medium-high heat. Boil for 4 to 5 minutes, or until the sauce is reduced by two-thirds (to about ¼ cup). Stir in the parsley. Drizzle the sauce over the turkey.

**per serving**

calories 190
total fat 4.5 g
  saturated fat 0.5 g
  trans fat 0.0 g
  polyunsaturated fat  0.5 g
  monounsaturated fat 2.5 g
cholesterol 71 mg

sodium 188 mg
carbohydrates 8 g
  fiber 0 g
  sugars 6 g
protein 28 g

dietary exchanges
½ other carbohydrate,
3 lean meat

Creamy country gravy tops lightly breaded turkey in this mouthwatering entrée.

# turkey cutlets and gravy

| serves 4 | 3 ounces turkey and 2 tablespoons gravy per serving |
|---|---|

¼ cup all-purpose flour and
2 teaspoons all-purpose flour,
divided use

1½ teaspoons salt-free all-purpose
seasoning blend

2 large egg whites

¼ cup fat-free milk

½ cup plain dry bread crumbs (lowest
sodium available)

4 turkey breast cutlets (about 4 ounces
each), all visible fat discarded, or
1 pound boneless, skinless turkey
breast, cut crosswise into 4 slices,
cutlets or slices flattened to ½-inch
thickness

Cooking spray

1 tablespoon canola or corn oil

¼ cup fat-free half-and-half

⅓ cup fat-free, low-sodium chicken
broth

⅛ teaspoon pepper

**per serving**

calories 268
total fat 5.0 g
  saturated fat 0.5 g
  trans fat 0.0 g
  polyunsaturated fat 1.5 g
  monounsaturated fat 2.5 g
cholesterol 71 mg

sodium 209 mg
carbohydrates 20 g
  fiber 1 g
  sugars 3 g
protein 34 g

**dietary exchanges**
1½ starch, 3 lean
meat

1. In a medium shallow dish, stir together ¼ cup flour and the seasoning blend. In a separate medium shallow dish, whisk the egg whites until foamy. Whisk in the milk. Put the bread crumbs in a third medium shallow dish. Set the dishes and a large plate in a row, assembly-line fashion.

2. Dip the turkey in the flour mixture, then in the egg white mixture, and finally in the bread crumbs, turning to coat at each step and gently shaking off any excess. Using your fingertips, gently press the coating so it adheres to the turkey. Transfer to the plate. Sprinkle any remaining bread crumb mixture over the turkey. Lightly spray both sides with cooking spray.

3. In a large nonstick skillet, heat the oil over medium-high heat, swirling to coat the bottom. Cook the turkey for 4 minutes on each side, or until no longer pink in the center. Transfer to serving plates, leaving any pan drippings in the skillet. Reduce the heat to medium.

4. Meanwhile, in a small bowl, whisk together the half-and-half and the remaining 2 teaspoons flour. Whisk in the broth and pepper. Whisk into the pan drippings, scraping to dislodge any browned bits. Cook for 1 minute, whisking constantly. Spoon the gravy over the turkey.

Turkey and cranberries are a common pairing, but most prepared cranberry sauces and relishes are filled with added sugar. Our recipe brings together turkey cutlets with a relish that relies on the sweetness of a fresh orange and less than a teaspoon of sugar to temper the tartness of the cranberries.

# turkey cutlets with fresh cranberry-orange relish

**serves 4** : 3 ounces turkey and ¼ cup relish per serving

½ teaspoon grated orange zest

½ cup diced orange sections (about 1 medium orange)

½ cup fresh cranberries, finely chopped

½ teaspoon sugar

1 teaspoon ground cumin

½ teaspoon ground allspice

½ teaspoon onion powder

¼ teaspoon pepper

4 turkey breast cutlets (about 4 ounces each), about ½ inch thick, all visible fat discarded

1 teaspoon canola or corn oil and 1 teaspoon canola or corn oil, divided use

¼ teaspoon salt

1. In a small bowl, stir together the orange zest, orange, cranberries, and sugar. Set aside.

2. In a separate small bowl, stir together the cumin, allspice, onion powder, and pepper. Sprinkle the mixture over both sides of the turkey. Using your fingertips, gently press the mixture so it adheres to the turkey.

3. In a large nonstick skillet, heat 1 teaspoon oil over medium-high heat, swirling to coat the bottom. Cook half the turkey for 2 minutes on each side, or until no longer pink in the center. Transfer to a large plate. Cover to keep warm. Repeat with the remaining 1 teaspoon oil and the remaining turkey.

4. Sprinkle the turkey with the salt. Serve the relish on the side.

**cook's tip:** If you crave cranberries, buy extra packages when they're in season and freeze them in an airtight container or a resealable plastic freezer bag. They will last about a year.

### per serving

| | |
|---|---|
| calories 169 | sodium 202 mg |
| total fat 3.5 g | carbohydrates 6 g |
|   saturated fat 0.5 g |   fiber 1 g |
|   trans fat 0.0 g |   sugars 3 g |
|   polyunsaturated fat 1.0 g | **protein 28 g** |
|   monounsaturated fat 1.5 g | **dietary exchanges** |
| cholesterol 70 mg | ½ fruit, 3 lean meat |

Italian spices enliven traditional stuffed peppers, while lean ground turkey stands in for the more commonly used ground beef. To heighten the visual appeal of this dish, use a variety of bell pepper colors.

# italian stuffed peppers

**serves 4** | 1 stuffed pepper per serving

1 tablespoon olive oil

1 cup finely chopped onion

¾ cup sliced carrots

½ cup diced green bell pepper

3 medium garlic cloves, minced

1 pound ground skinless turkey breast

1½ teaspoons dried Italian seasoning, crumbled

1 28-ounce can no-salt-added crushed tomatoes, drained

¾ cup uncooked long-grain rice

¼ teaspoon pepper, or to taste

4 medium bell peppers (a variety of colors preferred), tops sliced off and discarded, seeds and ribs discarded

1. In a medium nonstick skillet, heat the oil over medium-high heat, swirling to coat the bottom. Cook the onion, carrots, and diced bell pepper for 3 minutes, or until the onion is soft, stirring frequently. Stir in the garlic. Cook for 2 minutes, stirring frequently.

2. Stir in the turkey and Italian seasoning. Reduce the heat to medium. Cook for 3 to 5 minutes, or until the turkey is no longer pink in the center, stirring occasionally to turn and break up the turkey. Stir in the tomatoes, rice, and pepper. Cook for 20 to 25 minutes, or until the rice is tender.

3. Meanwhile, blanch the bell peppers in boiling water for 5 minutes. Drain well in a colander. Pat the insides dry with paper towels. Transfer the peppers to plates. Spoon the filling into the peppers.

**per serving**

calories 406
total fat 5.5 g
  saturated fat 1.0 g
  trans fat 0.0 g
  polyunsaturated fat 1.0 g
  monounsaturated fat 3.0 g
cholesterol 70 mg

sodium 116 mg
carbohydrates 53 g
  fiber 9 g
  sugars 13 g
protein 36 g

dietary exchanges
2 starch, 5 vegetable, 3 lean meat

Shepherd's pie is a traditional Irish comfort food consisting of a meat filling topped with mashed potatoes. In our healthier version of this pub staple, a blanket of mashed cauliflower conceals a creamy mixture of lean ground turkey, peas, carrots, and hearty winter squash.

# individual shepherd's pies

| serves 4 | 1 pie per serving |
|----------|-------------------|

1 teaspoon canola or corn oil

1 pound ground skinless turkey breast

2 cups diced acorn or butternut squash

1 medium onion, diced

3 tablespoons whole-wheat flour

1½ cups fat-free milk

½ cup fat-free, low-sodium chicken broth and ¼ cup fat-free, low-sodium chicken broth, divided use

¼ teaspoon poultry seasoning

⅛ teaspoon pepper and ¹⁄₁₆ teaspoon pepper, divided use

1 cup frozen green peas and carrots, thawed

½ head (about 1 pound) cauliflower, cut into pieces

½ cup water

2 medium garlic cloves

½ teaspoon chopped fresh rosemary

1. In a large skillet, heat the oil over medium-low heat, swirling to coat the bottom. Cook the turkey for 3 minutes, stirring occasionally to turn and break up the turkey. Stir in the squash and onion. Cook, covered, for 7 minutes, or until the onion begins to soften and the turkey is no longer pink in the center, stirring occasionally.

2. Stir in the flour. Cook for 3 minutes, stirring frequently.

3. Stir in the milk, ½ cup broth, poultry seasoning, and ⅛ teaspoon pepper. Cook for 2 to 3 minutes, stirring constantly. Reduce the heat and simmer for 15 minutes, stirring occasionally.

4. Stir in the peas and carrots. Cook for 3 minutes, stirring occasionally.

5. Meanwhile, in a 4-quart saucepan, bring the cauliflower, water, garlic, rosemary, and the remaining ¼ cup broth to a simmer over low heat. Simmer, covered, for 15 minutes, or until the cauliflower is tender when pierced with a fork. Uncover and cook for 5 minutes. Drain well in a colander.

## per serving

| | |
|---|---|
| calories 281 | sodium 170 mg |
| total fat 2.5 g | carbohydrates 30 g |
|   saturated fat 0.5 g |   fiber 7 g |
|   trans fat 0.0 g |   sugars 10 g |
|   polyunsaturated fat 0.5 g | protein 36 g |
|   monounsaturated fat 1.0 g | dietary exchanges |
| cholesterol 72 mg | 1½ starch, 2 vegetable, 3½ lean meat |

**6.** In a food processor or blender, process the cauliflower mixture and the remaining $1/16$ teaspoon pepper for 1 minute, or until thick and smooth.

**7.** Preheat the broiler.

**8.** Spoon the turkey mixture into four 16-ounce ceramic ramekins or a $1^{1}/_{2}$-quart glass casserole dish. Top with the cauliflower mixture, making sure the turkey mixture is completely covered. Broil about 6 inches from the heat for 5 minutes, or until the topping becomes firmer. Serve immediately.

**cook's tip:** Almost any starchy vegetable can stand in for the cauliflower. In addition to traditional potatoes, you can try sweet potatoes, butternut squash, or pumpkin.

This Cuban favorite usually contains ground beef, but our version uses ground skinless turkey breast instead. Sweet golden raisins contrast with briny capers and tangy green olives to provide layers of complex flavors. Serve the picadillo over brown rice to soak up the sauce. Sautéed plantains are a traditional accompaniment.

# turkey picadillo

**serves 4** · **1 cup per serving**

1 tablespoon olive oil

1 medium onion, minced

1 medium red bell pepper, minced

3 medium garlic cloves, minced

¼ teaspoon pepper (freshly ground preferred)

1 pound ground skinless turkey breast

1 8-ounce can no-salt-added tomato sauce

¼ cup marsala or dry red wine (regular or nonalcoholic)

2 tablespoons golden raisins

2 tablespoons capers, drained

1 tablespoon no-salt-added tomato paste (optional)

1½ teaspoons ground cumin

1 teaspoon dried oregano, crumbled

¼ cup thinly sliced pimiento-stuffed green olives, drained

1. In a large skillet, heat the oil over medium-high heat, swirling to coat the bottom. Cook the onion and bell pepper for 3 minutes, or just until soft, stirring frequently. Stir in the garlic and pepper. Cook for 2 to 3 minutes, stirring frequently.

2. Reduce the heat to medium. Stir in the turkey. Cook for 8 to 10 minutes, or until lightly browned on the outside and no longer pink in the center, stirring occasionally to turn and break up the turkey.

3. Stir in the remaining ingredients except the olives. Bring the picadillo to a boil. Reduce the heat and simmer for 15 minutes, or until moist but not soupy, stirring occasionally.

4. Stir in the olives.

**cook's tip on plantains:** Plantains, which look like large bananas, are starchier and less sweet than bananas and are usually eaten cooked. To sauté them, halve 2 medium green plantains lengthwise. Cut them diagonally into ½-inch slices. In a large nonstick skillet, heat 1 tablespoon canola or corn oil, swirling to coat the bottom. Cook the plantains for 3 to 4 minutes on each side, or until the edges are golden brown.

**per serving**

| | |
|---|---|
| calories 251 | sodium 402 mg |
| total fat 5.5 g | carbohydrates 17 g |
| saturated fat 1.0 g | fiber 3 g |
| trans fat 0.0 g | sugars 10 g |
| polyunsaturated fat 0.5 g | protein 30 g |
| monounsaturated fat 3.5 g | |
| cholesterol 70 mg | dietary exchanges |
| | 2 vegetable, ½ fruit, 3 lean meat |

Packed with whole-grain pasta, cannellini beans, turkey sausage, and veggies including kale, escarole, and carrots, this soup is nutritious and rich tasting. Enjoy a hot bowlful with crusty whole-grain bread to fortify yourself on a cold or rainy day.

# greens-and-beans soup with pasta and sausage

**serves 8** | 1½ cups per serving

1 **tablespoon olive oil**

2 **large onions, chopped**

8 **ounces low-fat sweet or hot Italian turkey or chicken sausage, cut crosswise into ½-inch slices**

3 **medium carrots, diced**

2 **medium garlic cloves, minced**

6 **cups fat-free, low-sodium vegetable broth**

1 **14.5-ounce can no-salt-added diced tomatoes, undrained**

2 **cups dried whole-grain bowtie (farfalle) pasta**

1 **15.5-ounce can no-salt-added cannellini beans, rinsed and drained**

8 **ounces chopped kale, any large stems discarded**

8 **ounces chopped escarole, tough stems discarded**

½ **cup shredded Parmesan cheese**

**per serving**

calories 277
total fat 6.5 g
  saturated fat 2.0 g
  trans fat 0.0 g
  polyunsaturated fat 1.5 g
  monounsaturated fat 3.0 g
cholesterol 26 mg

sodium 403 mg
carbohydrates 41 g
  fiber 8 g
  sugars 6 g
protein 15 g

dietary exchanges
2 starch, 2 vegetable,
1½ lean meat

1. In a large stockpot or Dutch oven, heat the oil over medium-high heat, swirling to coat the bottom. Cook the onions for 3 minutes, or until soft, stirring frequently. Reduce the heat to medium low and cook for 15 minutes, or until caramelized, stirring frequently.

2. Stir in the sausage. Cook for 5 to 6 minutes, or until lightly browned, stirring frequently. Stir in the carrots and garlic. Cook for 3 minutes, stirring frequently.

3. Stir in the broth and tomatoes with liquid. Increase the heat to high and bring to a boil. Reduce the heat and simmer for 5 to 6 minutes, or until the carrots are just tender.

4. Stir in the pasta, beans, kale, and escarole. Cook for 7 to 10 minutes, or until the pasta is al dente, stirring frequently.

5. Ladle the soup into bowls. Sprinkle with the Parmesan.

**cook's tip:** Substitute Swiss chard, collards, or any hearty green for the escarole or kale. This soup freezes well for a quick and filling meal.

If you haven't experimented with fresh fennel yet, this substantial pilaf is a great way to start. The fennel bulb has an earthy taste—not quite the strong "licorice" flavor of fennel seeds, but more like an onion with some attitude.

# turkey sausage, fennel, and bulgur pilaf

**serves 4** | 1¼ cups per serving

6 ounces low-fat sweet or hot Italian turkey sausage, casings discarded

¾ cup uncooked instant, or fine-grain, bulgur

1 tablespoon canola or corn oil

1 medium fennel bulb, diced

½ cup diced onion

½ cup thinly sliced carrot

¼ cup dried tart cherries

¼ cup chopped walnuts, dry-roasted

¼ cup water

1. Heat a large skillet over medium-high heat. Cook the sausage for 3 to 4 minutes, or until no longer pink, stirring occasionally to turn and break up the sausage. Transfer to a plate. Set aside.

2. Meanwhile, prepare the bulgur using the package directions, omitting the salt. Fluff with a fork.

3. In the same skillet, still over medium-high heat, heat the oil, swirling to coat the bottom. Cook the fennel, onion, and carrot for 7 to 8 minutes, or until the fennel and onion are richly browned and the carrot is tender, stirring occasionally. Remove from the heat.

4. Stir in the cherries, walnuts, water, sausage, and bulgur.

**per serving**

calories 291
total fat 12.0 g
  saturated fat 1.5 g
  trans fat 0.0 g
  polyunsaturated fat 5.5 g
  monounsaturated fat 4.0 g
cholesterol 33 mg

sodium 274 mg
carbohydrates 35 g
  fiber 8 g
  sugars 6 g
protein 13 g

dietary exchanges
1½ starch, ½ fruit,
1 vegetable, 1 lean
meat, 2 fat

# meats

This roast is seasoned with paprika and onion and garlic powders, browned on the stovetop, and then cooked "low and slow" in the oven. It's served topped with sweet and sautéed shallots.

# eye-of-round roast with browned shallots

**serves 8** | 3 ounces beef and 2 tablespoons shallots per serving

Cooking spray

1½ teaspoons paprika

1 teaspoon onion powder

1 teaspoon garlic powder

½ teaspoon pepper (coarsely ground preferred)

¼ teaspoon salt and ¼ teaspoon salt, divided use

1 2-pound eye-of-round roast, all visible fat discarded

1 teaspoon canola or corn oil and 2 teaspoons canola or corn oil, divided use

6 to 8 medium shallots, peeled and thinly sliced

2 teaspoons sugar

1. Preheat the oven to 300°F. Lightly spray a 13 × 9 × 2-inch baking dish with cooking spray.

2. In a small bowl, stir together the paprika, onion powder, garlic powder, pepper, and ¼ teaspoon salt. Sprinkle over both sides of the beef. Using your fingertips, gently press the mixture so it adheres to the beef.

3. In a large nonstick skillet, heat 1 teaspoon oil over medium-high heat, swirling to coat the bottom. Cook the beef for 6 minutes, browning on all sides. Transfer to the baking dish, leaving the drippings in the skillet.

4. Roast the beef for 1 hour for medium rare, or to the desired doneness. Transfer the beef to a cutting board. Let stand for 15 minutes before slicing thinly.

5. Meanwhile, in the same skillet, over medium heat, stir the remaining 2 teaspoons oil into the pan drippings. Cook the shallots for 8 minutes, or until richly browned, stirring frequently. Remove from the heat.

6. Stir in the sugar and the remaining ¼ teaspoon salt. Serve the shallots over the beef.

**per serving**

| | |
|---|---|
| calories 160 | sodium 188 mg |
| total fat 4.0 g | carbohydrates 4 g |
| saturated fat 1.0 g | fiber 0 g |
| trans fat 0.0 g | sugars 2 g |
| polyunsaturated fat 0.5 g | **protein 25 g** |
| monounsaturated fat 2.5 g | |
| cholesterol 48 mg | **dietary exchanges** |
| | 3 lean meat |

**italian meatball sliders**  page 26

**crunchy apple-carrot slaw** page 53

**fresh garden soup** page 36

**crunchy chicken fingers with yogurt sauce** page 111

**kale salad with
citrus dressing** page 46

**asparagus and mushroom
soup** page 44

**salmon-corn chowder**  page 70

**spicy shrimp and grits** page 87

chinese chicken stir-fry page 107

**turkey medallions with sweet potato-walnut mash** page 116

**beef manicotti** page 142

**pork and green onion tacos** page 159

**garlicky greek salad pizza**   page 164

**thai red curry**
page 190

**amaranth and green peas with mint** page 200

roasted radishes page 216

**spanish-style potato tortilla**   page 233

**chocolate and red wine mini cupcakes**   page 245

**sangría-style punch**   page 239

**lemon mini cheesecakes** page 254

True to its name, beef tenderloin has the ultimate melt-in-your-mouth texture, and a slathering of Dijon mustard, garlic, rosemary, and thyme enhances its meaty flavor. Serve this with Roasted Radishes (page 216) and baked sweet potatoes.

# herb-crusted beef tenderloin

| serves 4 | 3 ounces beef per serving |
|---|---|

Cooking spray

2 tablespoons Dijon mustard (lowest sodium available)

1 tablespoon chopped fresh rosemary or 1 teaspoon dried rosemary, crushed

1 tablespoon chopped fresh thyme or 1 teaspoon dried thyme, crumbled

4 medium garlic cloves, chopped

½ teaspoon pepper (freshly ground preferred)

1 1-pound beef tenderloin, all visible fat discarded

**per serving**

calories 166
total fat 5.5 g
  saturated fat 2.5 g
  trans fat 0.0 g
  polyunsaturated fat 0.5 g
  monounsaturated fat 2.5 g
cholesterol 53 mg
sodium 204 mg
carbohydrates 3 g
  fiber 1 g
  sugars 1 g
protein 25 g

dietary exchanges
3 lean meat

**cook's tip on beef doneness:** An instant-read thermometer is the best way to test the doneness of beef and other meats. Medium-rare beef will register 145°F. Remove the beef from the oven when it's 5 to 10 degrees below the desired doneness. The beef will continue to cook while it stands.

1. Preheat the oven to 425°F. Lightly spray an 8-inch square baking dish with cooking spray.

2. In a small bowl, whisk together the mustard, rosemary, thyme, garlic, and pepper.

3. Using 2 feet of kitchen twine, wrap it around one end of the beef. Tie a knot. Pull the twine diagonally over one side, pressing it down with your fingers, and wrap around the beef. Bring it up beneath the twine on top. Pull gently to tighten and form a cross shape. Repeat at 2-inch intervals (3 or 4 times). When you reach the other end, pull the twine over the end and up the length of the underside beneath the loops. Knot securely at the original end to help the beef keep its shape during roasting.

4. Using the back of a spoon or a pastry brush, spread the mustard mixture all over the beef. Transfer to the pan.

5. Roast for 30 to 40 minutes, or to the desired doneness. Transfer the beef to a cutting board. Let stand for 10 minutes. Discard the twine before cutting the beef crosswise into slices.

Lean eye-of-round steaks become tender and tasty as they slowly simmer in a rosemary-scented blend of beef broth and red wine. Potatoes and carrots cook to perfection in the same pan, making cleanup a breeze.

# braised beef with potatoes and carrots

| serves 4 | 3 ounces beef, ½ cup vegetables, and 2 tablespoons sauce per serving |
| --- | --- |

1 tablespoon chopped fresh rosemary

½ teaspoon pepper

4 eye-of-round steaks (about 4 ounces each), all visible fat discarded

Cooking spray

1 cup fat-free, low-sodium beef broth

½ cup dry red wine (regular or nonalcoholic)

2 tablespoons no-salt-added tomato paste

1 medium dried bay leaf

8 ounces fingerling potatoes, halved lengthwise

8 ounces baby carrots

1. Sprinkle the rosemary and pepper over both sides of the beef. Using your fingertips, gently press the seasonings so they adhere to the beef.

2. Lightly spray a large skillet with cooking spray. Heat over medium-high heat. Cook the beef for 4 to 5 minutes, or until browned, turning once halfway through.

3. In a small bowl, stir together the broth, wine, tomato paste, and bay leaf. Pour the broth mixture over the beef. Arrange the potatoes and carrots around and over the beef. Reduce the heat to low. Cook, covered, for 45 minutes to 1 hour, or until the beef and vegetables are tender (no stirring needed). Transfer the beef and vegetables to a platter. Cover to keep warm.

4. If there is more than ½ cup of liquid in the skillet, increase the heat to high and bring it to a boil. Boil until the liquid is reduced to ½ cup. Discard the bay leaf. Pour the sauce over the beef and vegetables.

**per serving**

calories 223
total fat 3.0 g
    saturated fat 1.5 g
    trans fat 0.0 g
    polyunsaturated fat 0.5 g
    monounsaturated fat 1.5 g
cholesterol 54 mg

sodium 134 mg
carbohydrates 16 g
    fiber 3 g
    sugars 5 g
protein 29 g

dietary exchanges
½ starch, 1 vegetable, 3 lean meat

The sweet-tartness of dried cherries is a perfect complement to the robust beefiness of flank steak. Serve with Oregano Brussels Sprouts (page 205) or Broccoli with Caramelized Walnuts (page 203) to add a contrast of color to your plate.

# flank steak with cherry-wine sauce

**serves 4** : 3 ounces beef and 3 tablespoons sauce per serving

¼ teaspoon salt

¼ teaspoon pepper

1 1-pound flank steak, all visible fat discarded

2 teaspoons olive oil

1 medium shallot, finely chopped

½ cup fat-free, low-sodium beef broth

½ cup dry red wine (regular or nonalcoholic) or 100% cherry juice

⅓ cup coarsely chopped dried tart cherries

1 tablespoon balsamic vinegar

1 tablespoon chopped fresh thyme

**per serving**

calories 235
total fat 9.0 g
  saturated fat 3.0 g
  trans fat 0.5 g
  polyunsaturated fat 0.5 g
  monounsaturated fat 4.5 g
cholesterol 65 mg

sodium 208 mg
carbohydrates 10 g
  fiber 1 g
  sugars 6 g
protein 24 g

dietary exchanges
1 fruit, 3 lean meat

1. Sprinkle the salt and pepper over both sides of the beef.

2. In a large nonstick skillet, heat the oil over medium-high heat, swirling to coat the bottom. Cook the beef for 7 to 8 minutes on each side for medium rare, or until the desired doneness. Transfer to a cutting board. Cover to keep warm.

3. In the same skillet, still over medium-high heat, cook the shallot for 1 to 2 minutes, or until tender, stirring frequently. Stir in the broth, wine, cherries, and vinegar. Bring to a boil. Boil for 4 to 5 minutes, or until the liquid is reduced by half (to about ½ cup).

4. Stir in the thyme.

5. Thinly slice the beef diagonally across the grain and transfer to plates. Spoon the sauce over the beef.

Everything is grilled in this tangy salad—even the lettuce! The rich warmth of the components pairs perfectly with the tart lemon-feta dressing.

# grilled greek steak salad

| serves 4 | 3 ounces beef, 1¼ cups salad, 1 heaping tablespoon dressing, and 2 pita wedges per serving |
|---|---|

2 tablespoons fresh lemon juice

2 tablespoons olive oil (extra virgin preferred)

2 tablespoons crumbled fat-free feta cheese

1 teaspoon chopped fresh oregano

1 small garlic clove, minced

¼ teaspoon pepper

Cooking spray

½ medium red or sweet onion, such as Vidalia, Maui, or Oso Sweet, cut into 2 thick slices

1 pint (about 24) cherry or grape tomatoes

1 head of romaine

2 6-inch whole-grain pita pockets

1 teaspoon salt-free Greek seasoning blend, crumbled

1 1-pound flank steak, all visible fat discarded

1. Soak six 10-inch wooden skewers for at least 10 minutes in cold water to keep them from charring, or use metal skewers.

2. Meanwhile, in a small bowl, whisk together the lemon juice, oil, feta, oregano, garlic, and pepper. Set aside.

3. Lightly spray the grill rack with cooking spray. Preheat the grill on medium.

4. Put the onion slices on a flat surface. Hold one down with your palm while carefully working the skewer sideways through the middle of the layers (the result will look like an onion lollipop). Repeat with a second skewer and the remaining slice. Thread the tomatoes onto the remaining four skewers. Transfer the skewers to a platter. Place the romaine and pita pockets on the platter. Lightly spray both sides of the onion and tomato skewers, romaine, and pita pockets with cooking spray.

5. Sprinkle the seasoning blend over both sides of the beef. Using your fingertips, gently press the seasoning so it adheres to the beef. Grill the beef for 6 to 8 minutes on each side for medium rare, or until the desired doneness. Transfer to a cutting board. Let stand for 5 minutes.

**per serving**

calories 354 g
total fat 15.0 g
    saturated fat 4.0 g
    trans fat 0.5 g
    polyunsaturated fat 1.5 g
    monounsaturated fat 8.0 g
cholesterol 65 mg

sodium 300 mg
carbohydrates 28 g
    fiber 6 g
    sugars 7 g
protein 29 g

dietary exchanges
1 starch, 2 vegetable, 3 lean meat, 1 fat

6. Meanwhile, grill the onion and tomato skewers and the romaine for 3 to 4 minutes on each side, or until the onion is tender-crisp and the tomatoes and romaine are lightly charred. Transfer to a cutting board.

7. Grill the pita pockets for 1 to 2 minutes on each side, or until grill marks appear. Transfer to a cutting board.

8. Thinly slice the beef diagonally across the grain. Slide the onion and tomatoes off the skewers. Coarsely chop the onion and romaine. Halve the tomatoes if desired. Cut each pita pocket into four wedges.

9. Arrange the romaine on plates. Top with the beef, onion, and tomatoes. Drizzle with the dressing. Serve with the pita wedges.

**cook's tip:** Skewering the onion slices allows you to grill them easily without the rings falling through the grill rack.

**cook's tip on greek seasoning blend:** To make your own salt-free Greek seasoning blend, stir together 1 tablespoon dried oregano, 2 teaspoons dried mint, 2 teaspoons dried thyme, 1 teaspoon dried basil, 1 teaspoon dried marjoram, 1 teaspoon dried minced onion, and 1 teaspoon garlic powder. Store the mixture in an airtight container in a cool, dry place. Crumble the mixture just before use.

Named for the Mexican city of Tampico, where it originated, this steak dish has south-of-the-border flavor and flair with all of the onion, tomato, and green chile trimmings. Chili powder gives the meat a beautiful red sheen, and the smoked paprika heightens its flavor. Serve with brown rice and a vegetable side dish, such as Fiesta Veggies (page 221).

# steak tampiqueña

| serves 4 | 3 ounces beef per serving |
|---|---|

1 teaspoon olive oil

½ medium onion, thinly sliced

2 medium garlic cloves, thinly sliced

1 medium tomato, peeled, seeded if desired, and diced

1 4-ounce can chopped green chiles, drained

Cooking spray

1 teaspoon chili powder

1 1-pound boneless top sirloin steak, about 1 inch thick, all visible fat discarded, cut into 4 pieces

½ teaspoon smoked paprika

¼ cup shredded low-fat Monterey Jack cheese

**per serving**

calories 192
total fat 7.0 g
  saturated fat 2.5 g
  trans fat 0.0 g
  polyunsaturated fat 0.5 g
  monounsaturated fat 3.0 g
cholesterol 59 mg

sodium 210 mg
carbohydrates 5 g
  fiber 2 g
  sugars 2 g
protein 26 g

dietary exchanges
1 vegetable, 3 lean meat

1. In a small saucepan, heat the oil over medium heat, swirling to coat the bottom. Cook the onion and garlic for 3 to 4 minutes, or until the onion begins to soften. Stir in the tomato and green chiles. Increase the heat to medium high and bring to a simmer. Reduce the heat and simmer for 6 to 8 minutes so the flavors blend, stirring occasionally.

2. Lightly spray the grill rack or a broiler pan and rack with cooking spray. Preheat the grill on medium high or preheat the broiler.

3. Sprinkle the chili powder over both sides of the beef. Using your fingertips, gently press the chili powder so it adheres to the beef.

4. Grill, or broil 5 to 6 inches from the heat, for 10 to 15 minutes, or until the beef is the desired doneness, turning once halfway through. Transfer the beef to plates.

5. Sprinkle each piece of beef with the paprika. Spoon the onion mixture over each. Sprinkle with the Monterey Jack.

If you're searching for a gourmet entrée that's rich in flavor and super-fast, look no further. These piquant steaks are cooked with a light coating of fennel seeds and instant coffee granules that melts into the meat and enhances its beefy flavor. Diced tomato and a drizzle of an intense balsamic vinegar reduction are the finishing touches.

# coffee and fennel rubbed sirloin with tomato

| serves 4 | 3 ounces beef, ¼ cup tomato, and 1½ teaspoons sauce per serving |
|---|---|

2 teaspoons instant coffee granules

½ teaspoon garlic powder

¼ teaspoon dried fennel seeds

¼ teaspoon salt and ⅛ teaspoon salt, divided use

4 boneless sirloin steaks (about 4 ounces each), all visible fat discarded

1 teaspoon canola or corn oil

¼ cup water

¼ cup balsamic vinegar

2 teaspoons Worcestershire sauce (lowest sodium available)

1 medium tomato, seeded and diced

¼ teaspoon pepper (coarsely ground preferred)

**per serving**

calories 178
total fat 5.5 g
   saturated fat 2.0 g
   trans fat 0.0 g
   polyunsaturated fat 0.5 g
   monounsaturated fat 3.0 g
cholesterol 60 mg

sodium 304 mg
carbohydrates 4 g
   fiber 1 g
   sugars 3 g
protein 26 g

dietary exchanges
3 lean meat

1. In a small bowl, stir together the coffee granules, garlic powder, fennel seeds, and ¼ teaspoon salt. Sprinkle the mixture over both sides of the beef. Using your fingertips, gently press the seasonings so they adhere to the beef.

2. In a large nonstick skillet, heat the oil over medium-high heat, swirling to coat the bottom. Cook the beef for 4 minutes on each side, or to the desired doneness. Transfer to a platter. Cover to keep warm.

3. Stir the water, vinegar, and Worcestershire sauce into the pan drippings, scraping to dislodge any browned bits. Bring to a boil, still over medium-high heat. Boil for 2 to 2½ minutes, or until the mixture is reduced by three-fourths (to about 2 tablespoons), stirring frequently.

4. Just before serving, drizzle the sauce over the beef. Sprinkle with the tomato, pepper, and the remaining ⅛ teaspoon salt.

The name of this dish translates from the Spanish to mean "old clothes," a phrase that vividly describes the way the shreds of beef, bell pepper, and onion look in this traditional aromatic Cuban entrée.

# ropa vieja

**serves 6** | 1 cup per serving

1½ **pounds flank steak, all visible fat discarded**

1 **large onion, chopped, and 1 medium onion, thinly sliced, divided use**

2 **medium carrots, chopped**

2 **medium ribs of celery, chopped**

2 **medium garlic cloves, minced, and 2 medium garlic cloves, minced, divided use**

¾ **teaspoon dried oregano, crumbled, and ½ teaspoon dried oregano, crumbled, divided use**

¾ **teaspoon ground cumin and ½ teaspoon ground cumin, divided use**

½ **teaspoon pepper (freshly ground preferred)**

1 **14.5-ounce can no-salt-added diced tomatoes, undrained**

1 **tablespoon olive oil**

1 **medium red bell pepper, sliced**

½ **medium green bell pepper, sliced**

¼ **cup minced Italian (flat-leaf) parsley**

**per serving**

calories 206
total fat 9.0 g
  saturated fat 3.0 g
  trans fat 0.0 g
  polyunsaturated fat 0.5 g
  monounsaturated fat 5.0 g
cholesterol 48 mg

sodium 47 mg
carbohydrates 6 g
  fiber 2 g
  sugars 4 g
protein 24 g

dietary exchanges
1 vegetable, 3 lean meat

1. Put the beef, chopped onion, carrots, celery, 2 garlic cloves, ³/₄ teaspoon oregano, ³/₄ teaspoon cumin, and the pepper in a large Dutch oven or saucepan. Add the tomatoes with liquid. Add enough water to cover the beef by 1 to 2 inches.

2. Bring to a boil over medium-high heat. Reduce the heat and simmer for 1¹/₂ hours, or until the beef is fork-tender. Turn off the heat. Let stand for 15 minutes. Transfer the beef to a large plate or a cutting board. Let stand for 20 to 30 minutes, or until cool.

3. Meanwhile, strain the onion mixture and discard the solids. Set the broth aside. Using two forks or your fingers, shred the beef.

4. In a large skillet, heat the oil over medium-high heat, swirling to coat the bottom. Cook the bell peppers and sliced onion for 3 minutes, or until just soft, stirring frequently. Stir in the remaining 2 garlic cloves, ¹/₂ teaspoon oregano, and ¹/₂ teaspoon cumin. Cook for 1 to 2 minutes.

5. Stir the beef and 1¹/₂ cups of the broth into the bell pepper mixture. Reduce the heat and simmer for 10 to 15 minutes, or until the liquid is absorbed, stirring occasionally. Just before serving, sprinkle with the parsley.

Tender flank steak is briefly marinated in a savory, slightly spicy mixture of soy sauce, chili oil, garlic, and ginger before it's stir-fried. Crisp snow peas, earthy mushrooms, and crunchy water chestnuts bring more Asian flavors to the dish.

# chinese flank steak

**serves 4** | **1 cup per serving**

2 teaspoons cornstarch

½ cup dry sherry or fresh orange juice

2 tablespoons soy sauce (lowest sodium available)

2 medium garlic cloves, finely minced

1 teaspoon grated peeled gingerroot

⅛ teaspoon cayenne

1 pound flank steak, all visible fat discarded, frozen for 30 minutes, then sliced across the grain into strips 2 to 3 inches long and ½ to 1 inch wide

Cooking spray

1 teaspoon toasted sesame oil and 1 teaspoon toasted sesame oil, divided use

8 ounces mushrooms, sliced

6 ounces snow peas, trimmed

1 cup sliced green onions

1 8-ounce can sliced water chestnuts, drained

1. Put the cornstarch in a shallow glass dish. Add the sherry, soy sauce, garlic, gingerroot, and cayenne, whisking to dissolve. Add the beef, turning to coat. Cover and refrigerate for 30 minutes, turning occasionally.

2. Lightly spray a large skillet or wok with cooking spray. Pour in 1 teaspoon sesame oil, swirling to coat the bottom. Heat over high heat until very hot. Cook the mushrooms and snow peas for 1 to 2 minutes, or until tender-crisp and lightly browned, stirring constantly. Transfer to a plate. Cover to keep warm.

3. In the same skillet, still over high heat, heat the remaining 1 teaspoon sesame oil until very hot, swirling to coat the bottom. Cook the beef with the marinade and green onions for 5 minutes, or until the beef is browned, stirring constantly. Stir in the mushroom mixture and water chestnuts. Cook for 1 to 2 minutes, or until heated through, stirring constantly.

**per serving**

calories 287
total fat 11.5 g
  saturated fat 4.0 g
  trans fat 0.5 g
  polyunsaturated fat 1.5 g
  monounsaturated fat 5.5 g
cholesterol 53 mg

sodium 287 mg
carbohydrates 14 g
  fiber 5 g
  sugars 5 g
protein 28 g

dietary exchanges
3 vegetable, 3 lean meat, ½ fat

Succulent chunks of beef cook in a rich tomato stock spiked with beer, balsamic vinegar, and a touch of Louisiana-style hot sauce. Simply brown the beef and stir in the remaining ingredients; the long, slow simmering will do the rest.

# pub house beef stew

**serves 4** | **1¼ cups per serving**

Cooking spray

1 pound boneless top round steak, all visible fat discarded, cut into 1-inch cubes

2 medium garlic cloves, minced

1 14.5-ounce can no-salt-added stewed tomatoes, undrained

2 medium onions, cut into 4 wedges each

1 large green bell pepper, cut into 1-inch cubes

6 ounces light beer (regular or nonalcoholic)

1 tablespoon balsamic vinegar

2 teaspoons Worcestershire sauce (lowest sodium available)

1 medium dried bay leaf

2 teaspoons mild Louisiana-style hot-pepper sauce

¼ teaspoon salt

1. Lightly spray a Dutch oven with cooking spray. Heat over medium-high heat. Cook the beef for 5 minutes, or until browned, stirring frequently. Stir in the garlic. Cook for 15 seconds, stirring constantly.

2. Stir in the tomatoes with liquid, onions, bell pepper, beer, vinegar, Worcestershire sauce, and bay leaf. Increase the heat to high and bring to a boil. Reduce the heat and simmer, covered, for 1½ hours, or until the beef is very tender, stirring occasionally. Remove from the heat.

3. Discard the bay leaf. Stir in the hot sauce and salt.

**cook's tip:** For a thicker stew, put 2 teaspoons cornstarch in a small bowl. Add 2 tablespoons water, whisking to dissolve. Stir into the beef mixture at the end of the cooking time. Increase the heat to high and bring the stew to a boil. Boil for 1 minute, or until thickened slightly.

## per serving

calories 215
total fat 2.5 g
  saturated fat 1.0 g
  trans fat 0.0 g
  polyunsaturated fat 0.0 g
  monounsaturated fat 1.0 g
cholesterol 58 mg

sodium 364 mg
carbohydrates 17 g
  fiber 4 g
  sugars 11 g
protein 28 g

dietary exchanges
3 vegetable, 3 lean meat

Melt-in-your-mouth sirloin strips are stir-fried with crisp broccoli and red bell pepper in our lower-sodium version of the Chinese classic.

# beef and broccoli

**serves 4** : 1 cup beef mixture and ½ cup rice per serving

1 cup uncooked instant brown rice

2 teaspoons minced peeled gingerroot

2 medium garlic cloves, minced

1 1-pound boneless top sirloin steak, all visible fat discarded, cut into ¼-inch strips

1 tablespoon cornstarch

1 cup fat-free, low-sodium beef broth

2 tablespoons soy sauce (lowest sodium available)

2 tablespoons hoisin sauce (lowest sodium available)

1 teaspoon toasted sesame oil

¼ teaspoon crushed red pepper flakes

1 teaspoon canola or corn oil

3 cups broccoli florets

1 medium red bell pepper, cut into thin strips

**per serving**

calories 316
total fat 8.0 g
  saturated fat 2.0 g
  trans fat 0.0 g
  polyunsaturated fat 1.5 g
  monounsaturated fat 3.5 g
cholesterol 60 mg

sodium 362 mg
carbohydrates 29 g
  fiber 3 g
  sugars 5 g
protein 31 g

**dietary exchanges**
1½ starch,
1 vegetable, 3 lean meat

1. Prepare the rice using the package directions, omitting the salt and margarine. Set aside. Cover to keep warm.

2. In a medium bowl, stir together the gingerroot and garlic. Add the beef, turning to coat. Cover and refrigerate for at least 20 minutes (or up to 8 hours), turning occasionally.

3. Put the cornstarch in a small bowl. Add the broth, soy sauce, hoisin sauce, sesame oil, and red pepper flakes, whisking until the cornstarch is dissolved. Set aside.

4. In a large nonstick skillet or wok, heat the canola oil over medium-high heat, swirling to coat the bottom. Cook the beef for 4 to 6 minutes, stirring constantly. Transfer to a plate. (The beef won't be done at this point.)

5. In the same skillet, still over medium-high heat, cook the broccoli and bell pepper for 2 to 3 minutes, or until tender-crisp, stirring constantly.

6. Stir in the broth mixture. Bring to a simmer. Reduce the heat and simmer for 1 to 2 minutes, or until thickened, stirring occasionally.

7. Stir in the beef. Cook for 2 minutes, or to the desired doneness, stirring frequently. Serve over the rice.

meats

This is a bowl of soup you can really sink your teeth into. Chunks of mushroom and eggplant and tiny meatballs are simmered in an herb-enhanced, tomato-based broth. The delicate chiffonade of basil adds a bright, fresh flavor.

# italian vegetable soup with mini meatballs

**serves 8** | 1 cup per serving

Cooking spray

1 pound extra-lean ground beef

¼ cup shredded or grated Parmesan cheese

¼ cup egg substitute or 1 large egg

1 teaspoon dried oregano, crumbled, and ½ teaspoon dried oregano, crumbled, divided use

½ teaspoon dried fennel seeds, crushed with a mortar and pestle

1 teaspoon olive oil

4 ounces brown (cremini) mushrooms, quartered (about 1 cup)

1 medium eggplant, peeled and cut into ½-inch cubes

2 tablespoons water

1 8-ounce can no-salt-added tomato sauce

1 teaspoon paprika

½ teaspoon dried basil, crumbled

*(continued)*

1. Preheat the oven to 350°F. Lightly spray a broiler pan or a mesh rack with cooking spray. If using the rack, place it on a nonstick baking sheet or a baking sheet lined with aluminum foil for easy cleanup.

2. In a medium bowl, using your hands or a spoon, combine the beef, Parmesan, egg substitute, 1 teaspoon oregano, and fennel seeds. Shape into 56 ³/₄-inch meatballs. Transfer to the broiler pan. Bake for 15 minutes, or until the meatballs are no longer pink in the center.

3. Meanwhile, in a large saucepan, heat the oil over medium-high heat, swirling to coat the bottom. Cook the mushrooms for 2 to 3 minutes, or until slightly soft, stirring occasionally.

4. Stir in the eggplant and water. Cook for 4 minutes, or until the eggplant is slightly soft, stirring occasionally.

**5.** Stir in the tomato sauce, paprika, basil, onion powder, garlic powder, sugar, salt, pepper, and the remaining ¹/₂ teaspoon oregano. Increase the heat to high and bring the mixture to a boil. Reduce the heat and simmer, partially covered, for 10 minutes so the flavors blend, stirring occasionally.

**6.** Add the meatballs and green beans. Cook for 10 minutes, or until the green beans are tender, stirring occasionally. Ladle the soup into bowls. Garnish with the basil.

¹/₂ **teaspoon onion powder**

¹/₂ **teaspoon garlic powder**

¹/₂ **teaspoon sugar**

¹/₂ **teaspoon salt**

¹/₄ **teaspoon pepper**

 3 **ounces green beans, trimmed and cut into ¹/₂-inch pieces**

¹/₂ **cup fresh basil, rolled and cut into thin strips**

.............................................................

**per serving**

calories 127
**total fat 4.5 g**
 saturated fat 1.5 g
 trans fat 0.0 g
 polyunsaturated fat 0.5 g
 monounsaturated fat 2.0 g
**cholesterol 33 mg**

sodium 253 mg
**carbohydrates 8 g**
 fiber 3 g
 sugars 4 g
**protein 16 g**

**dietary exchanges**
2 vegetable, 2 lean meat

Lighten up classic baked manicotti with the addition of spinach and fat-free ricotta cheese. Broccolini and Red Bell Pepper with Garlic and Wine (page 204) or Oregano Brussels Sprouts (page 205) work well as side dishes that echo the Italian flavors of this entrée. *(See photo insert.)*

# beef manicotti

| serves 6 | 2 stuffed manicotti shells per serving |
|----------|----------------------------------------|

12 **large manicotti shells**

**sauce**

 1 **tablespoon olive oil**

1½ **cups chopped onions**

 1 **medium garlic clove, minced**

 2 **14.5-ounce cans no-salt-added whole Italian plum (Roma) tomatoes, undrained**

 1 **8-ounce can no-salt-added tomato sauce**

 1 **6-ounce can no-salt-added tomato paste**

½ **cup chopped fresh parsley**

½ **cup dry red wine (regular or nonalcoholic)**

 1 **teaspoon chopped fresh basil**

¼ **teaspoon pepper (freshly ground preferred), or to taste**

*(continued)*

1. Prepare the pasta using the package directions, omitting the salt. (The shells should be soft but not limp.) Drain well in a colander. Transfer to a large plate. Set aside.

2. In a large saucepan, heat 1 tablespoon oil over medium-high heat, swirling to coat the bottom. Cook 1½ cups onions and 1 garlic clove for about 3 minutes, or until the onion is soft, stirring frequently. Stir in the remaining sauce ingredients. Reduce the heat and simmer for 20 to 30 minutes, or until thickened.

3. Meanwhile, in a large skillet, heat the remaining 1 tablespoon oil over medium-high heat, swirling to coat the bottom. Cook the remaining ½ cup onion and 1 garlic clove for 3 minutes, or until the onion is soft, stirring frequently. Stir in the beef. Cook for 8 to 10 minutes, or until browned on the outside and no longer pink in the center, stirring occasionally to turn and break up the beef. Drain and discard any fat. Stir in the spinach, oregano, and the remaining ½ teaspoon pepper. Remove from the heat.

4. Preheat the oven to 350°F. Lightly spray a 13 × 9 × 2-inch glass baking dish with cooking spray.

5. Meanwhile, spoon the filling into the shells. Spread a little of the sauce in the baking dish. Arrange the manicotti in rows in the dish. Spoon any leftover filling around the manicotti. Spread the ricotta over the top. Pour the remaining sauce over all.

6. Bake for 20 minutes, or until bubbly.

### filling

- 1 tablespoon olive oil
- ½ cup chopped onion
- 1 medium garlic clove, minced
- 1 pound extra-lean ground beef
- 10 ounces frozen chopped spinach, thawed and squeezed dry
- ½ teaspoon dried oregano, crumbled
- ½ teaspoon pepper (freshly ground preferred), or to taste

---

Cooking spray

- 1 cup fat-free ricotta cheese

..............................................................

### per serving

| | |
|---|---|
| calories 410 | sodium 180 mg |
| total fat 9.5 g | carbohydrates 51 g |
| saturated fat 2.5 g | fiber 6 g |
| trans fat 0.0 g | sugars 14 g |
| polyunsaturated fat 1.0 g | protein 29 g |
| monounsaturated fat 5.0 g | dietary exchanges |
| cholesterol 48 mg | 2 starch, 4 vegetable, 3 lean meat |

Meat loaf is quintessential American comfort food. This version serves up savory flavor with a sweet heat from a peachy glaze and crushed red pepper flakes that are mixed into the loaf, along with oatmeal for a whole-grain boost. Butternut Squash and Swiss Chard Gratin (page 207) makes an elegant side dish that can bake right alongside the meat loaf.

# spicy meat loaf with peach glaze

| serves 4 | 1 slice per serving |
| --- | --- |

Cooking spray

1 pound extra-lean ground beef

½ medium green bell pepper, diced

½ cup diced onion

½ cup uncooked quick-cooking oatmeal

2 large egg whites

4 ounces no-salt-added tomato sauce and 4 ounces no-salt-added tomato sauce, divided use

2 teaspoons soy sauce and 2 teaspoons soy sauce (lowest sodium available), divided use

¼ teaspoon salt

⅛ teaspoon crushed red pepper flakes

⅓ cup peach or apricot all-fruit spread

2 teaspoons sugar

2 teaspoons cider vinegar

1. Preheat the oven to 350°F. Line a baking sheet with aluminum foil. Lightly spray the foil with cooking spray. Set aside.

2. Crumble the beef into a large bowl. Add the bell pepper, onion, oatmeal, egg whites, 4 ounces tomato sauce, 2 teaspoons soy sauce, the salt, and red pepper flakes. Using your hands or a spoon, combine the ingredients.

3. Transfer the beef mixture to the baking sheet. Shape into a loaf about 8 × 5 inches. Spoon the remaining 4 ounces tomato sauce over the top and sides of the meat loaf.

4. Bake for 55 minutes, or until the internal temperature of the meat loaf registers 160°F on an instant-read thermometer.

## per serving

calories 290
total fat 6.5 g
  saturated fat 2.5 g
  trans fat 0.5 g
  polyunsaturated fat 1.0 g
  monounsaturated fat 2.5 g
cholesterol 62 mg
sodium 397 mg

carbohydrates 30 g
  fiber 3 g
  sugars 18 g
protein 29 g

dietary exchanges
1 fruit, 1 vegetable, ½ other carbohydrate, 3 lean meat

5. About 5 minutes before the meat loaf is ready, prepare the glaze: In a small saucepan, cook the peach spread over medium heat for 2 minutes, or until just slightly melted. Remove from the heat. (You can also microwave the peach spread in a small microwaveable bowl on 100 percent power [high] for 20 to 30 seconds.)

6. Stir in the sugar, vinegar, and the remaining 2 teaspoons soy sauce. Spoon the glaze over the meat loaf.

7. Bake for 5 minutes, or until the glaze is hot. Transfer the baking sheet to a cutting board. Let the meat loaf stand for 10 minutes before slicing.

**cook's tip:** For an even spicier meat loaf, substitute 1 medium poblano pepper, seeds and ribs discarded, for the bell pepper and red pepper flakes.

**lunchbox tip:** To make this meat loaf more appealing to kids, leave out the red pepper flakes. Leftovers make great sandwiches.

Mix up your weeknight routine with a beautiful, easy-to-make meal by filling tender eggplant with a savory mixture of ground beef and mushrooms, then baking it to perfection. To accompany this Italian-style meal, serve Fresh Tomato and Cucumber Salad (page 51) or Lemon-Bulgur Salad (page 56).

# beefy stuffed eggplant

| serves 4 | 2 stuffed eggplant halves per serving |
| --- | --- |

Cooking spray

4 medium Japanese eggplants

1 tablespoon olive oil

12 ounces extra-lean ground beef

1 cup chopped onion

1 cup chopped mushrooms, such as button, brown (cremini), portobello, or shiitake (stems discarded)

1½ teaspoons dried basil, crumbled

½ teaspoon dried parsley, crumbled

½ teaspoon pepper (freshly ground preferred)

¼ cup no-salt-added tomato paste

¼ cup wheat germ

2 tablespoons chopped fresh parsley

1. Preheat the oven to 350°F. Lightly spray a 13 × 9 × 2-inch baking dish with cooking spray.

2. Halve the eggplants lengthwise. Scoop out the pulp, leaving a ¼-inch border of the shell all the way around. Place the shells in the baking dish. Dice the pulp. Set aside.

3. In a large skillet, heat the oil over medium-high heat. Cook the beef, onion, mushrooms, basil, parsley, and pepper for 8 to 10 minutes, or until the beef begins to brown, stirring constantly to turn and break up the beef. Stir in the tomato paste, wheat germ, and eggplant pulp. Cook for 5 minutes, or just until heated through.

4. Spoon the beef mixture into the eggplant shells. Bake for 20 to 30 minutes. Just before serving, sprinkle with the parsley.

**cook's tip on japanese eggplant:** Smaller than globe eggplants, Japanese eggplants have a thin skin and sweet, delicate flavor. They are sold in most supermarkets and Asian markets.

**per serving**

calories 249
total fat 8.5 g
  saturated fat 2.5 g
  trans fat 0.5 g
  polyunsaturated fat 1.0 g
  monounsaturated fat 4.0 g
cholesterol 47 mg

sodium 82 mg
carbohydrates 24 g
  fiber 10 g
  sugars 10 g
protein 23 g

dietary exchanges
4 vegetable, 2½ lean meat

Fragrant fresh basil is the star in this one-skillet dish. Pair this entrée with steamed broccoli or a leafy green salad, such as Kale Salad with Citrus Dressing (page 46).

# basil beef with noodles

| serves 6 | 1½ cups per serving |
|----------|---------------------|

2 teaspoons olive oil

1 pound extra-lean ground beef

¾ cup minced onion

2 medium garlic cloves, minced

1 28-ounce can no-salt-added diced tomatoes, undrained

2 cups water

1¼ cups fat-free, low-sodium beef broth

½ cup dry red wine (regular or nonalcoholic)

½ cup chopped fresh basil or 3 tablespoons dried basil, crumbled

8 ounces dried whole-grain no-yolk noodles

½ teaspoon pepper

¼ teaspoon salt

1. In a large skillet, heat the oil over medium heat, swirling to coat the bottom. Cook the beef, onion, and garlic for 3 to 5 minutes, or until the beef is browned on the outside and no longer pink in the center, stirring occasionally to turn and break up the beef.

2. Stir in the tomatoes with liquid, water, broth, wine, and basil. Increase the heat to high and bring to a boil. Stir in the pasta, pepper, and salt. Reduce the heat and simmer for 8 to 10 minutes, or until the pasta is tender.

**per serving**

calories 307
total fat 6.5 g
   saturated fat 1.5 g
   trans fat 0.0 g
   polyunsaturated fat 1.0 g
   monounsaturated fat 3.0 g
cholesterol 42 mg

sodium 199 mg
carbohydrates 37 g
   fiber 6 g
   sugars 6 g
protein 23 g

dietary exchanges
2 starch, 1 vegetable, 2½ lean meat

This slight twist on traditional chili packs the taste of tamales into every heartwarming bowl of red, thanks to the inclusion of chewy hominy, which adds a distinctive flavor similar to that of masa harina (a corn flour best known for its use in tamales). Hominy is hulled white or yellow corn kernels, sold either canned or dried. When the dried hominy is ground, it is known as grits.

# beef and hominy chili

**serves 4**  |  **1½ cups per serving**

Cooking spray

1 pound extra-lean ground beef

½ 15.5-ounce can yellow or white hominy, rinsed and drained

1 14.5-ounce can no-salt-added diced tomatoes, undrained

1 large green bell pepper, chopped

1 cup water

¾ cup frozen whole-kernel corn

2 medium fresh jalapeños, seeds and ribs discarded, finely chopped (see cook's tip on page 109)

2 packets (2 teaspoons) salt-free instant beef bouillon

2 teaspoons chili powder

1 teaspoon ground cumin

¼ cup chopped fresh cilantro

1. Lightly spray a Dutch oven with cooking spray. Heat over medium-high heat. Cook the beef for 3 to 5 minutes, or until browned on the outside and no longer pink in the center, stirring occasionally to turn and break up the beef.

2. Stir in the remaining ingredients except the cilantro. Increase the heat to high and bring to a boil. Reduce the heat and simmer, covered, for 30 minutes. Stir in the cilantro.

**per serving**

calories 255
total fat 6.5 g
    saturated fat 2.5 g
    trans fat 0.5 g
    polyunsaturated fat 1.0 g
    monounsaturated fat 2.5 g
cholesterol 62 mg

sodium 350 mg
carbohydrates 25 g
    fiber 4 g
    sugars 6 g
protein 28 g

dietary exchanges
1 starch, 2 vegetable,
3 lean meat

The marinade for this pork has it all: spiciness, tanginess, and sweetness. Use more or less chili sauce depending on your boldness. Pair it with an Asian-flavored vegetable dish, such as Marinated Asparagus (page 201) or Snow Pea and Sesame Stir-Fry (page 220).

# grilled sweet chile pork tenderloin

**serves 4**  :  3 ounces pork per serving

¼ cup plain rice vinegar

2 tablespoons honey

2 teaspoons toasted sesame oil

1 to 2 teaspoons hot-chile sauce (sriracha preferred)

1 teaspoon canola or corn oil

1 medium garlic clove, minced

1 1-pound pork tenderloin, all visible fat discarded

Cooking spray

¼ cup chopped fresh cilantro

1. In a large shallow glass dish, whisk together the vinegar, honey, sesame oil, chile sauce, canola oil, and garlic. Add the pork, turning to coat. Cover and refrigerate for 1 to 4 hours, turning occasionally.

2. When the pork has marinated, lightly spray the grill rack with cooking spray. Preheat the grill on medium.

3. Drain the pork, discarding the marinade. Grill the pork for 18 to 20 minutes, or until it registers 145°F on an instant-read thermometer, turning the pork every 5 minutes. Transfer to a cutting board. Let stand for 3 minutes. Cut the pork crosswise into slices. Transfer to plates. Sprinkle with the cilantro.

**per serving**

calories 126
total fat 2.5 g
  saturated fat 1.0 g
  trans fat 0.0 g
  polyunsaturated fat 0.5 g
  monounsaturated fat 1.0 g
cholesterol 74 mg

sodium 98 mg
carbohydrates 0 g
  fiber 0 g
  sugars 0 g
protein 24 g

dietary exchanges
3 lean meat

Fruit chutney adds just the right touch of sweetness to tender pork coated with a savory combination of spices. Try this entrée with Ethiopian Cracked Wheat (page 223) and North African Spiced Carrots (page 209) for a taste of the exotic.

# pork tenderloin with apricot and fig chutney

**serves 4** : 3 ounces pork and ¼ cup chutney per serving

1 teaspoon olive oil and 1 tablespoon olive oil, divided use

2 medium shallots, chopped

½ cup water

½ cup quartered fresh figs

¼ cup chopped dried apricot halves

2 tablespoons light brown sugar

2 tablespoons cider vinegar

Cooking spray

2 teaspoons garlic powder

1 teaspoon dried oregano, crumbled

½ teaspoon pepper

¼ teaspoon salt

1 1-pound pork tenderloin, all visible fat discarded

1. In a small saucepan, heat 1 teaspoon oil over medium heat, swirling to coat the bottom. Cook the shallots for 1 to 2 minutes, or until tender-crisp, stirring occasionally.

2. Gently stir in the water, figs, apricots, brown sugar, and vinegar. Bring to a simmer over medium-high heat, stirring occasionally but gently, so the figs retain their shape. Reduce the heat and simmer for 15 to 20 minutes, or until the mixture is thickened. Remove from the heat. Cover to keep warm.

3. Meanwhile, preheat the oven to 375°F. Lightly spray a rimmed baking sheet with cooking spray. Set aside.

4. In a small bowl, stir together the garlic powder, oregano, pepper, and salt. Sprinkle all over the pork. Using your fingertips, gently press the mixture so it adheres to the pork.

### per serving

calories 239
total fat 7.0 g
  saturated fat 1.5 g
  trans fat 0.0 g
  polyunsaturated fat 1.0 g
  monounsaturated fat 4.0 g
cholesterol 74 mg

sodium 212 mg
carbohydrates 19 g
  fiber 2 g
  sugars 15 g
protein 25 g

dietary exchanges
½ fruit, ½ other
carbohydrate, 3 lean
meat

**5.** In a large skillet, heat the remaining 1 tablespoon oil over medium-high heat, swirling to coat the bottom. Cook the pork for 6 to 8 minutes, or until golden brown, turning to brown all sides. (The pork won't be done at this point.) Transfer to the baking sheet.

**6.** Roast for 20 to 25 minutes, or until the pork registers 145°F on an instant-read thermometer. Transfer to a cutting board. Let stand for 3 minutes. Cut the pork crosswise into slices. Transfer to plates. Spoon the chutney over the pork.

**cook's tip on figs:** Fresh figs have a short shelf life. It's optimal to use them within a day or two of purchase. Handle fresh figs with care because their delicate skin bruises easily. Carefully wrap them in paper towels and transfer them to a covered container. Refrigerate them in the coldest part of your refrigerator. If figs aren't in season, try substituting coarsely chopped plums.

**cook's tip on sticky foods:** To cut dried apricots or other sticky foods easily, use kitchen shears lightly sprayed with cooking spray.

Ancho powder comes from the sweetest of the dried chiles, providing a rich, slightly fruity taste rather than a deep heat. Aïoli, a creamy, mayonnaise-based sauce made with fresh garlic, balances out the flavors.

# ancho-rubbed pork tenderloin with rosemary aïoli

| serves 4 | 3 ounces pork and 2 tablespoons aïoli per serving |
|---|---|

1½ teaspoons ancho powder

1 teaspoon smoked paprika

½ teaspoon pepper (coarsely ground preferred)

¼ teaspoon ground cumin

1 1-pound pork tenderloin, all visible fat discarded

1 teaspoon canola or corn oil

⅛ teaspoon salt

### aïoli

¼ cup light mayonnaise

¼ cup fat-free sour cream

1 medium garlic clove, minced

½ teaspoon dried rosemary, crushed

⅛ teaspoon salt

1. Preheat the oven to 425°F.

2. In a small bowl, stir together the ancho powder, paprika, pepper, and cumin. Sprinkle the mixture all over the pork. Using your fingertips, gently press the mixture so it adheres to the pork.

3. In a large nonstick skillet, heat the oil over medium-high heat, swirling to coat the bottom. Cook the pork for 6 to 8 minutes, or until golden brown, turning to brown on all sides. (The pork won't be done at this point.)

4. Transfer the pork to an 11 × 7 × 2-inch glass baking dish. Sprinkle with ⅛ teaspoon salt.

5. Roast for 15 to 20 minutes, or until the pork registers 145°F on an instant-read thermometer. Transfer to a cutting board. Let stand for 3 minutes. Cut the pork crosswise into slices.

6. Meanwhile, in a small bowl, whisk together the aïoli ingredients. Serve with the pork.

### per serving

calories 184
total fat 8.0 g
  saturated fat 1.5 g
  trans fat 0.0 g
  polyunsaturated fat 3.5 g
  monounsaturated fat 2.5 g
cholesterol 67 mg

sodium 352 mg
carbohydrates 5 g
  fiber 1 g
  sugars 1 g
protein 23 g

dietary exchanges
½ other carbohydrate,
3 lean meat

The flavor of greens can range from the mild sweetness of Bibb lettuce to the dark pepperiness of arugula and everything in between. This salad uses mustard greens, whose sharp taste is tempered by a sweet-tart citrus vinaigrette.

# pork and mustard greens salad

| serves 4 | 2¼ cups salad, 3 ounces pork, and 2 tablespoons dressing per serving |
|---|---|

Cooking spray

### salad

2 butterflied pork chops (about 8 ounces each), all visible fat discarded

2 teaspoons salt-free steak grilling blend

¼ teaspoon salt

8 cups loosely packed torn mustard greens

1 11-ounce can mandarin oranges in juice, drained

½ cup thinly sliced red onion, separated into rings and halved

### dressing

¼ cup fresh orange juice

3 tablespoons white balsamic vinegar

1 tablespoon sugar

⅛ teaspoon salt

2 tablespoons canola or corn oil

1 to 2 teaspoons grated peeled gingerroot

1. Lightly spray a grill pan or large skillet with cooking spray. Heat over medium-high heat.

2. Sprinkle both sides of the pork with the grilling blend and ¼ teaspoon salt. Using your fingertips, gently press the seasonings so they adhere to the pork. Cook for 4 minutes on each side, or until the pork registers 145°F on an instant-read thermometer. Transfer to a cutting board. Let stand for 3 minutes. Cut into thin slices.

3. Meanwhile, arrange the greens on plates. Place the oranges and onion on the greens.

4. In a small bowl, whisk together the orange juice, vinegar, sugar, and ⅛ teaspoon salt.

5. Pour the oil into the orange juice mixture in a fine stream, whisking constantly until smooth. Whisk in the gingerroot.

6. Arrange the pork on the oranges and onion. Pour the dressing over all.

### per serving

calories 288
total fat 13.0 g
  saturated fat 2.0 g
  trans fat 0.0 g
  polyunsaturated fat 2.5 g
  monounsaturated fat 6.5 g
cholesterol 66 mg

sodium 298 mg
carbohydrates 19 g
  fiber 5 g
  sugars 14 g
protein 25 g

dietary exchanges
1 fruit, 1 vegetable, 3 lean meat, 1 fat

When you braise pork chops, you end up with fork-tender and delicious meat that has soaked up the braising liquid and the moisture from the sautéed mushrooms, onion, and celery. The dry rub and chopped herbs add a zesty flavor to the chops.

# southern-style smothered pork chops

| serves 4 | 3 ounces pork, ¼ cup vegetables, and ½ cup rice per serving |
| --- | --- |

1 cup uncooked instant brown rice

2 teaspoons chopped fresh thyme and 1 teaspoon chopped fresh thyme, divided use

1 teaspoon salt-free Creole or Cajun seasoning blend (see cook's tip on page 75)

4 boneless pork loin chops (about 4 ounces each), about ½ inch thick, all visible fat discarded

1 teaspoon olive oil and 1 teaspoon olive oil, divided use

2 cups sliced button mushrooms

½ cup sliced onion

1 medium rib of celery, chopped

1 cup fat-free, low-sodium chicken broth

1 tablespoon coarse-grain Dijon mustard (lowest sodium available)

**1.** Prepare the rice using the package directions, omitting the salt and margarine. Remove from the heat. Cover to keep warm.

**2.** Meanwhile, sprinkle 2 teaspoons thyme and the seasoning blend over both sides of the pork. Using your fingertips, gently press the seasonings so they adhere to the pork.

**3.** In a large skillet, heat 1 teaspoon oil over medium-high heat, swirling to coat the bottom. Cook the pork for 2 minutes on each side, or until browned. (The pork won't be done at this point.) Transfer to a plate.

**4.** In the same skillet, still over medium-high heat, heat the remaining 1 teaspoon oil, swirling to coat the bottom. Cook the mushrooms, onion, and celery for 2 to 3 minutes, or until the mushrooms and onion are beginning to soften and the celery is tender-crisp, stirring occasionally.

**5.** Stir in the broth and mustard. Bring to a simmer. Return the pork to the skillet.

### per serving

calories 272
total fat 7.5 g
   saturated fat 1.5 g
   trans fat 0.0 g
   polyunsaturated fat 1.0 g
   monounsaturated fat 3.5 g
cholesterol 75 mg

sodium 163 mg
carbohydrates 21 g
   fiber 2 g
   sugars 2 g
protein 30 g

dietary exchanges
1½ starch, 3 lean meat

Reduce the heat and simmer, covered, for 20 to 30 minutes, or until the pork is no longer pink in the center. Transfer the pork to a serving platter. Cover to keep warm.

6. Increase the heat to high and bring the mushroom mixture to a boil. Boil for 3 to 5 minutes, or until reduced to 1 cup of liquid and vegetables. Spoon the mushroom mixture over the pork. Sprinkle with the remaining 1 teaspoon thyme. Serve with the rice.

**cook's tip on fresh thyme:** Simply pull your fingers down the stem and the leaves will detach.

Red cabbage cooked with red wine vinegar, brown sugar, and cinnamon makes an irresistible contrast to crunchy-on-the-outside, tender-on-the-inside pork chops. Serve with low-fat mashed potatoes or spaetzle. To really round out this Viennese meal, serve Borscht (page 38) as a complementary starter.

# pork schnitzel with sweet-and-sour red cabbage

| serves 4 | 3 ounces pork and ¾ cup cabbage per serving |

½ teaspoon canola or corn oil and 1 teaspoon canola or corn oil, divided use

1 medium onion, thinly sliced

3 cups thinly sliced red cabbage

3 tablespoons red wine vinegar

2 tablespoons light brown sugar

1 cinnamon stick (about 3 inches long)

1 medium red apple, any variety, peeled and thinly sliced

¼ teaspoon salt and ⅛ teaspoon salt, divided use

⅛ teaspoon pepper

1 large egg white, lightly beaten

1 tablespoon water

*(continued)*

1. In a large saucepan, heat ½ teaspoon oil over medium heat, swirling to coat the bottom. Cook the onion for 6 minutes, or until soft, stirring frequently.

2. Stir in the cabbage, vinegar, brown sugar, and cinnamon stick. Bring to a simmer and simmer, covered, for 15 minutes, or until the cabbage is tender, stirring occasionally.

3. Stir in the apple, ¼ teaspoon salt, and the pepper. Return to a simmer and simmer, covered, for 10 minutes. Remove from the heat.

4. Discard the cinnamon stick. Set the cabbage mixture aside, uncovered (so the cabbage doesn't become soggy).

5. Meanwhile, in a medium shallow dish, whisk together the egg white and water. Put the panko in a separate medium shallow dish. Set the dishes and a large plate in a row, assembly-line fashion. Dip the pork in the egg white mixture, then the panko, turning

to coat at each step and gently shaking off any excess. Using your fingertips, gently press the coating so it adheres to the pork. Transfer to the plate.

6. In a large nonstick skillet, heat the remaining 1 teaspoon oil over medium-high heat, swirling to coat the bottom. Cook the pork for 3 to 4 minutes on each side, or until it registers 145°F on an instant-read thermometer. Transfer the pork to a separate large plate. Sprinkle with the remaining ⅛ teaspoon salt. Let stand for 3 minutes.

7. Reduce the heat to medium. Cook the cabbage mixture for 1 to 2 minutes, or until heated through. Serve with the pork.

⅔ cup whole-wheat panko (Japanese-style bread crumbs)

4 boneless center loin pork chops (about 4 ounces each), about ½ inch thick, all visible fat discarded

. . . . . . . . . . . . . . . . . . . . . . . . . . . . . . . . . . . . . . . . . . . . . . . . . .

### per serving

calories 281
total fat 6.5 g
   saturated fat 1.5 g
   trans fat 0.0 g
   polyunsaturated fat 1.0 g
   monounsaturated fat 2.5 g
cholesterol 78 mg

sodium 329 mg
carbohydrates 27 g
   fiber 4 g
   sugars 15 g
protein 29 g

dietary exchanges
1 starch, ½ fruit, 1 vegetable, 3 lean meat

Dried dates have a caramel-like flavor that marries well with the zing of onion and the tang of vinegar. If you want more sweetness, cook the onion a bit longer, until it caramelizes.

# honey-balsamic pork chops with dates

**serves 4** | 3 ounces pork and 2 tablespoons sauce per serving

¼ teaspoon salt

¼ teaspoon pepper

4 boneless pork loin chops (about 4 ounces each), about ½ inch thick, all visible fat discarded

2 teaspoons olive oil

½ medium onion, thinly sliced

½ cup fat-free, low-sodium chicken broth

¼ cup pitted dried dates, chopped

1 tablespoon balsamic vinegar

2 teaspoons honey

1 teaspoon chopped fresh thyme

1. Sprinkle the salt and pepper over both sides of the pork.

2. In a large nonstick skillet, heat the oil over medium-high heat, swirling to coat the bottom. Cook the pork for 3 to 4 minutes on each side, or until it registers 145°F on an instant-read thermometer. Transfer the pork to plates. Cover to keep warm.

3. In the same skillet, still over medium-high heat, cook the onion for 3 to 4 minutes, or until soft, stirring frequently. Stir in the broth and dates. Bring to a boil. Boil for 3 to 4 minutes, or until the liquid is reduced by half (to about ¼ cup).

4. Stir in the vinegar, honey, and thyme. Cook for 1 minute, stirring constantly. Spoon the sauce over the pork.

**per serving**

calories 214
total fat 6.0 g
  saturated fat 1.5 g
  trans fat 0.0 g
  polyunsaturated fat 0.5 g
  monounsaturated fat 3.5 g
cholesterol 75 mg

sodium 211 mg
carbohydrates 13 g
  fiber 1 g
  sugars 12 g
protein 26 g

dietary exchanges
1 fruit, 3 lean meat

Grilling lean pork chops and thinly slicing them is a fast way to get that classic pork flavor found in many Mexican dishes. Grilling the green onions gives them a charred, smoky taste that contrasts with the earthy spinach and sweet tomato. Enjoy this dish with a side of Cool Avocado-Cilantro Soup (page 45). *(See photo insert.)*

# pork and green onion tacos

| serves 4 | 2 tacos per serving |
|----------|---------------------|

Cooking spray

½ **cup fat-free sour cream**

¼ **cup chopped fresh cilantro**

1 **tablespoon fresh lime juice**

1 **small garlic clove, minced**

1 **teaspoon smoked paprika**

½ **teaspoon chipotle powder**

⅛ **teaspoon salt**

12 **ounces boneless pork loin chops (about ¾ inch thick), all visible fat discarded**

8 **medium green onions (6 to 8 inches long)**

8 **6-inch corn tortillas**

2 **cups loosely packed shredded spinach or romaine**

1 **medium tomato, cut into thin wedges**

1 **small lime, cut into 4 wedges**

1. Lightly spray the grill rack with cooking spray. Preheat the grill on medium.

2. In a small bowl, whisk together the sour cream, cilantro, lime juice, and garlic. Set aside.

3. In a separate small bowl, stir together the paprika, chipotle powder, and salt. Sprinkle over both sides of the pork. Using your fingertips, gently press the mixture so it adheres to the pork.

4. Grill the pork for 3 to 4 minutes on each side, or until it registers 145°F on an instant-read thermometer. Transfer to a cutting board. Let stand for 3 minutes.

5. Grill the green onions for 1 to 2 minutes on each side, or until they begin to brown. Transfer to the cutting board.

6. Warm the tortillas using the package directions.

7. Thinly slice the pork diagonally across the grain. Chop the green onions into 1-inch pieces. Layer as follows in the center of the tortillas: the pork, green onions, spinach, and tomato wedges. Spoon the sour cream mixture on top. Serve the tacos with the lime wedges.

**per serving**

calories 255
total fat 4.0 g
  saturated fat 1.0 g
  ·trans fat 0.0 g
  polyunsaturated fat 1.0 g
  monounsaturated fat 2.0 g
cholesterol 61 mg

sodium 176 mg
carbohydrates 29 g
  fiber 6 g
  sugars 7 g
**protein 24 g**

dietary exchanges
1½ starch,
1 vegetable, 3 lean
meat

A tangy marinade including pineapple juice, soy sauce, garlic, and gingerroot flavors the pork and keeps it moist. Chunks of fresh pineapple, crisp bell pepper, and sweet red onion add textural and flavor contrast. Serve this taste of the tropics on a bed of Almond Rice with Ginger (page 217).

# hawaiian-style pork kebabs

**serves 4** | 1 kebab per serving

½ cup 100% pineapple juice

2 tablespoons soy sauce (lowest sodium available)

2 medium garlic cloves, minced

1 teaspoon minced peeled gingerroot

1 teaspoon toasted sesame oil

1 pound boneless pork loin chops, all visible fat discarded, cut into 28 1-inch cubes

¾ cup pineapple chunks (28 ¾-inch pieces)

1 medium green bell pepper, cut into 28 ¾-inch squares

½ large red onion, cut into 28 ¾-inch squares

Cooking spray

¼ teaspoon coarse-grain sea salt (Hawaiian red preferred) or kosher salt (optional)

1. Soak four 10- to 12-inch wooden skewers for at least 10 minutes in cold water to prevent charring, or use metal skewers.

2. In a small glass bowl, whisk together the pineapple juice, soy sauce, garlic, gingerroot, and oil.

3. Thread 7 pieces each of the pork, pineapple, bell pepper, and red onion onto each skewer, alternating the ingredients. Transfer the kebabs to a 13 × 9 × 2-inch glass baking dish. Pour the marinade over the kebabs, turning to coat. Cover and refrigerate for 30 minutes to 8 hours, turning occasionally.

4. Lightly spray the grill rack or broiler rack and pan with cooking spray. Preheat the grill on medium high or preheat the broiler.

5. Meanwhile, drain the kebabs, discarding the marinade.

**per serving**

**WITHOUT COARSE-GRAIN SEA SALT**
calories 178
total fat 4.0 g
   saturated fat 1.5 g
   trans fat 0.0 g
   polyunsaturated fat 0.5 g
   monounsaturated fat 2.0 g
cholesterol 75 mg

sodium 253 mg
carbohydrates 8 g
   fiber 1 g
   sugars 6 g
protein 27 g

dietary exchanges
½ fruit, 3 lean meat

**6.** Grill the kebabs, or broil them 6 inches from the heat, for 2 minutes on each side, or until the pork registers 145°F on an instant-read thermometer and the pineapple, bell pepper, and onion are tender and golden brown. Transfer to a serving platter. Let stand for 3 minutes. Sprinkle with the salt.

**cook's tip:** All forms of salt—sea, kosher, or table—have the same amount of sodium, but a sprinkle of crunchy finishing salt can add more flavor than adding that same amount to a dish before it's cooked. Haleakala red sea salt from Hawaii has a briny, nutty flavor and slightly moist texture. Its red color is from the inclusion of a very small amount of volcanic clay, called alaea.

**WITH COARSE-GRAIN SEA SALT**

calories 178
total fat 4.0 g
    saturated fat 1.5 g
    trans fat 0.0 g
    polyunsaturated fat 0.5 g
    monounsaturated fat 2.0 g
cholesterol 75 mg

sodium 373 mg
carbohydrates 8 g
    fiber 1 g
    sugars 6 g
protein 27 g

dietary exchanges
½ fruit, 3 lean meat

# vegetarian entrées

This lightly seasoned noodle dish, filled with an array of vegetables that are quickly stir-fried with gingerroot and garlic, will fill you up as a lunch or dinner entrée. Edamame bumps up the protein.

# soba noodles with edamame

| serves 4 | 2 cups per serving |

1½ cups frozen shelled edamame

4 ounces dried soba noodles

½ cup fat-free, low-sodium vegetable broth

1 tablespoon soy sauce (lowest sodium available)

2 teaspoons toasted sesame oil

1 teaspoon canola or corn oil

2 teaspoons finely chopped peeled gingerroot

1 medium garlic clove, finely chopped

8 ounces bok choy or napa cabbage, thinly sliced

1 medium zucchini, cut into matchstick-size strips

1 medium red bell pepper, cut into matchstick-size strips

1 medium rib of celery, cut into matchstick-size strips

1 medium carrot, cut into matchstick-size strips

2 medium green onions, chopped

1. Prepare the edamame using the package directions, omitting the salt. Drain well in a colander. (You can prepare the edamame up to 24 hours in advance. Cover and refrigerate until needed.) Let cool.

2. Prepare the noodles using the package directions, omitting the salt. Drain well in a colander. Set aside.

3. In a small bowl, whisk together the broth, soy sauce, and sesame oil. Set aside.

4. In a large skillet or wok, heat the canola oil over high heat, swirling to coat the bottom. Working quickly, cook the gingerroot and garlic for 10 seconds, stirring constantly. Stir in the bok choy, zucchini, bell pepper, celery, carrot, and green onions. Cook for 3 to 4 minutes, or until the vegetables are tender-crisp, stirring constantly. Remove from the heat.

5. Stir the broth mixture, noodles, and edamame into the bok choy mixture.

**cook's tip:** Soba noodles can be found in the Asian section at some supermarkets or at specialty Asian markets, but if you can't find them, you can substitute whole-grain angel hair pasta.

## per serving

calories 245
total fat 6.5 g
  saturated fat 0.5 g
  trans fat 0.0 g
  polyunsaturated fat 2.5 g
  monounsaturated fat 2.5 g
cholesterol 0 mg

sodium 206 mg
carbohydrates 35 g
  fiber 7 g
  sugars 9 g
protein 14 g

dietary exchanges
2 starch, 1 vegetable, 1 lean meat, ½ fat

Salad and a slice? Why not combine them and enjoy your pizza and greens in the same bite? We top our honey-wheat pizza crust with a cool, fresh chopped Greek salad, complete with kalamata olives and feta. What a contrast of tastes, textures, and temperatures! Prepare the dough ahead of time so you'll be ready for an easy weeknight dinner. *(See photo insert.)*

# garlicky greek salad pizza

**serves 6** | **1 slice per serving**

**dough**

- 1 cup plus 2 tablespoons lukewarm water (105°F to 115°F)
- 1 ¼-ounce package active dry yeast
- 1½ cups all-purpose flour, 3 to 4 tablespoons all-purpose flour, and ¼ cup all-purpose flour (if needed), divided use
- 1 cup whole-wheat flour
- 1½ teaspoons honey
- ½ teaspoon olive oil
- ½ teaspoon salt
  Cooking spray

- 1 tablespoon finely chopped fresh oregano or 1 teaspoon dried oregano, crumbled
- 2 teaspoons olive oil
- 2 large garlic cloves, crushed
- ¼ teaspoon crushed red pepper flakes

*(continued)*

1. In a small bowl, combine the water and yeast, stirring to dissolve. Let stand for 5 minutes.

2. Meanwhile, in a large bowl, stir together 1½ cups all-purpose flour, the whole-wheat flour, honey, ½ teaspoon oil, and the salt.

3. When the yeast is ready, add it to the flour mixture, stirring until the dough starts to pull away from the side of the bowl. (You may need extra flour.)

4. Using the remaining 3 to 4 tablespoons all-purpose flour, lightly flour a flat surface. Turn out the dough. Knead for 5 minutes, gradually adding, if needed, enough of the final ¼ cup all-purpose flour to make the dough smooth and elastic. (The dough shouldn't be dry or stick to the surface. You may not need any of the final ¼ cup all-purpose flour, or you may need all of it if the dough is sticky.)

5. Lightly spray a separate large bowl and a piece of plastic wrap large enough to cover the top of the bowl with cooking spray.

Transfer the dough to the bowl, turning to coat with the cooking spray. Cover the bowl with the plastic wrap, with the sprayed side down. Let the dough rise in a warm, draft-free place (about 85°F) for about 1 hour, or until doubled in bulk. Punch the dough down. Using a small amount of all-purpose flour, lightly flour a flat surface. Roll the dough into a 12-inch circle. Transfer to a large pizza stone or baking sheet. Let the dough stand for 10 minutes.

6. Meanwhile, preheat the oven to 425°F.

7. In a small bowl, whisk together 1 tablespoon oregano, 2 teaspoons oil, the garlic, and red pepper flakes. Set aside.

8. Bake the pizza dough for 12 to 15 minutes, or until lightly browned.

9. Meanwhile, in a third large bowl, toss together the romaine, tomato, bell pepper, cucumber, onion, olives, and 1 tablespoon oregano. Transfer the mixture to a cutting board. Using a large chef's knife, chop the mixture into bite-size pieces. Return to the bowl. Add the lemon juice and 2 teaspoons oil to the salad, tossing to coat.

10. When the crust is baked, remove from the oven. Immediately brush with the oregano mixture.

11. Arrange the salad on the crust. Sprinkle with the feta.

## salad

- 4 cups chopped romaine
- 1 medium tomato, chopped
- ½ medium green bell pepper, chopped
- ½ medium cucumber, peeled, seeded, and chopped
- ⅓ cup chopped red onion
- 5 kalamata olives, drained and coarsely chopped
- 1 tablespoon finely chopped fresh oregano or 1 teaspoon dried oregano, crumbled
- 1 tablespoon fresh lemon juice
- 2 teaspoons olive oil
- 2 ounces crumbled fat-free feta cheese

........................................................

### per serving

calories 295
total fat 5.5 g
  saturated fat 1.0 g
  trans fat 0.0 g
  polyunsaturated fat 1.0 g
  monounsaturated fat 3.0 g
cholesterol 0 mg

sodium 400 mg
carbohydrates 53 g
  fiber 5 g
  sugars 4 g
protein 10 g

dietary exchanges
3 starch, 1 vegetable, ½ fat

cook's tip: To make the dough ahead of time, let it rise, punch it down, and then transfer it to a resealable plastic bag to refrigerate or freeze it. When preparing refrigerated dough, give it enough time to come to room temperature before forming it into a crust. When preparing frozen dough, let it thaw at room temperature before using it. Refrigerated dough will keep for three to four days. Frozen dough will keep for three months.

The vegetable possibilities for this dish range from A for asparagus to Z for zucchini. As your favorites come into season, substitute them for some of the options here.

# pasta primavera

**serves 4** | **2 cups per serving**

1 cup fat-free ricotta cheese

1 tablespoon fresh lemon juice

8 ounces dried whole-grain thin spaghetti

1 teaspoon olive oil

½ cup chopped onion

¼ cup chopped green onions

2 teaspoons minced garlic

1 teaspoon dried Italian seasoning, crumbled

¼ teaspoon pepper, or to taste

2 cups sliced mushrooms, such as button, brown (cremini), portobello, or shiitake (stems discarded)

1½ cups sliced carrots

10 ounces frozen chopped broccoli, thawed

1 cup sliced bell pepper (any color)

¼ teaspoon crushed red pepper flakes, or to taste (optional)

¼ cup shredded or grated Parmesan cheese

1. In a small bowl, whisk together the ricotta and lemon juice. Set aside.

2. Prepare the pasta using the package directions, omitting the salt. Drain well in a colander. Set aside.

3. Meanwhile, in a large skillet, heat the oil over medium-high heat, swirling to coat the bottom. Cook the onion, green onions, garlic, Italian seasoning, and pepper for 1 minute, stirring frequently. Stir in the mushrooms. Cook for 1 minute, stirring occasionally. Stir in the carrots, broccoli, bell pepper, and red pepper flakes. Cook for 3 to 4 minutes, or until the vegetables are tender-crisp, stirring constantly.

4. In a large bowl, stir together the pasta and ricotta mixture. Top with the vegetable mixture. Sprinkle with the Parmesan.

**per serving**

calories 347
total fat 4.5 g
   saturated fat 1.0 g
   trans fat 0.0 g
   polyunsaturated fat 1.0 g
   monounsaturated fat 2.0 g
cholesterol 14 mg

sodium 204 mg
carbohydrates 60 g
   fiber 11 g
   sugars 10 g
protein 18 g

dietary exchanges
3 starch, 3 vegetable,
1 lean meat

These lasagna stacks are prepared ahead of time and microwaved individually, so they're especially convenient on nights when the family can't eat together. They're not only super-fast and easy but nutritious as well, with a healthy spectrum of veggies!

# no-bake mini lasagne

| serves 4 | 1 lasagna per serving |
|---|---|

4 dried whole-grain lasagna noodles

1 tablespoon olive oil

4 ounces broccoli florets

4 ounces button mushrooms, sliced

4 ounces zucchini or yellow summer squash, thinly sliced

4 ounces asparagus, trimmed and cut into ½-inch pieces

2 ounces baby spinach

2 medium garlic cloves, minced

½ teaspoon dried oregano, crumbled

¼ teaspoon pepper

⅛ teaspoon salt

½ cup fat-free ricotta cheese

1 cup shredded or grated low-fat mozzarella cheese

2 tablespoons shredded or grated Parmesan cheese

**per serving**

calories 255
total fat 7.5 g
   saturated fat 2.0 g
   trans fat 0.0 g
   polyunsaturated fat 0.5 g
   monounsaturated fat 4.0 g
cholesterol 17 mg

sodium 374 mg
carbohydrates 30 g
   fiber 6 g
   sugars 5 g
protein 17 g

dietary exchanges
1½ starch,
1 vegetable, 1½ lean
meat

1. Prepare the pasta using the package directions, omitting the salt. Drain well in a colander. Carefully arrange the pasta in a single layer on a large piece of wax paper and pat dry with paper towels. Cut each noodle crosswise into 3 pieces. Set aside.

2. Meanwhile, in a large nonstick skillet, heat the oil over medium heat, swirling to coat the bottom. Cook the broccoli, mushrooms, and zucchini for 4 to 5 minutes, or until tender, stirring occasionally.

3. Stir in the asparagus, spinach, garlic, oregano, pepper, and salt. Cook for 1 to 2 minutes, or until the asparagus is tender, stirring occasionally. Remove from the heat.

4. Place a piece of pasta on a microwaveable dinner plate. Spoon 1 tablespoon of the ricotta on top. Spoon ½ cup of the broccoli mixture over the ricotta. Sprinkle with 2 tablespoons mozzarella. Repeat. Place a third piece of pasta on top. Sprinkle with 1½ teaspoons Parmesan. Repeat on three separate plates with the remaining ingredients.

5. Microwave each plate of lasagna on 100 percent power (high) for 1 minute, or until the Parmesan is melted.

Mild eggplant is simmered with tomatoes, mushrooms, and onions in this rich, stewlike summery sauce. It's finished with fresh basil, lemon zest, red pepper flakes, and a sprinkle of pine nuts, then served over whole-grain pasta for a robust meatless meal.

# linguine with eggplant and cannellini sauce

| serves 6 | 1 cup pasta and 1 cup sauce per serving |

12 ounces peeled eggplant, cut into ½-inch cubes

½ teaspoon salt

1 tablespoon olive oil

1 large onion, chopped into ½-inch pieces

1 cup chopped mushrooms, such as button, brown (cremini), portobello, or shiitake (stems discarded)

2 medium garlic cloves, finely chopped

¼ cup dry red wine (regular or nonalcoholic)

2 medium tomatoes, chopped into ½-inch pieces

1 cup fat-free, low-sodium vegetable broth and ½ cup fat-free, low-sodium vegetable broth, divided use

12 ounces dried whole-grain linguine, fettuccine, or other whole-grain pasta

1 cup canned no-salt-added cannellini beans, rinsed and drained

*(continued)*

1. Put the eggplant in a colander. Sprinkle with the salt. Let stand for 30 minutes. Rinse well. Pat dry with paper towels.

2. In a large skillet, heat the oil over medium-high heat, swirling to coat the bottom. Cook the onion for 5 minutes, or until beginning to brown, stirring frequently. Stir in the mushrooms, garlic, and eggplant. Cook for 10 minutes, stirring frequently. There will be browned bits in the skillet; don't let them burn. Stir in the wine, scraping to dislodge the browned bits. Stir in the tomatoes and 1 cup broth. Reduce the heat and simmer, covered, for 20 minutes, or until the eggplant is tender, stirring occasionally.

3. Meanwhile, prepare the pasta using the package directions, omitting the salt. Drain well in a colander.

**4.** Stir the beans, lemon zest, red pepper flakes, and the remaining 1/2 cup broth into the sauce. Cook for 5 minutes. Remove from the heat. Gently stir the basil into the sauce.

**5.** Transfer the pasta to plates. Top with the sauce. Sprinkle with the pine nuts. Serve immediately.

**cook's tip:** Salting the eggplant before cooking removes some of its moisture and bitterness. If you would like to further reduce the sodium in this dish, select smaller eggplants, which are sweeter and do not need to be salted.

1½ teaspoons grated lemon zest

¼ teaspoon crushed red pepper flakes (optional)

1 cup tightly packed fresh basil, rolled and cut into thin strips

2 tablespoons pine nuts, coarsely chopped

......................................................

**per serving**

calories 312
**total fat 5.5 g**
   saturated fat 0.5 g
   trans fat 0.0 g
   polyunsaturated fat 1.5 g
   monounsaturated fat 2.5 g
**cholesterol 0 mg**

**sodium 219 mg**
**carbohydrates 56 g**
   fiber 11 g
   sugars 6 g
**protein 12 g**

**dietary exchanges**
3 starch, 2 vegetable, ½ fat

Harira, a soup that's often served during Ramadan to break the daytime fast, is redolent with sweet and savory Middle Eastern spices, such as cinnamon and cumin. Potatoes, lentils, and chickpeas make this vegetarian soup hearty.

# moroccan harira

**serves 6** | **1½ cups per serving**

1 tablespoon olive oil

1 medium onion, thinly sliced

1 28-ounce can no-salt-added diced tomatoes, undrained

3 tablespoons chopped fresh cilantro

½ teaspoon salt

¼ teaspoon pepper

½ teaspoon ground cinnamon

½ teaspoon ground cumin

¼ teaspoon ground ginger

¼ teaspoon ground turmeric

5 cups water

1 cup dried lentils, sorted for stones and shriveled lentils, rinsed, and drained

2 medium white potatoes, peeled and cut into ½-inch cubes

1 15.5-ounce can no-salt-added chickpeas, rinsed and drained

1 medium lemon, cut into 6 wedges

1. In a large stockpot or Dutch oven, heat the oil over medium-high heat, swirling to coat the bottom. Cook the onion for about 3 minutes, or until soft, stirring frequently.

2. Meanwhile, in a food processor or blender, process the tomatoes with liquid, cilantro, salt, and pepper until smooth. Set aside.

3. Stir the cinnamon, cumin, ginger, and turmeric into the onion. Cook for 1 minute, stirring constantly.

4. Stir in the tomato mixture. Bring to a boil, still over medium-high heat.

5. Stir in the water and lentils. Reduce the heat and simmer for 15 minutes.

6. Stir in the potatoes. Cook over low heat for 15 to 20 minutes, or until the lentils and potatoes are just tender, stirring occasionally.

7. Stir in the chickpeas. Bring to a low boil. Remove from the heat. Serve the soup with the lemon wedges.

**per serving**

calories 289
total fat 3.0 g
   saturated fat 0.5 g
   trans fat 0.0 g
   polyunsaturated fat 0.0 g
   monounsaturated fat 1.5 g
cholesterol 0 mg

sodium 233 mg
carbohydrates 52 g
   fiber 10 g
   sugars 9 g
protein 16 g

dietary exchanges
3 starch, 2 vegetable, 1 lean meat

Cardamom has a pungent aroma and a warm, spicy-sweet flavor that characterizes a lot of East Indian cooking. Together with smoky cumin, spicy cayenne, sweet golden raisins, and toasty nuts, it adds an exotic richness to tender lentils and bulgur.

# cardamom-scented lentils with bulgur

**serves 4** | 1¼ cups per serving

4 cups water

⅓ cup dried green lentils, sorted for stones and shriveled lentils, rinsed, and drained

½ cup uncooked instant, or fine-grain, bulgur

1 tablespoon canola or corn oil

1½ cups diced onion

1 medium carrot, thinly sliced

1 medium red bell pepper, diced

2 medium garlic cloves, minced

1¼ teaspoons ground cumin

½ teaspoon ground cardamom

⅛ teaspoon cayenne

½ cup golden raisins

⅓ cup chopped walnuts or pecans, dry-roasted

½ teaspoon salt

2 tablespoons chopped fresh parsley

1. In a large saucepan, bring the water and lentils to a boil over high heat. Reduce the heat and simmer, covered, for 15 minutes.

2. Stir in the bulgur. Return to a simmer. Simmer, covered, for 12 minutes, or until the lentils and bulgur are tender. Drain well in a fine-mesh sieve. Transfer to a large bowl. Gently fluff with a fork.

3. Meanwhile, in a large nonstick skillet, heat the oil over medium-high heat, swirling to coat the bottom. Cook the onion, carrot, and bell pepper for 8 minutes, or until the edges of the onion are lightly browned, stirring occasionally. Stir in the garlic, cumin, cardamom, and cayenne. Cook for 15 seconds, stirring constantly.

4. Stir the onion mixture, raisins, walnuts, and salt into the lentil mixture.

5. Just before serving, sprinkle with the parsley.

**per serving**

calories 324
total fat 10.5 g
   saturated fat 1.0 g
   trans fat 0.0 g
   polyunsaturated fat 6.0 g
   monounsaturated fat 3.0 g
cholesterol 0 mg

sodium 317 mg
carbohydrates 52 g
   fiber 9 g
   sugars 18 g
protein 11 g

dietary exchanges
1 fruit, 2 vegetable,
2 starch, 2 fat

Meaty portobello mushrooms and sweet onions, simmered with fresh garlic, basil, and a splash of balsamic vinegar, make a rich topping for creamy polenta flavored with chewy, sweet sun-dried tomatoes.

# portobello ragout with sun-dried tomato polenta

serves 6 | ¾ cup mushroom mixture and ½ cup polenta per serving

### ragout

- 1 tablespoon plus 2 teaspoons olive oil
- 3 medium portobello mushrooms, cut into ½-inch slices
- 2 medium sweet onions, such as Vidalia, Maui, or Oso Sweet, cut into ¼-inch rings
- 2 large garlic cloves, thickly sliced
- ¼ cup coarsely chopped fresh Italian (flat-leaf) parsley
- ¼ cup tightly packed fresh basil, coarsely chopped
- 2 teaspoons balsamic vinegar
- ¼ teaspoon salt
- Pepper to taste

*(continued)*

1. In a large skillet or Dutch oven, heat the oil over medium heat, swirling to coat the bottom. Cook the mushrooms, onions, and garlic, covered, for 10 to 20 minutes, or until the mushrooms release their liquid, stirring occasionally.

2. Stir in the remaining ragout ingredients. Cook, covered, for 5 minutes, or until the onions are soft, stirring occasionally.

3. Meanwhile, in a large saucepan or stockpot, whisk together the water, milk, and tomato paste. Bring to a boil over high heat. Stir in the tomatoes.

4. Reduce the heat to medium. Using a long-handled whisk, carefully whisk the mixture to create a swirl. Slowly pour the cornmeal in a steady stream into the swirl, whisking constantly. After all the cornmeal is added, hold the pan steady and continue whisking for 1 to 2 minutes, or until the polenta is the desired consistency.

**5.** Pour the polenta onto a large serving platter or into a large, deep serving bowl. Spoon the ragout on top. Sprinkle with the Parmesan and the remaining pepper to taste.

**cook's tip on sweet onions:** When the sweet onions you like are in season, you may want to freeze a big batch to have on hand the rest of the year. Chop the onions, spread them on a baking sheet, and freeze them. Seal the frozen onions in an airtight container or a resealable plastic freezer bag.

**cook's tip on tomato paste:** Tubes of tomato paste are convenient when you need only a spoonful, but they can be costly. You can get that same convenience by buying canned no-salt-added tomato paste and freezing small portions of it. Line a baking sheet with wax paper or aluminum foil. Place tablespoon-size dollops of tomato paste on the baking sheet. Freeze for 4 to 6 hours, or until the paste is firm. (This step will keep the portions from sticking together later.) Transfer the portions to an airtight container or a resealable plastic freezer bag and freeze for up to three months.

## polenta

**2½ cups water**

**1  12-ounce can fat-free evaporated milk**

**1  tablespoon no-salt-added tomato paste**

**5  dry-packed sun-dried tomatoes, thinly sliced**

**1  cup cornmeal**

**2  tablespoons shredded or grated Parmesan cheese**

**Pepper to taste**

.......................................................

### per serving

| | |
|---|---|
| calories 202 | sodium 201 mg |
| total fat 5.0 g | carbohydrates 34 g |
| saturated fat 1.0 g | fiber 3 g |
| trans fat 0.0 g | sugars 11 g |
| polyunsaturated fat 0.5 g | protein 8 g |
| monounsaturated fat 3.0 g | dietary exchanges |
| cholesterol 4 mg | 2 starch, 1 vegetable, ½ fat |

Protein-packed quinoa gives this chili a lighter texture. It's still warm and satisfying without the heaviness of some meat chilis, and the peppers give a depth of flavor.

# quinoa and roasted pepper chili

**serves 6** | 1½ cups per serving

2 teaspoons olive oil

1 medium onion, chopped

2 medium garlic cloves, minced

5 cups fat-free, low-sodium vegetable broth

1 15.5-ounce can no-salt-added pinto beans, rinsed and drained

1 14.5-ounce can no-salt-added diced tomatoes, undrained

1½ teaspoons chili powder

½ teaspoon ground cumin

¼ teaspoon salt

¼ teaspoon crushed red pepper flakes

1 cup uncooked quinoa, rinsed and drained

2 medium poblano peppers, roasted and diced

1 medium red bell pepper, roasted and diced

¼ cup plus 2 tablespoons fat-free sour cream

¼ cup plus 2 tablespoons shredded low-fat mozzarella cheese

1. In a large saucepan or stockpot, heat the oil over medium-high heat, swirling to coat the bottom. Cook the onion and garlic for 3 minutes, or until soft, stirring frequently. Stir in the broth, beans, tomatoes with liquid, chili powder, cumin, salt, and red pepper flakes. Bring to a simmer, still over medium-high heat.

2. Stir in the quinoa, poblanos, and bell pepper. Simmer, covered, for 20 minutes, or until the quinoa has absorbed most of the liquid (no stirring needed). Top each serving with the sour cream and mozzarella.

**cook's tip on roasted peppers:** To prepare roasted peppers, lightly spray a broiler pan and rack with cooking spray. Preheat the broiler. Broil the peppers on the broiler pan about 4 inches from the heat, turning until they are charred all over. Put the peppers in a small bowl and let stand, covered, for at least 5 minutes. (It won't hurt the peppers to stand for as long as 20 minutes.) Wearing plastic gloves if you're roasting hot chiles, rinse the chiles with cold water, removing and discarding the blackened skin, ribs, seeds, and stems.

**per serving**

calories 257
total fat 4.0 g
   saturated fat 0.5 g
   trans fat 0.0 g
   polyunsaturated fat 1.0 g
   monounsaturated fat 2.0 g
cholesterol 5 mg

sodium 203 mg
carbohydrates 42 g
   fiber 7 g
   sugars 10 g
protein 13 g

dietary exchanges
2½ starch, 2 vegetable, 1 lean meat

Surprisingly hearty and filling, this dish gets its natural sweetness from artichoke hearts and sun-dried tomatoes. Fresh lemon juice, a dash of hot-pepper sauce, and crumbled feta cheese add their assertive flavors.

# quinoa pilaf with artichokes and chickpeas

**serves 4** | 2 cups per serving

1 cup dry-packed sun-dried tomatoes

1¼ cups boiling water

1 cup uncooked quinoa, rinsed and drained

1 teaspoon olive oil

9 ounces frozen artichoke hearts, thawed and chopped

1 teaspoon dried oregano, crumbled

1 medium garlic clove, minced

½ teaspoon crushed red pepper flakes

1 15.5-ounce can no-salt-added chickpeas, rinsed and drained

1 tablespoon fresh lemon juice

½ teaspoon red hot-pepper sauce

¼ teaspoon salt-free lemon pepper

⅛ teaspoon salt

2 ounces fat-free feta cheese, crumbled

1. Put the tomatoes in a small bowl. Pour in the water to cover. Let stand for about 10 minutes, or until softened.

2. Drain the tomatoes, reserving the liquid in a 2-cup measuring cup. Chop the tomatoes. Set aside.

3. Add enough water to the measuring cup to equal 2 cups. Pour into a medium saucepan. Stir in the quinoa. Bring to a boil over high heat. Reduce the heat and simmer, covered, for about 15 minutes, or until all the liquid is absorbed. Transfer to a large bowl. Fluff with a fork. Set aside.

4. Meanwhile, in a large nonstick skillet, heat the oil over medium heat, swirling to coat the bottom. Cook the artichokes, oregano, garlic, and red pepper flakes for 2 minutes, stirring frequently. Stir in the chickpeas. Cook for 5 minutes, or until heated through, stirring occasionally. Remove from the heat.

5. Stir the lemon juice, hot-pepper sauce, lemon pepper, salt, tomatoes, and artichoke mixture into the quinoa until combined. Spoon the pilaf onto a serving platter. Sprinkle with the feta.

## per serving

calories 368
total fat 5.0 g
  saturated fat 0.5 g
  trans fat 0.0 g
  polyunsaturated fat 2.0 g
  monounsaturated fat 2.0 g
cholesterol 0 mg

sodium 365 mg
carbohydrates 63 g
  fiber 14 g
  sugars 6 g
protein 19 g

dietary exchanges
3 starch, 3 vegetable, 1 lean meat

Chewy brown rice mingles with fluffy quinoa, crisp edamame, fresh vegetables, sweet dried apricots, and crunchy almonds to make an intriguing main-dish salad.

# rice, quinoa, and edamame salad

**serves 4** | 1¼ cups per serving

2 cups water

⅓ cup uncooked instant brown rice

⅓ cup uncooked quinoa, rinsed and drained

**dressing**

2 tablespoons fresh lime juice

2 tablespoons plain rice vinegar

2 teaspoons minced peeled gingerroot

2 teaspoons canola or corn oil

1 teaspoon sugar

½ teaspoon salt

⅛ teaspoon crushed red pepper flakes

————

1 cup frozen shelled edamame, thawed and patted dry

½ medium cucumber, seeded and diced

½ medium red bell pepper, chopped

8 dried apricot halves, thinly sliced

½ cup chopped fresh cilantro

⅓ cup finely chopped red onion

⅓ cup slivered almonds, dry-roasted

1. In a large saucepan, bring the water, rice, and quinoa to a boil over high heat. Reduce the heat and simmer, covered, for 10 minutes, or until the rice is tender. Transfer to a fine-mesh sieve. Rinse with cold water for 1 to 2 minutes, or until cool. Drain well. Fluff with a fork.

2. Meanwhile, in a small bowl, whisk together the dressing ingredients. Set aside.

3. In a large bowl, stir together the edamame, cucumber, bell pepper, apricots, cilantro, onion, and almonds. Stir in the rice mixture.

4. Pour the dressing over the salad, tossing to coat.

**cook's tip:** The components of this salad can be prepared in advance, but don't combine them until serving time so your salad will be at its freshest and crispest.

**per serving**

calories 243
total fat 10.0 g
   saturated fat 0.5 g
   trans fat 0.0 g
   polyunsaturated fat 3.0 g
   monounsaturated fat 5.5 g
cholesterol 0 mg

sodium 301 mg
carbohydrates 30 g
   fiber 6 g
   sugars 9 g
protein 10 g

dietary exchanges
2 starch, ½ lean meat, 1 fat

This satiating pilaf combines a triple threat of whole grains with grape tomatoes, edamame, and feta. Its light, lemony dressing gets a little heat from hot-chile sauce and lots of herbaceous flavor from fresh basil and cilantro.

# three-grain pilaf

**serves 4** | 1¼ cups per serving

1½ cups water

½ cup uncooked wild rice

¼ cup uncooked quinoa, rinsed and drained

¼ cup uncooked instant, or fine-grain, bulgur

1 cup grape tomatoes, quartered

¾ cup frozen shelled edamame or green peas, thawed and patted dry

1 tablespoon canola or corn oil

2 to 3 teaspoons grated lemon zest

1½ tablespoons fresh lemon juice

2 medium garlic cloves, minced

½ teaspoon hot-chile sauce, such as sriracha

¼ cup chopped fresh basil

¼ cup chopped fresh cilantro

¾ cup crumbled low-fat feta cheese

1. In a large saucepan, bring the water and rice to a boil over high heat. Reduce the heat and simmer, covered, for 20 minutes. Stir in the quinoa and bulgur. Simmer, covered, for 15 minutes, or until the bulgur is tender.

2. Put the tomatoes and edamame in a fine-mesh sieve. Pour the rice mixture into the sieve. Drain well.

3. In a large bowl, whisk together the oil, lemon zest, lemon juice, garlic, and chile sauce. Stir in the rice mixture, tomato mixture, basil, and cilantro.

4. Gently stir in the feta.

## per serving

calories 277
total fat 9.0 g
  saturated fat 2.5 g
  trans fat 0.0 g
  polyunsaturated fat 2.5 g
  monounsaturated fat 3.5 g
cholesterol 10 mg

sodium 398 mg
carbohydrates 36 g
  fiber 6 g
  sugars 4 g
protein 15 g

dietary exchanges
2½ starch, 1½ lean meat

Americans have turned ancient flatbreads into an ultramodern way to serve a meal. In this dish, whole-grain tortillas envelop a filling of nutty brown rice and hot curried vegetables that pick up smokiness from cumin and sweetness from dried currants.

# curried vegetable and rice wraps

serves 6 | 1 wrap per serving

¾ cup uncooked brown rice

Cooking spray

1 teaspoon canola or corn oil

1 medium onion, halved lengthwise, then cut into thin half-moon slices

3 medium zucchini, cut into ½-inch cubes

2 medium bell peppers (any color), cut into ½-inch squares

3 medium tomatoes, peeled and diced, or 1 14.5-ounce can no-salt-added diced tomatoes, drained

¼ cup dried currants or raisins

2 teaspoons curry powder

1 teaspoon ground cumin

¾ teaspoon red hot-pepper sauce

6 8-inch whole-grain tortillas (lowest sodium available)

1. Prepare the rice using the package directions, omitting the salt and margarine. Set aside.

2. Meanwhile, lightly spray a large skillet with cooking spray. Pour in the oil, swirling to coat the bottom. Heat over high heat. Cook the onion for 2 minutes, or until it begins to soften, stirring occasionally.

3. Reduce the heat to medium. Stir in the zucchini and bell peppers. Cook for 10 minutes, or until soft, stirring occasionally.

4. Stir in the remaining ingredients except the tortillas.

5. Spoon the rice onto the tortillas, keeping it toward the center. Top with the zucchini mixture. Roll up the tortillas. Secure each wrap with a wooden toothpick.

cook's tip: The currants add sweetness to this dish without being noticeably fruity. If you're using raisins, they'll be just as subtle if you cut them into small pieces. Lightly spray your kitchen shears with cooking spray to prevent the raisins from sticking to the blades.

## per serving

calories 287
total fat 5.5 g
    saturated fat 1.5 g
    trans fat 0.0 g
    polyunsaturated fat 1.5 g
    monounsaturated fat 2.0 g
cholesterol 0 mg

sodium 342 mg
carbohydrates 54 g
    fiber 8 g
    sugars 11 g
protein 9 g

dietary exchanges
2½ starch, ½ fruit, 2 vegetable, ½ fat

Bring a taste of the islands to your table with this lightened-up version of a popular Hawaiian dish. Fluffy scrambled egg substitute, sweet red bell pepper, tender snow peas, creamy tofu, and juicy pineapple blend with brown rice for a vegetarian entrée that's sure to satisfy.

# hawaiian fried rice

| serves 4 | 1½ cups per serving |
|---|---|

1½ cups uncooked instant brown rice

2 teaspoons canola or corn oil and 1 teaspoon canola or corn oil, divided use

½ cup egg substitute

1 cup snow peas, trimmed and cut crosswise into ½-inch pieces

1 medium red bell pepper, diced

4 medium green onions, thinly sliced

2 medium garlic cloves, minced

1 teaspoon minced peeled gingerroot

12 ounces light firm tofu, drained, patted dry, and diced

1 8-ounce can pineapple chunks in their own juice, drained

2 tablespoons soy sauce (lowest sodium available)

1 teaspoon toasted sesame oil

**per serving**

calories 289
total fat 7.5 g
  saturated fat 0.5 g
  trans fat 0.0 g
  polyunsaturated fat 3.0 g
  monounsaturated fat 3.5 g
cholesterol 0 mg

sodium 302 mg
carbohydrates 41 g
  fiber 5 g
  sugars 11 g
protein 15 g

dietary exchanges
2 starch, ½ fruit,
1 vegetable, 1½ lean
meat

1. Prepare the rice using the package directions, omitting the salt and margarine. Spread the rice in an even layer on a rimmed baking sheet or in a 13 × 9 × 2-inch baking dish. Refrigerate, uncovered, for 15 to 20 minutes, or until cool.

2. In a large nonstick skillet or wok, heat 2 teaspoons canola oil over medium heat, swirling to coat the bottom. Pour in the egg substitute. Cook for 1 minute, or until almost set, without stirring. Rapidly stir to break the egg substitute into pieces. Transfer to a plate.

3. In the same skillet, still over medium heat, heat the remaining 1 teaspoon canola oil, swirling to coat the bottom. Cook the snow peas, bell pepper, green onions, garlic, and gingerroot for 2 minutes, or until the vegetables are tender-crisp, stirring frequently.

4. Gently stir in the tofu, pineapple, soy sauce, and sesame oil. Cook for 2 to 3 minutes, or until the tofu is heated through, gently stirring occasionally.

5. Stir in the rice and egg substitute pieces. Cook for 2 to 3 minutes, or until heated through, stirring occasionally.

A traditional Southern dish that's frequently served on New Year's Day, Hoppin' John is thought to bring great prosperity to those who eat it. The black-eyed peas symbolize coins, and the collard greens represent wealth. Regardless of what you believe, this dish will help you stick to your resolution to eat heart healthy.

# hoppin' john

**serves 6** | 1½ cups per serving

1 teaspoon olive oil

½ cup chopped onion

1 medium rib of celery, chopped

½ medium red bell pepper, chopped

½ medium yellow bell pepper, chopped

2 medium garlic cloves, minced

4 cups fat-free, low-sodium vegetable broth

3 cups coarsely chopped collard greens, any large stems discarded

16 ounces frozen black-eyed peas (no need to thaw)

1 14.5-ounce can no-salt-added diced tomatoes, undrained

¾ cup uncooked brown rice

2 teaspoons salt-free Creole or Cajun seasoning blend (see cook's tip on page 75)

½ teaspoon salt

¼ teaspoon crushed red pepper flakes

1. In a large stockpot or Dutch oven, heat the oil over medium-high heat, swirling to coat the bottom. Cook the onion, celery, bell peppers, and garlic for 5 to 6 minutes, or until the vegetables are soft, stirring occasionally.

2. Stir in the remaining ingredients and bring to a simmer. Reduce the heat and simmer, covered, for 40 to 45 minutes, or until the rice is tender, stirring once halfway through.

**per serving**

calories 248
total fat 2.5 g
  saturated fat 0.5 g
  trans fat 0.0 g
  polyunsaturated fat 0.5 g
  monounsaturated fat 1.0 g
cholesterol 0 mg

sodium 266 mg
carbohydrates 48 g
  fiber 7 g
  sugars 4 g
protein 11 g

dietary exchanges
2½ starch,
2 vegetable, ½ lean meat

Brimming with okra, red beans, zucchini, and a host of supporting vegetables, this hearty meal is sure to please. Serve it over a whole grain, or enjoy a bowl on its own.

# vegetarian gumbo

| serves 5 | heaping 1½ cups per serving |
| --- | --- |

¼ cup all-purpose flour

3 tablespoons canola or corn oil

2 medium ribs of celery, diced

1 medium onion, diced

1 medium carrot, diced

½ medium red bell pepper, diced

¼ medium green bell pepper, diced

4 medium garlic cloves, minced

2 medium tomatoes, diced

1 cup fat-free, low-sodium vegetable broth

2½ cups frozen sliced okra, thawed

2 cups canned no-salt-added small red beans, rinsed and drained

1 medium zucchini, diced

½ cup tomato puree

2 medium dried bay leaves

1 teaspoon dried thyme, crumbled

1 teaspoon filé powder (optional)

1 teaspoon salt-free Creole or Cajun seasoning blend (see cook's tip on page 75)

¼ teaspoon cayenne

1. In a large skillet, stir together the flour and oil. Cook over medium-low heat for 10 minutes, or until the mixture is chocolate brown and fragrant, stirring constantly. Stir in the celery, onion, carrot, bell peppers, and garlic. Cook for 3 to 4 minutes, or until the vegetables begin to release their liquid, stirring occasionally.

2. Stir in the tomatoes and broth. Increase the heat to medium. Cook, covered, for 10 minutes, or until the tomatoes begin to soften and release their liquid, stirring occasionally.

3. Stir in the remaining ingredients. Bring to a simmer and simmer, covered, for 15 minutes, or until the vegetables are tender. Discard the bay leaves before serving the gumbo.

cook's tip: Filé powder, sometimes known as gumbo filé, is made from the dried leaves of the sassafras tree. It adds a distinctive, earthy flavor and also acts as a thickening agent.

**per serving**

calories 248
total fat 9.5 g
   saturated fat 0.5 g
   trans fat 0.0 g
   polyunsaturated fat 2.5 g
   monounsaturated fat 5.5 g
cholesterol 0 mg

sodium 95 mg
carbohydrates 34 g
   fiber 9 g
   sugars 9 g
protein 9 g

dietary exchanges
1½ starch,
3 vegetable, 1½ fat

This salad pops with flavor and crunch, thanks to a parade of colorful fresh vegetables, including bell pepper, grape tomatoes, spinach, and onion. A sprinkle of nutty Asiago cheese is the crowning touch!

# penne salad with white beans and asiago

**serves 4** : 1½ cups per serving

4 ounces dried whole-grain penne

1 cup canned no-salt-added navy beans, rinsed and drained

½ 14-ounce can quartered artichoke hearts, drained

½ medium yellow bell pepper, diced

½ cup grape tomatoes, quartered

½ cup tightly packed spinach, chopped

¼ cup diced onion

1 tablespoon plus 1 teaspoon capers, drained

3 tablespoons red wine vinegar

2 tablespoons olive oil

2 medium garlic cloves, minced

¼ teaspoon salt

―――

¼ cup chopped fresh basil

¼ cup shredded Asiago cheese

**1.** Prepare the pasta using the package directions, omitting the salt. Transfer to a colander. Rinse with cold water to cool. Drain well.

**2.** Meanwhile, in a large bowl, stir together the beans, artichoke hearts, bell pepper, tomatoes, spinach, onion, and capers.

**3.** In a small bowl, whisk together the vinegar, oil, garlic, and salt.

**4.** Stir the pasta into the bean mixture. Pour the dressing over the salad, tossing gently to coat.

**5.** Just before serving, stir in the basil. Sprinkle with the Asiago.

**per serving**

calories 271
total fat 10.0 g
 saturated fat 2.5 g
 trans fat 0.0 g
 polyunsaturated fat 1.0 g
 monounsaturated fat 5.5 g
cholesterol 6 mg
sodium 384 mg
carbohydrates 37 g
 fiber 7 g
 sugars 5 g
protein 10 g
dietary exchanges
2 starch, 1 vegetable,
½ lean meat, 1 fat

This is a veggie version of five-way chili (chili, beans, spaghetti, cheese, and onions).

# cincinnati chili

| serves 6 | ⅔ cup spaghetti and heaping ¾ cup chili per serving |
|---|---|

1 tablespoon canola or corn oil

½ cup diced white onion

1 tablespoon chili powder

1 tablespoon unsweetened cocoa powder

2 teaspoons sugar

½ teaspoon ground cinnamon

½ teaspoon ground cumin

¼ teaspoon pepper

⅛ teaspoon salt

1 15.5-ounce can no-salt-added pinto beans, rinsed and drained

1 15.5-ounce can no-salt-added red kidney beans, rinsed and drained

1 14.5-ounce can no-salt-added diced tomatoes, undrained

1 8-ounce can no-salt-added tomato sauce

½ cup water

1 4-ounce can diced green chiles

6 ounces dried whole-grain spaghetti

¼ cup sliced green onions

¼ cup shredded fat-free Cheddar cheese

1. In a large saucepan, heat the oil over medium heat, swirling to coat the bottom. Cook the onion for 4 to 6 minutes, or until soft, stirring occasionally. Stir in the chili powder, cocoa powder, sugar, cinnamon, cumin, pepper, and salt. Cook for 1 minute, stirring constantly. Stir in the pinto beans, kidney beans, tomatoes with liquid, tomato sauce, water, and chiles.

2. Increase the heat to medium high and bring the chili to a boil. Reduce the heat and simmer for 20 minutes, or until slightly thickened, stirring occasionally.

3. Meanwhile, prepare the pasta using the package directions, omitting the salt. Drain well in a colander. Transfer to plates or bowls. Ladle the chili over the pasta. Sprinkle with the green onions and Cheddar.

**lunchbox tip:** Mix the chili and spaghetti together or pack just the chili in a thermos to send your child off to school with a hot, healthy lunch.

**per serving**

calories 338
total fat 4.0 g
    saturated fat 0.0 g
    trans fat 0.0 g
    polyunsaturated fat 1.0 g
    monounsaturated fat 2.0 g
cholesterol 1 mg

sodium 205 mg
carbohydrates 62 g
    fiber 12 g
    sugars 11 g
protein 16 g

dietary exchanges
3½ starch, 1 vege-
table, 1 lean meat

vegetarian entrées

183

This hearty vegetarian stew is loaded with flavor from onion, garlic, allspice, cloves, coriander, and gingerroot. Sweet potatoes and golden raisins add sweetness to the chickpeas and tomatoes, while a touch of lemon zest adds a note of brightness. Serve the stew over couscous to soak up the delicious, fragrant liquid.

# moroccan sweet potato and chickpea stew

**serves 8** | 1¼ cups per serving

½ teaspoon ground allspice

½ teaspoon ground cloves

½ teaspoon ground coriander

½ teaspoon pepper (freshly ground preferred)

⅛ teaspoon cayenne (optional)

1 tablespoon olive oil

2 large onions, chopped

3 to 4 medium garlic cloves, finely minced

1 tablespoon grated peeled gingerroot

2 pounds unpeeled sweet potatoes, chopped

2 cups fat-free, low-sodium vegetable broth

1 14.5-ounce can no-salt-added diced tomatoes, undrained

*(continued)*

1. In a small bowl, stir together the allspice, cloves, coriander, pepper, and cayenne.

2. In a Dutch oven or large saucepan, heat the oil over medium-high heat, swirling to coat the bottom. Cook the onions for 6 to 8 minutes, or until light golden brown, stirring frequently. Stir in the garlic and gingerroot. Cook for 2 to 3 minutes, stirring frequently. Stir in the allspice mixture. Cook for 2 minutes, or until the spices are toasted and fragrant, stirring constantly.

3. Stir in the sweet potatoes, broth, tomatoes with liquid, tomato sauce, and raisins. Gently stir in the chickpeas. Increase the heat to high and bring to a boil. Reduce the heat and simmer, covered, for 15 minutes, or until the sweet potatoes are just tender.

**4.** Uncover and simmer for 25 to 30 minutes, or until the stew is thickened.

**5.** Just before serving, stir in the parsley and lemon zest.

lunchbox tip: This stew is even better the next day, making it a delicious choice for a school lunch. Bring it to room temperature before reheating and packing it in a thermos.

1 8-ounce can no-salt-added tomato sauce

¾ cup golden raisins

2 15.5-ounce cans no-salt-added chickpeas, rinsed and drained

¼ cup chopped Italian (flat-leaf) parsley

1 tablespoon grated lemon zest

....................................................

**per serving**

calories 311
total fat 3.0 g
  saturated fat 0.5 g
  trans fat 0.0 g
  polyunsaturated fat 0.5 g
  monounsaturated fat 1.5 g
cholesterol 0 mg

sodium 108 mg
carbohydrates 64 g
  fiber 10 g
  sugars 19 g
protein 10 g

dietary exchanges
3 starch, 1 fruit,
1 vegetable

These tacos don't require any cooking, which makes them a perfect choice for the hottest of summer evenings. They pair well with a fuss-free salad or side, such as Cool Jícama-Cabbage Slaw (page 52).

# cool lettuce-wrap tacos

**serves 4** | 2 tacos per serving

1 cup canned no-salt-added black beans, rinsed and drained

½ cup frozen whole-kernel corn, thawed

1 small Italian plum (Roma) tomato, diced

½ small avocado, diced

2 tablespoons chopped fresh cilantro

1 tablespoon fresh lemon juice

½ teaspoon chili powder

8 Bibb lettuce leaves

½ cup shredded low-fat Monterey Jack cheese

½ cup salsa (lowest sodium available)

1. In a small bowl, stir together the beans, corn, tomato, avocado, cilantro, lemon juice, and chili powder.

2. Spoon ¼ cup of the bean mixture into the center of each lettuce leaf. Sprinkle with the Monterey Jack. Top with the salsa. For tacos, fold the sides of the lettuce over the filling. For burritos, roll the lettuce to enclose the filling, tucking in the ends. Secure each burrito with a wooden toothpick.

**lunchbox tip:** These tacos are perfect for eating at school because they don't need to be heated. Pack the lettuce and filling separately, and tuck some Cherry-Nut Trail Mix (page 32) into the sack to round out this portable meal.

**per serving**

calories 173
total fat 6.5 g
  saturated fat 2.0 g
  trans fat 0.0 g
  polyunsaturated fat 1.0 g
  monounsaturated fat 3.0 g
cholesterol 8 mg

sodium 214 mg
carbohydrates 20 g
  fiber 5 g
  sugars 5 g
protein 9 g

dietary exchanges
1 starch, 1 vegetable,
1 lean meat, ½ fat

A cornucopia of fresh vegetables simmers in a rich tomato sauce, then tops steaming spaghetti squash in this hearty, wholesome dish. Feel free to substitute veggies that are in season or your favorites for the ones listed.

# italian spaghetti squash

**serves 6** | 2½ cups per serving

1 4-pound spaghetti squash

1 tablespoon olive oil

1 medium onion, chopped

8 ounces mushrooms, such as button, brown (cremini), portobello, or shiitake (stems discarded), sliced

⅓ cup dry red wine (regular or nonalcoholic)

2 8-ounce cans no-salt-added tomato sauce

1 14.5-ounce can no-salt-added diced tomatoes, undrained

2 medium garlic cloves, minced

1 teaspoon dried Italian seasoning, crumbled

¼ teaspoon pepper

2 cups cooked broccoli florets

1 cup sliced carrots

1 small zucchini, sliced

¼ cup plus 2 tablespoons shredded or grated Parmesan cheese

2 tablespoons chopped fresh parsley

**per serving**

calories 193
total fat 5.0 g
   saturated fat 1.5 g
   trans fat 0.0 g
   polyunsaturated fat 1.0 g
   monounsaturated fat 2.0 g
cholesterol 4 mg

sodium 177 mg
carbohydrates 33 g
   fiber 8 g
   sugars 16 g
protein 8 g

dietary exchanges
1 starch, 3 vegetable,
1 fat

1. Preheat the oven to 350°F. Place the whole squash in a 13 × 9 × 2-inch glass baking dish. Pour in enough water to cover the bottom of the dish. Pierce the squash several times with a fork. Bake for 1 hour, or until the squash is tender and can easily be pierced with a sharp knife.

2. Meanwhile, in a large saucepan, heat the oil over medium heat, swirling to coat the bottom. Cook the onion for about 3 minutes, or until beginning to soften, stirring frequently. Stir in the mushrooms and wine. Cook for 2 to 3 minutes, stirring occasionally. Stir in the tomato sauce, tomatoes with liquid, garlic, Italian seasoning, and pepper. Increase the heat to medium-high and bring to a boil. Reduce the heat and simmer for 3 to 4 minutes, stirring occasionally. Stir in the broccoli, carrots, and zucchini. Simmer for 5 minutes, stirring occasionally.

3. When the squash is baked, halve it lengthwise and discard the seeds. Using a fork, scrape the squash lengthwise to release the strands, which resemble spaghetti. Transfer the strands to a serving platter. Pour the sauce over the squash. Sprinkle with the Parmesan and parsley.

Sweet bell peppers and tomatoes are the stars of this thick vegetable stew, which is spiked with fresh jalapeño. Green beans add extra color and texture, and browned tofu contributes protein. Serve this dish over brown rice or whole-grain pasta to sop up the molasses-based sauce.

# spicy smothered bell peppers with crisp tofu

**serves 4** | 2 cups per serving

1 teaspoon canola or corn oil and 1 teaspoon canola or corn oil, divided use

12 ounces light firm tofu, drained, patted dry, and diced

3 large bell peppers (1 green, 1 red, and 1 yellow preferred), sliced into thin strips

1 medium onion, diced

½ large or 1 small fresh jalapeño, seeds and ribs discarded, thinly sliced (see cook's tip on page 109)

8 ounces green beans, trimmed and cut into 2-inch pieces

3 tablespoons whole-wheat flour

1 cup water

½ cup fat-free, low-sodium vegetable broth

1 tablespoon molasses (dark preferred)

*(continued)*

**1.** In a large skillet, heat 1 teaspoon oil over medium-high heat, swirling to coat the bottom. Cook the tofu for 4 minutes, or until browned and crisp on all sides, turning at least once every minute. Watch carefully because it browns quickly. Transfer to a large plate. Set aside. Wipe the skillet with paper towels.

**2.** In the same skillet, heat the remaining 1 teaspoon oil, swirling to coat the bottom. Cook the bell peppers, onion, and jalapeño for 3 to 4 minutes, or until the bell peppers are tender-crisp and the onion is soft, stirring frequently. Stir in the green beans. Cook for 3 minutes, or until tender-crisp, stirring frequently. Stir in the flour. Cook for 1 minute, or until the flour is incorporated and begins to turn slightly brown, stirring constantly.

**3.** Meanwhile in a small bowl, whisk together the water, broth, molasses, soy sauce, oregano, and garlic.

**4.** When the flour is cooked, stir in the tomatoes and broth mixture. Increase the heat to high and bring to a boil. Gently stir in the tofu. Reduce the heat and simmer, covered, for 25 minutes, or until the sauce has thickened and the vegetables are tender, gently stirring occasionally (to avoid breaking up the tofu).

**cook's tip:** Tofu is a particularly effective ingredient in this dish because it soaks up the flavors from the sauce.

2 **teaspoons soy sauce (lowest sodium available)**

1 **teaspoon dried oregano, crumbled, or 1 tablespoon chopped fresh oregano**

2 **medium garlic cloves, minced**

2 **medium tomatoes, diced**

...................................................

### per serving

calories 171
total fat 4.5 g
   saturated fat 0.5 g
   trans fat 0.0 g
   polyunsaturated fat 2.0 g
   monounsaturated fat 2.0 g
cholesterol 0 mg

sodium 112 mg
carbohydrates 25 g
   fiber 6 g
   sugars 12 g
protein 11 g

dietary exchanges
½ starch, 3 vegetable, 1 lean meat

If you enjoy the layered flavors of Thai cuisine, you will love this easy dish that incorporates lemongrass, basil, coconut milk, and chiles. Pineapple Sorbet (page 257) or Almond-Mango Mousse (page 255) makes a fine finish for your meal. *(See photo insert.)*

# thai red curry

**serves 6** : 1 cup curry and ½ cup rice per serving

1 stalk lemongrass, 1 teaspoon lemongrass paste, 1 teaspoon ground dried lemongrass, or 1 teaspoon grated lemon zest

2½ cups fat-free, low-sodium vegetable broth

⅓ cup lite coconut milk

2 tablespoons Thai red curry paste (lowest sodium available)

1 tablespoon finely chopped peeled gingerroot

1 tablespoon soy sauce (lowest sodium available)

2 teaspoons sugar

3 medium garlic cloves, minced

¼ teaspoon crushed red pepper flakes (optional)

12 ounces light firm tofu, drained, patted dry, and cut into ¾-inch cubes

1 cup green beans, halved crosswise

1 cup thinly sliced red bell pepper

*(continued)*

1. Trim about 6 inches off the slender green end of the lemongrass stalk and discard. Remove the outer layer of leaves from the root of the stalk. Halve the stalk lengthwise. (Lemongrass stalks are slightly tough, so be careful as you slice.)

2. Place the lemongrass in a large saucepan. Stir in the broth, coconut milk, curry paste, gingerroot, soy sauce, sugar, garlic, and red pepper flakes. Bring to a simmer over medium-high heat, stirring occasionally.

3. Stir in the tofu, green beans, bell pepper, bamboo shoots, and carrot. Reduce the heat and simmer, covered, for 8 to 10 minutes, or until the vegetables are tender, stirring occasionally.

4. Meanwhile, prepare the rice using the package directions, omitting the salt and margarine. Remove from the heat. Cover to keep warm.

5. Stir the sliced basil into the tofu mixture. Simmer, covered, for 2 to 3 minutes, or until the curry is infused with basil flavor.

6. Put the cornstarch in a small bowl. Add the water, whisking to dissolve. Stir into the curry. Simmer for 2 to 3 minutes, or until the curry is thickened, stirring occasionally. Discard the lemongrass stalk.

7. Transfer the rice to plates. Spoon the curry over the rice. Garnish with the basil leaves.

**cook's tip on thai basil:** Thai basil has a thin green leaf with a purplish cast and its flavor is spicy and licorice-like. Look for it in Asian markets or specialty grocery stores, as well as at your local farmers' market. If it's not available, you can substitute sweet Italian basil, but the flavor will be different.

1 8-ounce can sliced bamboo shoots, drained

½ cup sliced carrot

1½ cups uncooked instant brown rice

½ cup loosely packed sliced fresh Thai basil and 18 fresh Thai basil leaves (optional), divided use

3 tablespoons cornstarch

⅓ cup water

............................................................

**per serving**

calories 178
total fat 2.5 g
   saturated fat 0.5 g
   trans fat 0.0 g
   polyunsaturated fat 1.0 g
   monounsaturated fat 0.5 g
cholesterol 0 mg

sodium 208 mg
carbohydrates 30 g
   fiber 3 g
   sugars 5 g
protein 9 g

dietary exchanges
1½ starch,
1 vegetable, ½ lean meat

These lasagnalike towers are layered with flavor. Tender white beans and green bell pepper, creamy ricotta, and a rich tomato sauce are all sandwiched between slices of broiled eggplant. Melted mozzarella tops each stack. Just add a dark leafy green salad and some whole-grain pasta or bread and you've got dinner under control.

# eggplant and ricotta stacks

**serves 4** : 1 stack per serving

Cooking spray

1 tablespoon olive oil

1 pound eggplant, trimmed and cut crosswise into 8 rounds

1 medium green bell pepper, chopped

⅓ cup chopped fresh basil

¼ cup fat-free ricotta

2 medium garlic cloves, minced

½ teaspoon dried fennel seeds

1 8-ounce can no-salt-added tomato sauce

½ 15.5-ounce can no-salt-added navy beans, rinsed and drained

½ cup shredded low-fat mozzarella cheese

1 tablespoon plus 1 teaspoon shredded or grated Parmesan cheese

1. Preheat the broiler. Line a baking sheet with aluminum foil. Lightly spray the foil with cooking spray.

2. Lightly brush the oil over both sides of the eggplant rounds. Arrange the rounds in a single layer on the baking sheet. Sprinkle the bell pepper around the eggplant. Broil about 4 to 6 inches from the heat for 6 minutes, or until the eggplant is beginning to lightly brown. Turn over the rounds. Gently stir the bell pepper. Broil for 6 minutes, or until the eggplant is tender and beginning to lightly brown. Remove the baking sheet from the oven.

3. Turn off the broiler. Preheat the oven to 350°F.

4. In a small bowl, stir together the basil, ricotta, garlic, and fennel seeds.

**per serving**

calories 176
total fat 5.5 g
   saturated fat 1.5 g
   trans fat 0.0 g
   polyunsaturated fat 0.5 g
   monounsaturated fat 3.0 g
cholesterol 8 mg

sodium 171 mg
carbohydrates 22 g
   fiber 8 g
   sugars 8 g
protein 12 g
dietary exchanges
½ starch, 3 vegetable,
1½ lean meat

**5.** Place 4 eggplant slices in an 11 × 7 × 2-inch glass baking dish. Spread half the tomato sauce over the eggplant. Top with, in order, the beans, bell pepper, ricotta mixture, and the remaining eggplant. Spoon the remaining tomato sauce over the stacks.

**6.** Bake for 20 minutes, or until heated through. Sprinkle with the mozzarella. Bake for 5 minutes, or until the mozzarella is melted. Remove from the oven.

**7.** Sprinkle with the Parmesan. Let stand for 10 minutes so the flavors blend.

**cook's tip:** Try to find an eggplant that is uniform in size so that the rounds are all about the same size.

Using Asian dumpling wrappers makes it a snap to prepare these healthy potato and cheese pierogi. Our recipe pairs them with cooked cabbage and onion, a traditional accompaniment. You can easily double the number of pierogi and freeze the extras for up to six months—no thawing necessary.

# polish pierogi

| serves 3 | 6 pierogi and 1 cup vegetables per serving |
|---|---|

1 teaspoon canola or corn oil

½ pound green cabbage, thinly sliced

1 large onion, thinly sliced

1 medium dried bay leaf

½ teaspoon coriander seeds, crushed

½ teaspoon black peppercorns, crushed

¼ cup dry white wine (regular or nonalcoholic)

¼ cup water (optional)

$\frac{1}{16}$ teaspoon salt and $\frac{1}{16}$ teaspoon salt, divided use

½ pound peeled white potatoes, diced

¼ cup no-salt-added fat-free cottage cheese

18 whole-wheat or white round dumpling wrappers or skins (about 3½ inches in diameter) (whole-wheat preferred)

1. In a medium skillet, heat the oil over medium-high heat, swirling to coat the bottom. Cook the cabbage, onion, bay leaf, coriander seeds, and peppercorns for about 5 minutes, or until the onion is slightly browned, stirring frequently. Stir in the wine, scraping to dislodge any browned bits. Reduce the heat and simmer, covered, for 30 minutes, or until the cabbage is tender and the onion is very soft. You may need to add ¼ cup water if the mixture gets too dry. Remove from the heat.

2. Discard the bay leaf. Stir $\frac{1}{16}$ teaspoon salt into the cabbage mixture.

3. Meanwhile, fill a 1½-quart saucepan three-fourths full with cold water. Add the potatoes. Bring to a boil over high heat. Reduce the heat and simmer for 15 minutes, or until tender when pierced with a fork. Drain well in a colander. Pat the potatoes dry. Transfer to a large bowl.

4. Stir in the cottage cheese and the remaining $\frac{1}{16}$ teaspoon salt. Using a potato masher, mash the potato mixture until smooth.

## per serving

calories 230
total fat 2.5 g
  saturated fat 0.5 g
  trans fat 0.0 g
  polyunsaturated fat 0.5 g
  monounsaturated fat 1.0 g
cholesterol 7 mg

sodium 343 mg
carbohydrates 42 g
  fiber 5 g
  sugars 6 g
protein 9 g

dietary exchanges
2 starch, 2 vegetable

**5.** To make the pierogi, place 2 teaspoons of potato mixture in the center of a wrapper. Dip your finger in warm water and trace it around the edge of the wrapper. Fold in half, pinching the edges together to seal them. Repeat with the remaining filling and wrappers. Transfer the pierogi to a large plate.

**6.** Fill a large saucepan two-thirds full with water. Bring to a boil over high heat. Gently lower the pierogi into the boiling water, being careful not to overcrowd the pan (you will probably need to cook them in batches). Bring to a low boil. Boil gently for 4 to 5 minutes, or until the pierogi float to the top. If they stick to the bottom of the pan, gently release them with a spatula. Using a slotted spoon, remove the pierogi from the water. Let drain. Transfer to plates. Serve immediately with the cabbage mixture on the side.

**cook's tip:** You can find dumpling wrappers in the refrigerator or freezer section of Asian or regular grocery stores. Or, you can make your own dough using 2½ cups white whole-wheat flour, ¼ teaspoon salt, ½ cup plus 2 tablespoons water, and 2 tablespoons fat-free plain yogurt. Stir the ingredients together until a dough forms. Roll out the dough to a thickness of ⅛ inch. Using a water glass, cut out 3½-inch circles. This recipe will make enough dough for 18 pierogi.

Celebrate a classic sandwich that's equally irresistible when it's vegetarian, with soy crumbles standing in for ground beef. Adding some grated carrots and zucchini is a great way to sneak in some extra veggies.

# veggie sloppy joes

**serves 4** | **1 sandwich per serving**

1 tablespoon olive oil

1 large onion, chopped

1 medium red bell pepper, chopped

1 large garlic clove, minced

8 ounces soy crumbles, thawed if frozen

3 medium carrots, grated

2 small zucchini or yellow summer squash, grated

½ cup no-salt-added ketchup

½ cup water

2 tablespoons light or dark brown sugar

2 tablespoons cider vinegar

1 teaspoon Worcestershire sauce (lowest sodium available)

1 teaspoon minced fresh thyme or ¼ teaspoon dried thyme, crumbled

⅛ teaspoon pepper (freshly ground preferred)

4 whole-grain hamburger buns (lowest sodium available)

1. In a large skillet, heat the oil over medium-high heat, swirling to coat the bottom. Cook the onion and bell pepper for about 3 minutes, or until just soft, stirring frequently. Stir in the garlic. Cook for 2 minutes.

2. Reduce the heat to medium. Stir in the soy crumbles. Cook for 5 minutes, or until heated through, stirring constantly.

3. Stir in the carrots and zucchini. Reduce the heat and simmer for 5 to 6 minutes, stirring frequently.

4. Stir in the ketchup, water, brown sugar, vinegar, and Worcestershire sauce. Increase the heat to high and bring to a boil. Reduce the heat and simmer for 3 to 5 minutes, stirring frequently.

5. Just before serving, stir in the thyme and pepper. Spoon the soy crumble mixture onto the buns.

**per serving**

calories 327
total fat 6.0 g
    saturated fat 1.0 g
    trans fat 0.0 g
    polyunsaturated fat 1.5 g
    monounsaturated fat 3.0 g
cholesterol 0 mg

sodium 431 mg
carbohydrates 54 g
    fiber 10 g
    sugars 24 g
protein 18 g

dietary exchanges
2 starch, 2 vegetable,
1 other carbohydrate,
2 lean meat

When zucchini is in abundance, purchase the small, tender ones and stuff them with soy crumbles, fresh veggies, and Italian seasonings. Add a spinach salad and a side of whole-wheat orzo or couscous for dinner.

# stuffed zucchini

## serves 4 : 2 stuffed zucchini halves per serving

4 small zucchini (about 8 ounces each)

2 teaspoons Worcestershire sauce (lowest sodium available)

Cooking spray

1 teaspoon olive oil

10 ounces frozen soy crumbles

½ cup finely chopped onion

1 medium garlic clove, minced

1 cup chopped seeded tomatoes

1 tablespoon chopped fresh oregano

¼ teaspoon pepper

⅓ cup shredded or grated Parmesan cheese

### per serving

| | |
|---|---|
| calories 185 | sodium 397 mg |
| total fat 4.0 g | carbohydrates 18 g |
|   saturated fat 1.5 g |   fiber 7 g |
|   trans fat 0.0 g |   sugars 8 g |
|   polyunsaturated fat 0.5 g | protein 21 g |
|   monounsaturated fat 1.5 g | dietary exchanges |
| cholesterol 5 mg | ½ starch, 2 vegetable, 2½ lean meat |

1. Halve the zucchini lengthwise. Scoop out the pulp, leaving a ¼-inch border of the shell all the way around. Dice the pulp. Set aside.

2. Place the shells with the cut sides down in a medium glass baking dish. Microwave, covered, on 100 percent power (high) for 4 to 6 minutes, or just until the zucchini is tender. Remove from the microwave. Uncover the dish carefully to avoid steam burns. Brush the insides of the zucchini shells with the Worcestershire sauce.

3. Preheat the broiler. Lightly spray a broiler pan with cooking spray.

4. Meanwhile, in a large nonstick skillet, heat the oil over medium heat, swirling to coat the bottom. Cook the soy crumbles, onion, garlic, and reserved zucchini pulp for 8 to 10 minutes, or until the onion is soft, stirring occasionally. Stir in the tomatoes, oregano, and pepper. Cook for 2 to 3 minutes, or until the tomatoes are tender, stirring occasionally. Spoon the soy crumble mixture into the zucchini shells. Sprinkle with the Parmesan.

5. Broil about 4 inches from the heat for 1 to 2 minutes, or until the Parmesan is melted.

Yellow squash shells are stuffed with a fresh filling of bell peppers, green onions, corn, and Monterey Jack cheese, then broiled to perfection. Add Fruit Salad with Cranberry-Ginger Dressing (page 54) or Confetti Rice Pilaf (page 219) for an easy, summery meal.

# savory stuffed squash

| serves 4 | 2 squash halves per serving |
| --- | --- |

Cooking spray

4 medium zucchini or yellow summer squash, halved lengthwise

2 tablespoons water

1 cup frozen whole-kernel corn, thawed and drained

¼ cup chopped red bell pepper

¼ cup chopped green bell pepper

2 medium green onions, chopped

1 tablespoon minced fresh oregano or 1 teaspoon dried oregano, crumbled

1 teaspoon salt-free lemon pepper

1 teaspoon salt-free all-purpose seasoning blend

¾ cup grated low-fat Monterey Jack cheese

**per serving**

calories 146
total fat 5.0 g
  saturated fat 2.5 g
  trans fat 0.0 g
  polyunsaturated fat 0.5 g
  monounsaturated fat 1.0 g
cholesterol 12 mg

sodium 155 mg
carbohydrates 18 g
  fiber 4 g
  sugars 7 g
protein 10 g

dietary exchanges
½ starch, 2 vegetable, 1 lean meat

1. Preheat the broiler. Lightly spray a broiler pan with cooking spray.

2. In a large saucepan, steam the zucchini for 5 to 7 minutes, or until tender-crisp. Immediately plunge into ice water to stop the cooking process and cool quickly. Drain the zucchini well, discarding the water. Scoop out the pulp, leaving a ¼-inch border of the shell all the way around. Place the shells on the broiler pan. Dice the pulp. Set aside.

3. Heat a medium nonstick skillet over medium-high heat. Pour in the water. Cook the corn, bell peppers, and green onions for 3 to 4 minutes, stirring frequently. Stir in the oregano, lemon pepper, seasoning blend, and diced zucchini pulp. Remove from the heat. Stir in the Monterey Jack until well combined.

4. Spoon the filling into the shells. Broil about 4 inches from the heat for 3 to 4 minutes, or until the filling is hot and the Monterey Jack is bubbly.

# side dishes

Amaranth is a grain that was domesticated more than 8,000 years ago. Iron rich, gluten free, and ever so versatile, it looks as if it could be a smaller cousin to couscous. In this side dish, amaranth is mixed with green peas and onion and then brightened with mint and lemon zest. *(See photo insert.)*

# amaranth and green peas with mint

**serves 4** | ½ cup per serving

½ cup uncooked amaranth

1 tablespoon canola or corn oil

1 cup finely chopped onion

½ cup frozen green peas, thawed

⅓ cup chopped fresh mint

2 teaspoons grated lemon zest

⅛ teaspoon salt

**per serving**

calories 154
total fat 5.5 g
   saturated fat 0.5 g
   trans fat 0.0 g
   polyunsaturated fat 1.5 g
   monounsaturated fat 2.5 g
cholesterol 0 mg

sodium 97 mg
carbohydrates 23 g
   fiber 4 g
   sugars 3 g
protein 5 g

dietary exchanges
1½ starch,
1 vegetable, ½ fat

1. Prepare the amaranth using the package directions, omitting the salt. Transfer to a fine-mesh sieve. Rinse with cold water. Drain well.

2. Meanwhile, in a medium skillet, heat the oil over medium heat, swirling to coat the bottom. Cook the onion for 6 minutes, or until browned on the edges, stirring occasionally. Stir in the peas and amaranth. Cook for 1 minute, or until the mixture is heated, stirring occasionally. Remove from the heat.

3. Add the mint, lemon zest, and salt, stirring gently to combine.

**cook's tip:** Rinsing the cooked amaranth with cold water helps it keep its shape and stops the cooking process. The amaranth will reheat gently and quickly when you stir it into the other ingredients in the skillet.

A cool change from the more familiar steamed or roasted asparagus, this dish is perfect as a sweet and savory complement to an Asian-inspired entrée such as Plank-Grilled Tuna Steaks (page 80).

# marinated asparagus

| serves 4 | 6 asparagus spears per serving |
|----------|-------------------------------|

1 pound asparagus spears (about 24), trimmed

### marinade

2 tablespoons finely chopped green onions

1 tablespoon white vinegar

1 tablespoon honey

2 teaspoons fresh orange juice

2 teaspoons soy sauce (lowest sodium available)

2 large garlic cloves, minced

1 teaspoon toasted sesame oil

1 teaspoon Worcestershire sauce (lowest sodium available)

1 teaspoon sesame seeds

½ teaspoon crushed red pepper flakes

1 teaspoon sesame seeds

1. In a skillet large enough to allow you to lay the asparagus flat, bring 2 inches of water to a boil over high heat. Add the asparagus, arranging the spears in a single layer. Cook for 2 minutes. Using tongs, immediately plunge the asparagus into a large bowl of ice water to stop the cooking process. Let soak for 2 to 3 minutes. Spread paper towels on a flat surface. Dry the asparagus well on the paper towels.

2. Meanwhile, in a small bowl, whisk together the marinade ingredients. Pour into a large, shallow glass casserole dish. Add the asparagus, turning several times to coat. Cover and refrigerate for 4 to 24 hours, turning occasionally.

3. Drain the asparagus, discarding the marinade. Arrange the asparagus on a platter. Garnish with the remaining 1 teaspoon sesame seeds.

### per serving

calories 29
total fat 0.5 g
  saturated fat 0.0 g
  trans fat 0.0 g
  polyunsaturated fat 0.0 g
  monounsaturated fat 0.0 g
cholesterol 0 mg

sodium 71 mg
carbohydrates 5 g
  fiber 2 g
  sugars 3 g
protein 3 g

dietary exchanges
1 vegetable

This simple, quick dish highlights the popular stir-fry flavors of soy, garlic, and gingerroot. Try it with Asian-accented entrées, such as Ginger-Lime Halibut (page 64) or Grilled Sweet Chile Pork Tenderloin (page 149).

# baby bok choy with ginger and garlic

**serves 4** | **1 head per serving**

2 teaspoons canola or corn oil

2 teaspoons grated peeled gingerroot

1 large garlic clove, thinly sliced

4 heads baby bok choy, bases trimmed, halved lengthwise

¼ cup water

1 tablespoon soy sauce (lowest sodium available)

In a large nonstick skillet, heat the oil over medium-high heat, swirling to coat the bottom. Cook the gingerroot and garlic for 1 to 2 minutes, or until fragrant, stirring constantly. Stir in the bok choy, water, and soy sauce. Reduce the heat and simmer, covered, for 2 to 3 minutes, or until the bok choy is tender-crisp.

**cook's tip:** If baby bok choy, which is the sweeter variety, is unavailable, you can use one small head of regular bok choy. Thinly slice the thick stems and coarsely chop the leaves.

**per serving**

calories 36
total fat 2.5 g
   saturated fat 0.0 g
   trans fat 0.0 g
   polyunsaturated fat 0.5 g
   monounsaturated fat 1.5 g
cholesterol 0 mg

sodium 154 mg
carbohydrates 3 g
   fiber 1 g
   sugars 2 g
protein 2 g

dietary exchanges
½ fat

Cooking sweet onion and walnuts "low and slow" gives them an intense flavor that permeates every bite of this simple and super-tasting side dish. Steamed green beans will benefit from the same treatment.

# broccoli with caramelized walnuts

**serves 8** | ¾ cup per serving

1 tablespoon olive oil

½ cup diced sweet onion, such as Vidalia, Maui, or Oso Sweet

¼ cup chopped walnuts

¼ teaspoon pepper

⅛ teaspoon salt

1 pound broccoli florets

**per serving**

| | |
|---|---|
| calories 62 | sodium 56 mg |
| total fat 4.5 g | carbohydrates 5 g |
| saturated fat 0.5 g | fiber 2 g |
| trans fat 0.0 g | sugars 2 g |
| polyunsaturated fat 2.0 g | protein 2 g |
| monounsaturated fat 1.5 g | dietary exchanges |
| cholesterol 0 mg | 1 vegetable, 1 fat |

1. In a large nonstick skillet, heat the oil over low heat, swirling to coat the bottom. Cook the remaining ingredients except the broccoli for 18 to 20 minutes, or until the onion and walnuts are browned and caramelized, stirring occasionally.

2. Meanwhile, in a large saucepan, steam the broccoli for 6 to 8 minutes, or just until tender. Drain well. Transfer the broccoli to the skillet, tossing with the onion mixture to combine.

**cook's tip:** The onion and walnuts can be prepared up to an hour in advance. Tossing them with the hot broccoli will reheat them.

Sweet red bell pepper and dry white wine highlight the delicate flavor of Broccolini—sometimes called baby broccoli. Broccolini is a hybrid of broccoli and gai lan, which is also called Chinese broccoli or Chinese kale. Its flavor is reminiscent of both broccoli and asparagus.

# broccolini and red bell pepper with garlic and wine

**serves 4**  :  **1 cup per serving**

1 tablespoon olive oil

1 medium red bell pepper, cut into matchstick-size strips

1 pound Broccolini, trimmed

2 medium garlic cloves, finely chopped

¼ teaspoon pepper

⅛ teaspoon salt

¼ cup dry white wine (regular or nonalcoholic)

**per serving**

calories 85
total fat 4.0 g
  saturated fat 0.5 g
  trans fat 0.0 g
  polyunsaturated fat 0.5 g
  monounsaturated fat 2.5 g
cholesterol 0 mg

sodium 112 mg
carbohydrates 10 g
  fiber 4 g
  sugars 3 g
protein 4 g

dietary exchanges
2 vegetable, 1 fat

1. In a large skillet, heat the oil over medium-high heat, swirling to coat the bottom. Cook the bell pepper for 2 minutes, stirring frequently.

2. Stir in the Broccolini. Cook for 2 minutes, stirring frequently.

3. Stir in the garlic, pepper, and salt. Cook for 1 minute, stirring frequently.

4. Reduce the heat to medium. Pour in the wine. Bring to a simmer and simmer, covered, for 2 minutes, or until the Broccolini is just tender, stirring frequently.

Fresh oregano sweeps brussels sprouts with flavor *à l'Italiano* in this easy side dish. Serve these with Trout Piccata (page 78) or Braised Beef with Potatoes and Carrots (page 130).

# oregano brussels sprouts

**serves 4** | ½ cup per serving

1 pound medium brussels sprouts, trimmed

   Cooking spray

4 medium green onions, sliced

2 medium ribs of celery, diced

2 medium garlic cloves, chopped

1 tablespoon water (optional)

2 tablespoons chopped fresh oregano

⅛ teaspoon salt

**per serving**

calories 66
total fat 0.5 g
  saturated fat 0.0 g
  trans fat 0.0 g
  polyunsaturated fat 0.0 g
  monounsaturated fat 0.0 g
cholesterol 0 mg

sodium 122 mg
carbohydrates 14 g
  fiber 6 g
  sugars 4 g
protein 4 g

dietary exchanges
3 vegetable

1. In a medium saucepan, steam the brussels sprouts for 6 minutes, or until tender. Transfer to a colander. Rinse with cold water to stop the cooking process. Drain well.

2. Lightly spray the same saucepan with cooking spray. Cook the green onions, celery, and garlic, covered, over medium-high heat for 3 minutes, stirring occasionally.

3. Stir in the brussels sprouts. Cook, covered, for 5 to 10 minutes, or until heated through, stirring occasionally. Stir in 1 tablespoon water, if needed, to keep the vegetables from sticking to the pan.

4. Just before serving, gently stir in the oregano and salt.

Bulgur is a mainstream whole grain that's easy to find in most grocery stores. Its nutty flavor and chewiness are complemented by the crunchiness of dry-roasted nuts, sweetness from golden raisins, and a hint of sharpness from orange zest.

# bulgur with nuts and raisins

### serves 4     ½ cup per serving

½ teaspoon grated orange zest

¼ cup fresh orange juice or water

¼ cup golden raisins

½ cup uncooked instant, or fine-grain, bulgur

¼ cup slivered almonds, dry-roasted

¼ cup chopped walnuts, dry-roasted

**per serving**

calories 185
total fat 8.5 g
   saturated fat 1.0 g
   trans fat 0.0 g
   polyunsaturated fat 4.5 g
   monounsaturated fat 3.0 g
cholesterol 0 mg

sodium 5 mg
carbohydrates 26 g
   fiber 5 g
   sugars 8 g
protein 5 g

dietary exchanges
1 starch, 1 fruit,
1½ fat

1. In a small saucepan, bring the orange juice to a boil over medium-high heat. Put the raisins in a small bowl. Pour in the juice. Set aside so the raisins can plump.

2. Meanwhile, prepare the bulgur using the package directions, omitting the salt. Transfer to a medium bowl. Fluff with a fork.

3. Drain the raisins, discarding the juice. Gently stir the raisins, almonds, walnuts, and orange zest into the bulgur. Serve warm, at room temperature, or chilled.

**Go Red brunch tip:** This side dish can be served chilled or at room temperature, making it an excellent choice for a brunch buffet. Try sweetened dried cranberries or dried tart cherries instead of the raisins to add a touch of red.

The sweet creaminess of butternut squash is layered in this gratin with the slightly pungent, mildly salty flavor of Swiss chard sautéed with onion. It's blanketed with a light white sauce and topped with browned panko and Parmesan for a side dish that makes any meal a special occasion.

# butternut squash and swiss chard gratin

**serves 6** : ½ cup per serving

Cooking spray

1 teaspoon canola or corn oil

1 medium onion, diced

8 cups chopped Swiss chard, tough stems discarded

2 medium garlic cloves, minced

1 cup fat-free milk

2 tablespoons white whole-wheat flour

⅛ teaspoon ground nutmeg

⅛ teaspoon dried thyme, crumbled, or ¼ teaspoon chopped fresh thyme (optional)

1 2-pound butternut squash, peeled, thinly sliced into rounds, seeds and strings discarded

¼ cup whole-wheat panko (Japanese-style bread crumbs)

1 tablespoon shredded or grated Parmesan cheese

⅛ teaspoon pepper

1. Preheat the oven to 350°F. Lightly spray a 1½-quart casserole dish with cooking spray. Set aside.

2. In a large skillet, heat the oil over medium-high heat, swirling to coat the bottom. Cook the onion for 5 minutes, or until beginning to brown, stirring frequently. Stir in the chard and garlic. Cook for 4 to 5 minutes, or until the chard is tender, stirring once halfway through. Drain well in a colander.

3. Meanwhile, in a small bowl, whisk together the milk, flour, nutmeg, and thyme until the mixture is smooth.

4. In the casserole dish, layer as follows: one-third of the squash rounds, half the chard mixture, one-third of the squash rounds, the remaining chard mixture, and the remaining squash rounds. Pour the milk mixture over all. Sprinkle with the panko, Parmesan, and pepper. Cover the dish with aluminum foil. Bake for 45 minutes. Uncover and bake for 10 minutes, or until bubbly and lightly browned.

**per serving**

| | |
|---|---|
| calories 120 | sodium 144 mg |
| total fat 1.5 g | carbohydrates 25 g |
| saturated fat 0.5 g | fiber 4 g |
| trans fat 0.0 g | sugars 7 g |
| polyunsaturated fat 0.5 g | protein 5 g |
| monounsaturated fat 0.5 g | **dietary exchanges** |
| cholesterol 1 mg | 1½ starch, 1 vegetable |

side dishes

Baby carrots are cooked in honey and orange juice, which glazes them to a sweet, glossy finish. Pair them with Creamed Spinach with Salmon (page 71) or Herb-Crusted Beef Tenderloin (page 129) for a meal that will please kids and adults alike.

# honey-orange glazed carrots

**serves 4** | ½ cup per serving

2 **cups baby carrots, halved lengthwise**

¼ **teaspoon grated orange zest**

½ **cup fresh orange juice**

1½ **tablespoons honey**

**Pinch of pepper (optional)**

### per serving

calories 65
total fat 0.5 g
  saturated fat 0.0 g
  trans fat 0.0 g
  polyunsaturated fat 0.0 g
  monounsaturated fat 0.0 g
cholesterol 0 mg

sodium 26 mg
carbohydrates 16 g
  fiber 1 g
  sugars 13 g
protein 1 g

dietary exchanges
1 vegetable, ½ other
carbohydrate

1. In a medium skillet, stir together the carrots, orange zest, orange juice, and honey. Bring to a boil, covered, over medium heat. Boil gently for 4 to 5 minutes, or until the carrots are tender-crisp, reducing the heat to medium low if necessary.

2. Uncover the skillet. Increase the heat to high. Boil for 3 to 4 minutes, or until the liquid has a syrupy consistency and is reduced by half (to about ¼ cup). Transfer the carrot mixture to a serving dish. Sprinkle with the pepper.

Everyday carrots become something special when they're cooked with a blend of common spices that creates the exotic warmth of a cuisine from a region halfway around the world. Adding both fresh lemon juice and lemon zest at the very end of the cooking time gives this side dish a burst of tartness.

# north african spiced carrots

**serves 6** | **½ cup per serving**

1 teaspoon olive oil

1 pound carrots, cut diagonally into ¼-inch pieces

½ teaspoon ground cumin

½ teaspoon coriander seeds, crushed, or ½ teaspoon ground coriander

¼ teaspoon paprika

¼ teaspoon salt

⅛ teaspoon pepper

½ cup fat-free, low-sodium chicken or vegetable broth

1 teaspoon grated lemon zest

2 tablespoons fresh lemon juice

1. In a large skillet, heat the oil over medium-high heat, swirling to coat the bottom. Cook the carrots for 2 to 3 minutes, or until tender-crisp, stirring occasionally.

2. Stir in the cumin, coriander seeds, paprika, salt, and pepper. Stir in the broth. Bring to a simmer over medium-high heat. Reduce the heat and simmer, covered, for 10 minutes, or until the carrots are tender.

3. Increase the heat to medium high. Cook for 1 to 2 minutes, or until the liquid is reduced by half (to about ¼ cup). Don't stir.

4. Just before serving, stir in the lemon zest and lemon juice.

**cook's tip on crushing seeds:** You can crush seeds by using a mortar and pestle or by spreading them in a single layer on a cutting board and either pressing them with the side of a chef's knife blade or rolling over them with a rolling pin.

**per serving**

calories 41
total fat 1.0 g
  saturated fat 0.0 g
  trans fat 0.0 g
  polyunsaturated fat 0.0 g
  monounsaturated fat 0.5 g
cholesterol 0 mg

sodium 155 mg
carbohydrates 8 g
  fiber 2 g
  sugars 4 g
protein 1 g

dietary exchanges
2 vegetable

Louisiana's Creole cuisine draws from French, Spanish, and African cuisine, to mention just a few. Traditional Creole dishes tend to rely heavily on butter and cream. This recipe is more like the nouvelle style, using lighter, fresher ingredients and seasonings.

# creole eggplant

| serves 6 | heaping ¾ cup per serving |
|----------|---------------------------|

1 tablespoon canola or corn oil

¼ cup sliced mushrooms, such as button, brown (cremini), portobello, or shiitake (stems discarded)

2 tablespoons chopped onion

2 tablespoons chopped green bell pepper

2 cups canned no-salt-added stewed tomatoes, undrained, or diced fresh tomatoes

Pepper to taste (freshly ground preferred)

1 medium eggplant, sliced into rounds or cubed

Cooking spray

½ cup plain dry bread crumbs (lowest sodium available)

1 tablespoon light tub margarine

1. In a medium saucepan, heat the oil over low heat, swirling to coat the bottom. Cook the mushrooms, onion, and bell pepper for 5 minutes, stirring occasionally. Stir in the tomatoes with liquid and the pepper. Cook for 30 minutes, or until the sauce is thickened, stirring occasionally.

2. Meanwhile, fill a large saucepan halfway with water. Bring to a boil over high heat. Cook the eggplant for 10 minutes, or until slightly tender. Drain well in a colander.

3. Preheat the oven to 350°F. Lightly spray a 2-quart casserole dish with cooking spray.

4. Arrange a layer of eggplant in the dish. Top with some of the sauce. Continue layering the eggplant and sauce until all the eggplant is used, finishing with a layer of sauce. Sprinkle with the bread crumbs. Dot with the margarine. Bake for 30 minutes, or until bubbling.

### per serving

calories 66
total fat 2.5 g
  saturated fat 0.0 g
  trans fat 0.0 g
  polyunsaturated fat 0.5 g
  monounsaturated fat 1.0 g
cholesterol 0 mg

sodium 56 mg
carbohydrates 10 g
  fiber 3 g
  sugars 4 g
protein 2 g

dietary exchanges
2 vegetable, ½ fat

Give basic steamed green beans some character with a tangy, spicy sauté. Serve this veggie side with your favorite grilled or roasted entrée, or with Mexican-flavored dishes such as Chicken and Black Bean Enchiladas (page 108).

# green beans with chile and lemon

**serves 8** ⋮ ½ cup per serving

1 pound green beans, trimmed and cut into 1½-inch pieces

1 teaspoon olive oil

1 medium garlic clove, minced

½ teaspoon chili powder

2 tablespoons chopped green onions

½ teaspoon grated lemon zest

⅛ teaspoon salt

**per serving**

calories 24
**total fat 0.5 g**
   saturated fat 0.0 g
   trans fat 0.0 g
   polyunsaturated fat 0.0 g
   monounsaturated fat 0.5 g
**cholesterol 0 mg**

sodium 43 mg
**carbohydrates 4 g**
   fiber 2 g
   sugars 2 g
**protein 1 g**

**dietary exchanges**
1 vegetable

1. In a large saucepan, steam the green beans for 7 to 9 minutes, or until tender. Drain well.

2. Meanwhile, in a large nonstick skillet, heat the oil over medium-low heat, swirling to coat the bottom. Cook the garlic and chili powder for 2 to 3 minutes, or until the garlic is fragrant, stirring frequently. (Don't let the garlic brown.)

3. Add the green beans, green onions, lemon zest, and salt, stirring to coat.

This fresh take on Southern-style greens gets its smoky, meaty taste from low-fat ham. A little bit of sugar tames the slight bitterness of the greens, while a last-minute addition of hot-pepper sauce turns up the heat. Try it alongside Spicy Shrimp and Grits (page 87) or Turkey Cutlets and Gravy (page 119).

# fiery kale with ham

**serves 5** | **½ cup per serving**

1 teaspoon canola or corn oil and 2 teaspoons canola or corn oil, divided use

⅓ cup diced lower sodium, low-fat ham, all visible fat discarded

1 medium onion, chopped

1 medium garlic clove, minced

2 cups water

8 ounces chopped kale, any large stems discarded

1½ teaspoons sugar

1½ teaspoons cider vinegar

1½ to 2 teaspoons Louisiana-style hot-pepper sauce or red hot-pepper sauce

**per serving**

calories 70
total fat 3.5 g
  saturated fat 0.5 g
  trans fat 0.0 g
  polyunsaturated fat 1.0 g
  monounsaturated fat 2.0 g
cholesterol 3 mg

sodium 122 mg
carbohydrates 9 g
  fiber 2 g
  sugars 3 g
protein 3 g

dietary exchanges
2 vegetable, ½ fat

1. In a Dutch oven or large saucepan, heat 1 teaspoon oil over medium-high heat, swirling to coat the bottom. Cook the ham for 2 to 3 minutes, or until browned, stirring frequently. Transfer to a small plate. Set aside.

2. In the same pot, heat the remaining 2 teaspoons oil, swirling to coat the bottom. Cook the onion for about 3 minutes, or until soft, stirring frequently. Stir in the garlic. Cook for 10 seconds, stirring constantly. Stir in the water, kale, and sugar. Bring to a simmer. Reduce the heat and simmer, covered, for 15 minutes, or until most of the water has evaporated and the kale is tender, stirring occasionally. Remove from the heat.

3. Stir in the vinegar and ham with any accumulated juices. Let stand, covered, for 3 minutes. Just before serving, sprinkle with the hot-pepper sauce.

**cook's tip:** You can substitute turnip greens, Swiss chard, or any other of your favorite greens for the kale. Just simmer the greens for about 5 minutes less.

Serve this sweet-and-sour bean dish, reminiscent of baked beans, as a side dish at a cookout, on a vegetarian buffet, or as a main dish over brown rice, bulgur, or farro.

# barbecued lima beans

| serves 8 | ¾ cup per serving |

32 ounces frozen baby lima beans

Cooking spray

1 small onion, minced

3 tablespoons light brown sugar

2 tablespoons Worcestershire sauce (lowest sodium available)

1 teaspoon chili powder

1 teaspoon pepper

1 teaspoon dry mustard

2 8-ounce cans no-salt-added tomato sauce

2 tablespoons cider vinegar

1. Prepare the lima beans using the package directions, omitting the salt and margarine. Drain well in a colander. Set aside.

2. Lightly spray a large skillet with cooking spray. Heat over medium-high heat. Cook the onion for 5 minutes, or until beginning to brown, stirring frequently.

3. Stir in the brown sugar, Worcestershire sauce, chili powder, pepper, and mustard. Cook for 3 minutes, stirring frequently.

4. Stir in the lima beans. Cook for 2 minutes, stirring to coat with the onion mixture.

5. Just before serving, stir in the tomato sauce and vinegar.

**per serving**

calories 195
total fat 0.5 g
  saturated fat 0.0 g
  trans fat 0.0 g
  polyunsaturated fat 0.0 g
  monounsaturated fat 0.0 g
cholesterol 0 mg

sodium 124 mg
carbohydrates 38 g
  fiber 11 g
  sugars 10 g
protein 9 g

dietary exchanges
2 starch, 1 vegetable, ½ lean meat

A natural with Coffee and Fennel Rubbed Sirloin with Tomato (page 135), this recipe features yellow potatoes, which provide a visually appealing golden hue and a rich, creamy texture without added fat.

# skillet potatoes with garlic

**serves 6**     ½ cup per serving

Cooking spray

4 **medium yellow potatoes, thinly sliced (about 6 cups)**

1 **medium leek (white part only), chopped, or ½ medium onion, chopped**

3 **medium garlic cloves, thinly sliced**

1 **teaspoon dried oregano, crumbled**

½ **teaspoon dried rosemary, crushed**

¼ **teaspoon salt**

¼ **teaspoon pepper**

¾ **cup water**

⅛ **teaspoon paprika**

**per serving**

calories 128
total fat 0.0 g
  saturated fat 0.0 g
  trans fat 0.0 g
  polyunsaturated fat 0.0 g
  monounsaturated fat 0.0 g
cholesterol 0 mg

sodium 110 mg
carbohydrates 29 g
  fiber 4 g
  sugars 2 g
protein 3 g

dietary exchanges
2 starch

1. Lightly spray a large skillet with cooking spray. Layer half the potatoes, half the leek, and half the garlic in the skillet.

2. In a small bowl, stir together the oregano, rosemary, salt, and pepper. Sprinkle half the oregano mixture over the potato mixture. Repeat the layers.

3. Pour the water around the edge of the potato mixture in the skillet. Bring to a boil over high heat. Reduce the heat and simmer, covered, for 30 minutes, or until the potatoes are tender and the liquid is absorbed. Add more water, if needed, during cooking.

4. Just before serving, sprinkle with the paprika.

**cook's tip:** Yellow potatoes are golden, thin-skinned potatoes with a moist yellow flesh and smooth texture. These potatoes are sold in your grocer's produce section under names such as Yukon Gold or Yellow Finn.

This side dish certainly pops with flavor and texture, from the fluffy quinoa to the crunchy pine nuts and tender corn. The cumin-scented dish pairs nicely with grilled foods such as Turkey and Bell Pepper Kebabs (page 113) or Plank-Grilled Tuna Steaks (page 80).

# quinoa-corn toss

### serves 4 | ½ cup per serving

1½ cups water

⅓ cup uncooked quinoa, rinsed and drained

1 teaspoon canola or corn oil

⅓ cup diced onion

1 small poblano pepper, seeds and ribs discarded, diced (see cook's tip on page 109)

½ cup frozen whole-kernel corn, thawed

¼ teaspoon ground cumin

¼ cup pine nuts, dry-roasted, or unsalted shelled pumpkin seeds, dry-roasted

⅛ teaspoon salt

**per serving**

calories 132
total fat 6.0 g
  saturated fat 1.0 g
  trans fat 0.0 g
  polyunsaturated fat 2.5 g
  monounsaturated fat 2.5 g
cholesterol 0 mg

sodium 77 mg
carbohydrates 17 g
  fiber 3 g
  sugars 3 g
**protein 5 g**

**dietary exchanges**
1 starch, 1 fat

1. In a medium saucepan, bring the water and quinoa to a boil over high heat. Reduce the heat and simmer, covered, for 10 minutes, or until the quinoa is tender. Transfer to a fine-mesh sieve. Rinse with cold water for 1 to 2 minutes, or until cool. Drain well. Transfer to a large bowl. Fluff with a fork.

2. Meanwhile, in a medium nonstick skillet, heat the oil over medium-high heat, swirling to coat the bottom. Cook the onion and poblano for 3 minutes, or until the onion is soft, stirring frequently. Stir in the corn and cumin. Cook for 1 minute, or until heated through, stirring constantly. Remove from the heat.

3. Stir the onion mixture into the quinoa. Stir in the pine nuts and salt.

Roasting mellows the radishes' peppery flavor. Stir them together with minced fresh thyme and shallots to create a unique and piquant side dish that helps boost roasted chicken, beef, or pork tenderloin to a whole new level of flavor. *(See photo insert.)*

# roasted radishes

**serves 4** | **½ cup per serving**

1 **pound radishes, trimmed and quartered**

2 **tablespoons minced fresh thyme**

2 **tablespoons minced shallots**

2 **teaspoons olive oil**

**Pepper to taste (freshly ground preferred)**

1. Preheat the oven to 425°F. Line a rimmed baking sheet with parchment paper.

2. In a large bowl, lightly stir together all the ingredients. Arrange the mixture in a single layer on the baking sheet. Place the baking sheet on the top rack of the oven. Roast for 20 to 25 minutes, or until the radishes are tender-crisp with edges that are beginning to turn golden brown, stirring occasionally.

**per serving**

calories 44
total fat 2.5 g
   saturated fat 0.5 g
   trans fat 0.0 g
   polyunsaturated fat 0.5 g
   monounsaturated fat 1.5 g
**cholesterol 0 mg**

sodium 45 mg
carbohydrates 5 g
   fiber 2 g
   sugars 3 g
**protein 1 g**

**dietary exchanges**
1 vegetable, ½ fat

Basic brown rice is spiked with almonds, gingerroot, and green onions. This speedy side is great served with Chinese Flank Steak (page 137).

# almond rice with ginger

**serves 4** | ½ cup per serving

½ cup uncooked quick-cooking brown rice

¼ cup sliced almonds, dry-roasted

2 to 3 tablespoons finely chopped green onions (green part only)

1 tablespoon light tub margarine

½ teaspoon grated peeled gingerroot

⅛ teaspoon salt

**1.** Prepare the rice using the package directions, omitting the salt and margarine. Remove from the heat.

**2.** Gently stir in the remaining ingredients.

**per serving**

calories 87
total fat 4.5 g
   saturated fat 0.0 g
   trans fat 0.0 g
   polyunsaturated fat 1.0 g
   monounsaturated fat 2.5 g
cholesterol 0 mg

sodium 99 mg
carbohydrates 10 g
   fiber 1 g
   sugars 0 g
protein 2 g

dietary exchanges
½ starch, 1 fat

Sweet raisins, honey, and dry-roasted pecans mix with brown basmati rice, which is then spiced with curry and cumin. It's an irresistible accompaniment for simply seasoned meat or poultry entrées and especially tasty with Rosemary-Garlic Roast Turkey Breast (page 114).

# curried pecan rice

**serves 4** | ½ cup per serving

1 cup water

½ cup uncooked brown basmati or brown jasmine rice

1 teaspoon canola or corn oil

½ cup diced onion

½ medium red or orange bell pepper, diced

¼ cup golden raisins

¼ cup chopped pecans, dry-roasted

1 teaspoon honey

1 teaspoon cider vinegar

½ teaspoon curry powder

½ teaspoon grated orange zest

¼ teaspoon ground cumin

1. In a medium saucepan, bring the water to a boil over high heat. Stir in the rice. Return to a boil. Reduce the heat and simmer, covered, for 22 minutes, or until the rice is tender and the liquid is absorbed.

2. Meanwhile, in a medium nonstick skillet, heat the oil over medium-high heat, swirling to coat the bottom. Cook the onion and bell pepper for 6 minutes, or until richly browned, stirring frequently.

3. Stir in the rice and the remaining ingredients.

**per serving**

calories 187
total fat 7.0 g
   saturated fat 0.5 g
   trans fat 0.0 g
   polyunsaturated fat 2.0 g
   monounsaturated fat 4.0 g
cholesterol 0 mg

sodium 7 mg
carbohydrates 31 g
   fiber 3 g
   sugars 10 g
protein 3 g

dietary exchanges
1½ starch, ½ fruit,
1 fat

Perfect for a buffet dinner, this dish can be prepared ahead and reheated. Its mild flavor makes it an excellent foil for assertive dishes such as Jerk Chicken with Mango-Avocado Salsa (page 99) or Coffee-Rubbed Salmon with Horseradish Sauce (page 65).

# confetti rice pilaf

**serves 6** : heaping ½ cup per serving

1 teaspoon light tub margarine

½ cup chopped onion

½ cup chopped bell pepper (combination of green, red, and yellow preferred)

¼ cup chopped celery

2 cups fat-free, low-sodium chicken broth, vegetable broth, or water

¾ cup uncooked brown rice

½ cup sliced mushrooms, such as button, brown (cremini), portobello, or shiitake (stems discarded)

2 tablespoons chopped fresh parsley

¾ teaspoon pepper, or to taste

**per serving**

calories 103
total fat 1.0 g
  saturated fat 0.0 g
  trans fat 0.0 g
  polyunsaturated fat 0.5 g
  monounsaturated fat 0.5 g
cholesterol 0 mg

sodium 34 mg
carbohydrates 20 g
  fiber 2 g
  sugars 1 g
protein 3 g

dietary exchanges
1½ starch

1. In a small skillet, melt the margarine over medium-high heat. Cook the onion, bell pepper, and celery for 3 minutes, or until the onion is soft and the bell pepper and celery are tender.

2. In a large saucepan, stir together the broth and rice. Stir in the onion mixture and mushrooms. Bring to a boil over medium-high heat. Reduce the heat and simmer, covered, for 45 to 50 minutes, or until the rice is tender and the liquid is absorbed. Remove from the heat.

3. Just before serving, stir in the parsley and pepper.

**lunchbox tip:** Kids love rice, and this mild yet flavorful and colorful version will be no exception. Reheat this whole-grain dish and use it as a bed for leftover chicken, pork, or beef in an insulated food jar.

An ideal accompaniment for Asian-influenced dishes such as Miso-Marinated Scallops on Soba Noodles (page 85), this veggie stir-fry gets its toasty, nutty flavor from sesame seeds and sesame oil.

# snow pea and sesame stir-fry

**serves 4** | **heaping ½ cup per serving**

1 teaspoon canola or corn oil

1 pound snow peas, trimmed

1 tablespoon minced peeled gingerroot

1 medium garlic clove, minced

1 tablespoon sesame seeds

½ teaspoon toasted sesame oil

¼ teaspoon salt

**per serving**

calories 80
total fat 3.5 g
   saturated fat 0.5 g
   trans fat 0.0 g
   polyunsaturated fat 1.5 g
   monounsaturated fat 1.5 g
cholesterol 0 mg

sodium 151 mg
carbohydrates 9 g
   fiber 3 g
   sugars 5 g
protein 4 g

dietary exchanges
2 vegetable, ½ fat

1. In a large nonstick skillet, heat the canola oil over medium-high heat, swirling to coat the bottom. Cook the snow peas, gingerroot, and garlic for 3 to 4 minutes, or until the snow peas are just tender-crisp, stirring constantly. Watch carefully so the mixture doesn't burn.

2. Stir in the sesame seeds, sesame oil, and salt. Cook for 30 seconds, stirring constantly.

**cook's tip:** Substitute almost any of your favorite vegetables for the snow peas. Try sliced zucchini, trimmed sugar snap peas, or very thin carrot "coins."

A spicy serrano chile and a splash of citrus perk up the summery combination of green beans, yellow squash, and corn. Serve this simple side with Pork and Green Onion Tacos (page 159) or Chicken and Black Bean Enchiladas (page 108).

# fiesta veggies

| serves 4 | ½ cup per serving |
|---|---|

1 teaspoon olive oil

1 large onion, halved lengthwise, then cut into thin half-moon slices

¾ cup sliced green beans (1-inch pieces)

1 small yellow summer squash, cut crosswise into ¼-inch slices

1 small serrano chile, seeds and ribs discarded, finely chopped (see cook's tip on page 109)

¾ cup frozen whole-kernel corn, thawed

2 tablespoons chopped fresh cilantro

1 tablespoon fresh lime juice

⅛ teaspoon pepper

1. In a medium nonstick skillet, heat the oil over medium heat, swirling to coat the bottom. Cook the onion and green beans for 2 minutes, stirring frequently.

2. Stir in the squash and serrano. Cook for 2 minutes, stirring frequently.

3. Stir in the corn. Cook for 2 to 3 minutes, or until the green beans, squash, serrano, and corn are tender-crisp.

4. Stir in the cilantro, lime juice, and pepper.

**per serving**

calories 73
total fat 1.5 g
  saturated fat 0.0 g
  trans fat 0.0 g
  polyunsaturated fat 0.5 g
  monounsaturated fat 1.0 g
cholesterol 0 mg

sodium 5 mg
carbohydrates 15 g
  fiber 3 g
  sugars 6 g
protein 2 g

dietary exchanges
½ starch, 1 vegetable, ½ fat

side dishes

Whip sweet potatoes and pineapple juice to a creamy consistency, mix them with crushed pineapple and spices, and then lightly sprinkle them with brown sugar. The result is a pillowy potato side that goes well with Chicken Oreganata (page 98) or Ancho-Rubbed Pork Tenderloin with Rosemary Aïoli (page 152). Use the rest of the crushed pineapple in Pineapple Sorbet (page 257).

# pineapple sweet potatoes

**serves 6** | ½ cup per serving

4 medium sweet potatoes, peeled (about 1 pound)

Cooking spray

¼ cup 100% pineapple juice

2 tablespoons light tub margarine and 1 teaspoon light tub margarine, divided use

2 tablespoons drained crushed pineapple in its own juice

¼ teaspoon ground cinnamon

¼ teaspoon ground nutmeg

¼ teaspoon ground allspice

2 tablespoons light brown sugar or 1 tablespoon light molasses

1. Put the sweet potatoes in a stockpot. Add enough water to cover. Bring to a boil. Boil for 30 minutes, or until tender.

2. Preheat the oven to 425°F. Lightly spray a 1-quart casserole dish with cooking spray.

3. In a large mixing bowl, using a potato masher, mash the sweet potatoes. Add the pineapple juice and 2 tablespoons margarine. Using an electric mixer on medium speed, beat until fluffy.

4. Stir in the pineapple, cinnamon, nutmeg, and allspice. Spread the mixture in the casserole dish. Sprinkle with the brown sugar. Dot with the remaining 1 teaspoon margarine.

5. Bake for 15 minutes, or until heated through.

**per serving**

| | |
|---|---|
| calories 107 | sodium 79 mg |
| total fat 2.0 g | carbohydrates 22 g |
| saturated fat 0.0 g | fiber 2 g |
| trans fat 0.0 g | sugars 9 g |
| polyunsaturated fat 0.5 g | protein 1 g |
| monounsaturated fat 1.0 g | |
| cholesterol 0 mg | dietary exchanges |
| | 1½ starch |

Although often served as a cooked breakfast cereal, cracked wheat makes an ideal pilaf-style side dish when mixed with brown rice, tomatoes, bell pepper, and onion. Here it's seasoned with a generous dose of berbere, an Ethiopian spice mix.

# ethiopian cracked wheat

| **serves 6** | ½ cup per serving |
|---|---|

1 teaspoon canola or corn oil

1 small onion, diced

¼ cup diced green bell pepper

1 medium garlic clove, minced

¼ cup uncooked instant brown rice

1½ cups water

1 medium tomato, diced

½ cup cracked wheat (cracked wheat berries) or bulgur

1 tablespoon plus 1 teaspoon berbere

1 tablespoon chopped fresh parsley

**per serving**

| | |
|---|---|
| calories 82 | sodium 6 mg |
| total fat 1.0 g | carbohydrates 16 g |
| saturated fat 0.0 g | fiber 3 g |
| trans fat 0.0 g | sugars 1 g |
| polyunsaturated fat 0.5 g | protein 2 g |
| monounsaturated fat 0.5 g | |
| cholesterol 0 mg | dietary exchanges |
| | 1 starch |

1. In a medium saucepan, heat the oil over medium-high heat, swirling to coat the bottom. Cook the onion, bell pepper, and garlic for 3 minutes, or until the onion is soft and the bell pepper is tender-crisp, stirring frequently.

2. Stir in the rice. Cook for 2 minutes, stirring frequently to separate the kernels and prevent them from burning. Stir in the water and tomato. Bring to a simmer. Reduce the heat and simmer, covered, for 15 minutes, or until the rice is tender.

3. Stir in the cracked wheat and berbere. Cook, covered, for 20 minutes. Remove from the heat.

4. Uncover and quickly stir in the parsley. Let stand, covered, for 10 minutes, or until the water is absorbed. Fluff with a fork. Serve immediately.

**cook's tip:** Berbere is sold in Middle Eastern markets and online. To make your own, stir together 3 teaspoons ground cumin, 1 teaspoon ground fennel, 1 teaspoon ground coriander, ½ teaspoon paprika, and ½ teaspoon cayenne. Use the leftovers for Pinto Beans and Eggs (page 234).

side dishes

This naturally sweet side dish easily dresses up roasted pork, chicken, or beef with almost no effort. The warm mix of autumnal spices highlights the fruits' own flavor and fills your home with an enticing aroma. Red pepper flakes add just a hint of heat to balance some of the sweetness. This dish also can be served at room temperature or cold.

# hot spiced fruit compote

**serves 4**    ½ cup per serving

1½ cups chopped fresh pineapple

½ medium firm pear, peeled and chopped

¼ cup water

½ teaspoon ground cinnamon

¼ teaspoon ground nutmeg

⅛ teaspoon ground cloves

⅛ teaspoon crushed red pepper flakes (optional)

2 apricots, quartered, or 4 canned or jarred apricot halves packed in their own juice, drained and halved

1 tablespoon dark brown sugar

1 tablespoon light tub margarine

½ teaspoon grated orange zest

½ teaspoon vanilla extract

1⁄16 teaspoon salt

1. In a medium saucepan, stir together the pineapple, pear, water, cinnamon, nutmeg, cloves, and red pepper flakes. Bring to a boil over high heat. Reduce the heat and simmer, covered, for 8 minutes, or until the pears are tender.

2. Stir in the remaining ingredients. Cook for 5 minutes, or until slightly thickened. Remove from the heat.

3. Let stand for 10 minutes so the flavors blend.

**per serving**

calories 79
total fat 1.5 g
   saturated fat 0.0 g
   trans fat 0.0 g
   polyunsaturated fat 0.5 g
   monounsaturated fat 0.5 g
cholesterol 0 mg

sodium 60 mg
carbohydrates 17 g
   fiber 2 g
   sugars 13 g
protein 1 g

dietary exchanges
1 fruit

# breads, breakfasts, and brunches

Moist and delicious, banana bread is a classic for good reason, but it can be loaded with way too many calories. Our version uses applesauce for natural moisture and sweetness and comes in at about 100 calories per serving.

# banana-nut bread

**serves 16** : 1 slice per serving

Cooking spray

⅓ cup sugar and ¼ cup sugar, divided use

⅓ cup unsweetened applesauce

1¼ cups mashed ripe banana

1¼ cups sifted all-purpose flour

2 teaspoons baking powder

¼ teaspoon ground cinnamon

⅛ teaspoon ground nutmeg

½ cup uncooked oatmeal

⅓ cup chopped walnuts, dry-roasted

3 large egg whites

**per serving**

calories 111
total fat 2.0 g
   saturated fat 0.0 g
   trans fat 0.0 g
   polyunsaturated fat 1.5 g
   monounsaturated fat 0.5 g
cholesterol 0 mg

sodium 61 mg
carbohydrates 22 g
   fiber 1 g
   sugars 10 g
protein 3 g

dietary exchanges
1½ other carbohydrate, ½ fat

**on-the-go breakfast tip:** For those mornings when you are running short on time, cut a slice of this bread in half and spread a tablespoon of low-sodium peanut butter between the slices to make a breakfast "sandwich."

1. Preheat the oven to 350°F. Lightly spray a 9 × 5 × 3-inch loaf pan with cooking spray.

2. In a large bowl, using an electric mixer on medium speed, beat ⅓ cup sugar and the applesauce for 1 minute, or until combined. Add the banana. Beat for 2 minutes, or until blended.

3. In a medium bowl, sift together the flour, baking powder, cinnamon, and nutmeg.

4. Stir in the oatmeal. Add the flour mixture to the banana mixture. Beat until the mixture is just moistened but no flour is visible. Don't overmix; the batter may be slightly lumpy. Gently stir in the walnuts.

5. In a separate medium bowl, beat the egg whites until foamy. Gradually add the remaining ¼ cup sugar, beating until stiff peaks form (the peaks don't fall when the beaters are lifted). Fold the egg white mixture into the flour mixture. Pour the batter into the loaf pan, gently smoothing the top.

6. Bake for 1 hour, or until a wooden toothpick inserted in the center comes out clean.

7. Transfer the pan to a cooling rack and let stand for 10 minutes. Invert the bread onto the rack. Let cool completely before slicing.

Ruby-red raspberries crown fruity and flavorful muffins, and a sprinkle of streusel adds just a hint of sweetness to counter the slight tartness of the berries.

# raspberry muffins

**serves 12** | 1 muffin per serving

Cooking spray

1½ cups white whole-wheat flour

1 teaspoon ground cinnamon

¾ teaspoon baking soda

¾ cup low-fat buttermilk

⅓ cup firmly packed light brown sugar

3 large egg whites

¼ cup canola or corn oil

2 teaspoons grated lemon zest

1 teaspoon vanilla extract

1 cup frozen unsweetened or fresh raspberries

2 tablespoons light brown sugar

2 tablespoons uncooked quick-cooking oatmeal

2 tablespoons chopped pecans

1 tablespoon light tub margarine

½ teaspoon ground cinnamon

1. Preheat the oven to 400°F. Lightly spray a standard 12-cup muffin pan with cooking spray.

2. In a large bowl, stir together the flour, 1 teaspoon cinnamon, and the baking soda.

3. In a medium bowl, whisk together the buttermilk, ⅓ cup brown sugar, egg whites, oil, lemon zest, and vanilla. Stir the buttermilk mixture into the flour mixture until the batter is just moistened but no flour is visible. Don't overmix; the batter may be slightly lumpy. Spoon the batter into the muffin cups. Top with the raspberries.

4. In a small bowl, stir together the remaining ingredients until the texture of coarse crumbs. Sprinkle over the muffins. Bake for 18 minutes, or until a wooden toothpick inserted in the center comes out clean.

5. Transfer the pan to a cooling rack and let stand for 10 minutes. Carefully transfer the muffins to the rack. Let cool completely, about 20 minutes.

**per serving**

calories 157
total fat 6.5 g
  saturated fat 0.5 g
  trans fat 0.0 g
  polyunsaturated fat 2.0 g
  monounsaturated fat 3.5 g
cholesterol 1 mg

sodium 118 mg
carbohydrates 21 g
  fiber 2 g
  sugars 11 g
protein 4 g

dietary exchanges
1½ other carbohydrate, 1 fat

These savory and slightly sweet cornbreadlike muffins are an ideal match for soups, stews, and chilis, such as Beef and Hominy Chili (page 148) or Vegetarian Gumbo (page 181).

# whole-wheat corn muffins

**serves 18** | 1 muffin per serving

Cooking spray

⅓ cup sugar

¼ cup plus 2 tablespoons canola or corn oil

1¼ cups fat-free milk

1 large egg

1 cup whole-wheat flour

1 tablespoon plus 1 teaspoon baking powder

½ teaspoon salt

1 cup cornmeal

**per serving**

calories 116
total fat 5.0 g
  saturated fat 0.5 g
  trans fat 0.0 g
  polyunsaturated fat 1.5 g
  monounsaturated fat 3.0 g
cholesterol 11 mg

sodium 165 mg
carbohydrates 16 g
  fiber 1 g
  sugars 5 g
protein 2 g

dietary exchanges
1 starch, 1 fat

1. Preheat the oven to 425°F. Lightly spray one standard 12-cup muffin pan and 6 cups of a second muffin pan with cooking spray.

2. In a medium bowl, whisk together the sugar and oil. Whisk in the milk and egg until well combined.

3. In a separate medium bowl, stir together the flour, baking powder, and salt. Stir the milk mixture into the flour mixture until the batter is just moistened but no flour is visible. Stir in the cornmeal until the batter is just moistened. Don't overmix or the muffins may be tough. Pour the batter into the muffin cups, filling each cup two-thirds full.

4. Bake for 25 minutes, or until a wooden toothpick inserted in the center of a muffin comes out clean.

5. Transfer the pan to a cooling rack and let stand for 10 minutes. Serve warm or remove the muffins from the pan, transfer to the rack, and let cool completely.

Scones, thought to have originated in Scotland, are similar to American biscuits. A combination of whole-wheat and all-purpose flour in the dough here results in a scone that's crisp on the outside and tender on the inside. Serve the scones with all-fruit spread or light tub margarine or just simply on their own.

# sweet potato scones

| serves 12 | 1 scone per serving |
| --- | --- |

Cooking spray

1 cup whole-wheat pastry flour, whole-wheat flour, or white whole-wheat flour

1 cup all-purpose flour and 2 to 3 tablespoons all-purpose flour, divided use

½ cup sweetened dried cranberries

⅓ cup firmly packed light brown sugar

2 tablespoons sugar

2 teaspoons baking powder

1 teaspoon pumpkin pie spice

¼ teaspoon baking soda

1 cup mashed cooked sweet potatoes

⅓ cup low-fat buttermilk

2 tablespoons canola or corn oil

1 large egg

**per serving**

| | |
| --- | --- |
| calories 179 | sodium 116 mg |
| total fat 3.0 g | carbohydrates 35 g |
|   saturated fat 0.5 g |   fiber 2 g |
|   trans fat 0.0 g |   sugars 13 g |
|   polyunsaturated fat 1.0 g | **protein 3 g** |
|   monounsaturated fat 1.5 g | **dietary exchanges** |
| cholesterol 16 mg | 2½ starch |

**1.** Preheat the oven to 400°F. Lightly spray a large baking sheet with cooking spray.

**2.** In a medium bowl, stir together the pastry flour, 1 cup all-purpose flour, the cranberries, sugars, baking powder, pumpkin pie spice, and baking soda.

**3.** In a separate medium bowl, whisk together the remaining ingredients except the remaining 2 to 3 tablespoons of all-purpose flour. Gradually stir the pastry flour mixture into the sweet potato mixture until the dough starts to pull away from the side of the bowl and forms a shaggy ball.

**4.** Using the remaining 2 to 3 tablespoons all-purpose flour, lightly flour a flat surface. Turn out the dough. Knead two to four times. Divide the dough in half and shape each half into a ball. Using your hands (lightly flour them) or a rolling pin, flatten each ball into a circle 5½ inches in diameter. Transfer the circles to the baking sheet. Using a pizza cutter or knife, cut each circle into 6 wedges, but don't separate the wedges.

**5.** Bake for 16 to 18 minutes, or until a wooden toothpick inserted in the center comes out clean. Separate into wedges before serving.

Apple juice and cinnamon flavor the batter for these pancakes, which are made with whole-wheat flour and contain less sodium than those made from a boxed mix. The spicy-sweet apple topping eliminates the need for sugar-laden syrup.

# apple-cinnamon pancakes

**serves 4** | 2 pancakes and ¼ cup apple mixture per serving

2 cups thinly sliced peeled tart or mildly tart cooking apples, such as Jonathan, Granny Smith, or McIntosh (about 2 medium)

3 tablespoons 100% apple juice and 2 tablespoons 100% apple juice, divided use

2 tablespoons light brown sugar

½ teaspoon ground cinnamon and ½ teaspoon ground cinnamon, divided use

1 cup whole-wheat flour

½ teaspoon baking soda

1 cup low-fat buttermilk

1 large egg white

½ teaspoon vanilla extract

1 teaspoon canola or corn oil

¼ cup fat-free plain Greek yogurt

1. In a small saucepan, stir together the apples, 3 tablespoons apple juice, brown sugar, and ½ teaspoon cinnamon. Cook, covered, over medium heat for 10 minutes, or until the apples are tender. Remove from the heat. Let stand, covered, while preparing the pancakes.

2. Meanwhile, preheat the oven to 200°F.

3. In a medium bowl, stir together the flour, baking soda, and the remaining ½ teaspoon cinnamon.

4. In a small bowl, whisk together the buttermilk and the remaining 2 tablespoons apple juice. Pour the buttermilk mixture, egg white, and vanilla into the flour mixture. Stir just until blended but no flour is visible.

5. Heat a large nonstick griddle or skillet over medium-high heat until a drop of water dripped on the griddle sizzles. Pour the oil onto the griddle. Using a heatproof pastry brush, spread the oil over the surface.

**per serving**

calories 213
total fat 2.5 g
    saturated fat 0.5 g
    trans fat 0.0 g
    polyunsaturated fat 0.5 g
    monounsaturated fat 1.0 g
cholesterol 3 mg

sodium 244 mg
carbohydrates 42 g
    fiber 4 g
    sugars 18 g
protein 8 g

dietary exchanges
2 starch, 1 fruit

**6.** Using a $^1/_4$-cup measure, pour the batter for 4 pancakes onto the griddle. Cook the pancakes for 1 minute, or until the tops begin to bubble and the bottoms are golden brown. Turn over. Cook for 1 minute, or until the bottoms are golden brown. Transfer the pancakes to a baking sheet, cover with aluminum foil, and put in the oven to keep warm while you cook the remaining batter. Just before serving, spread 1 tablespoon yogurt over each stack of pancakes. Top with the apple mixture.

**cook's tip on buying juice:** When buying fruit juice, be sure to read the label carefully and look for "100% juice"—not "fruit drink," "juice cocktail," or "juice beverage." There are no added sugars in 100% juice—just the natural sugars found in whole fruit.

Serve warm wedges of this wholesome morning delight—rolled oats baked with sweet ripe pears, golden raisins, and dry-roasted walnuts—for breakfast or brunch. Alongside, have some fat-free plain Greek yogurt mixed with fresh berries to get your day off to a healthy start.

# baked oatmeal "pie"

**serves 8**  |  1 wedge per serving

Cooking spray

2 cups uncooked oatmeal

⅓ cup golden raisins

¼ cup chopped walnuts, dry-roasted

2 teaspoons baking powder

½ teaspoon ground cinnamon

¼ teaspoon ground or grated nutmeg (freshly grated preferred)

¼ teaspoon salt

1 cup fat-free milk

½ cup fat-free plain yogurt

1 large egg

1 teaspoon vanilla extract

2 medium Bartlett pears, peeled and diced

2 tablespoons plus 2 teaspoons pure maple syrup

1. Preheat the oven to 375°F. Lightly spray a 9-inch pie pan with cooking spray. Set aside.

2. In a large bowl, stir together the oatmeal, raisins, walnuts, baking powder, cinnamon, nutmeg, and salt.

3. In a separate bowl, whisk together the milk, yogurt, egg, and vanilla. Pour into the oatmeal mixture, stirring to combine. Gently fold in the pears. Pour the oatmeal mixture into the pie pan.

4. Place the pie pan on the center rack of the oven. Bake for 35 to 40 minutes, or until the top of the oatmeal is browned and firm to the touch.

5. Remove the pie pan from the oven. Let cool for 5 to 10 minutes. Cut the "pie" into wedges. Drizzle each wedge with the maple syrup. Serve warm.

**cook's tip on pears:** Pears are ripe when the flesh just below the stem yields to gentle pressure.

**on-the-go breakfast tip:** Wrap a wedge in wax paper for a portable morning meal.

**per serving**

calories 196
total fat 4.5 g
  saturated fat 0.5 g
  trans fat 0.0 g
  polyunsaturated fat 2.5 g
  monounsaturated fat 1.0 g
cholesterol 24 mg

sodium 209 mg
carbohydrates 34 g
  fiber 4 g
  sugars 16 g
protein 7 g

dietary exchanges
1 starch, 1 fruit,
½ other carbohydrate,
½ lean meat

Not to be confused with Mexican tortillas, the Spanish tortilla is a traditional egg-and-potato dish similar to a thick, robust omelet or Italian frittata. Serve it as a breakfast entrée with a side of fresh fruit. *(See photo insert.)*

# spanish-style potato tortilla

| serves 6 | 1 wedge per serving |
|---|---|

1 tablespoon olive oil

1 pound potatoes, quartered lengthwise, then thinly sliced crosswise

1 medium onion, chopped

1½ cups egg substitute

½ cup shredded manchego curado cheese

1 4-ounce jar diced pimiento, drained well

**per serving**

calories 152
total fat 4.5 g
   saturated fat 2.0 g
   trans fat 0.0 g
   polyunsaturated fat 0.5 g
   monounsaturated fat 2.0 g
cholesterol 7 mg

sodium 183 mg
carbohydrates 18 g
   fiber 2 g
   sugars 4 g
protein 10 g

**dietary exchanges**
1 starch, 1 lean meat

1. Preheat the oven to 400°F.

2. In a medium ovenproof skillet, heat the oil over medium-high heat, swirling to coat the bottom.

3. In a large bowl, stir together the potatoes and onion. Transfer the mixture to the skillet. Using a spatula, gently spread and press it into an even layer. Reduce the heat to low. Cook, covered, for 10 to 12 minutes, or until the potatoes are just tender.

4. Meanwhile, in a large bowl, whisk together the egg substitute, manchego, and pimiento. Pour over the potato mixture. Don't stir. Bake for 10 to 15 minutes, or until the tortilla is set.

5. Slide the tortilla onto a serving plate, or serve directly from the skillet. Cut into 6 wedges.

**cook's tip on manchego cheese:** Manchego is a Spanish cheese made of sheep's milk. The curado version has been aged and has a mild, nutty flavor and creamy texture. It is commonly found in grocery stores.

**on-the-go breakfast tip:** To eat this tortilla on the move, stuff a wedge into half of a whole-grain pita pocket or wrap it in a corn tortilla. Then wrap wax paper around it or place the bottom half in a sandwich-size plastic bag with the top sticking out.

Mashed spicy pinto beans sidle up to eggs in a hearty dish inspired by *ful medames*, an ancient Egyptian breakfast bean dish.

# pinto beans and eggs

serves 4 ⦙ ½ cup beans and ½ cup eggs per serving

1 tablespoon plus 1 teaspoon olive oil and ½ teaspoon olive oil, divided use

½ cup thinly sliced red onion

2 medium tomatoes, chopped

1/16 teaspoon salt and 1/16 teaspoon salt, divided use

1 teaspoon berbere and 1 teaspoon berbere, divided use (see cook's tip on page 223)

½ teaspoon ground cumin

3 cups canned no-salt-added pinto beans, rinsed and drained

¼ cup water

2 teaspoons fresh lemon juice

Pinch of cayenne (optional)

2 large eggs

4 large egg whites

Cooking spray

1 tablespoon plus 1 teaspoon chopped green bell pepper

### per serving

| | |
|---|---|
| calories 282 | sodium 168 mg |
| total fat 7.5 g | carbohydrates 35 g |
| saturated fat 1.5 g | fiber 9 g |
| trans fat 0.0 g | sugars 9 g |
| polyunsaturated fat 1.0 g | protein 18 g |
| monounsaturated fat 4.5 g | dietary exchanges |
| cholesterol 93 mg | 2 starch, 1 vegetable, 2 lean meat |

1. In a medium skillet, heat 1 tablespoon plus 1 teaspoon oil over medium-high heat, swirling to coat the bottom. Cook the onion for 2 minutes, or until it begins to soften, stirring occasionally. Stir in the tomatoes. Cook for 1 minute. Sprinkle with 1/16 teaspoon salt. Transfer the mixture to a bowl. Wipe the skillet with paper towels.

2. In a medium saucepan, heat the remaining ½ teaspoon oil over medium-high heat, swirling to coat the bottom. Cook 1 teaspoon berbere and the cumin for 20 seconds, or until fragrant, stirring constantly. Stir in the beans, water, lemon juice, cayenne, and the remaining 1/16 teaspoon salt. Increase the heat to high and bring to a simmer, mashing the beans until they are the texture of coarse refried beans. Set aside.

3. In a medium bowl, using a fork, beat the eggs, egg whites, and the remaining 1 teaspoon berbere until combined.

4. Lightly spray the same medium skillet with cooking spray. Pour the egg mixture and half the onion mixture into the skillet. Cook for 3 to 4 minutes, or until the eggs are scrambled, stirring constantly.

5. Transfer the bean mixture and egg mixture to plates. Sprinkle with the bell pepper and the remaining onion mixture.

Just a hint of honey is all you need in this parfait that's layered with freshness—the natural sweetness of the fruit does the rest. Fat-free Greek yogurt adds creaminess as well as powerful protein, and crisp cereal contributes crunch and healthy fiber.

# honeyed berry-kiwi cereal parfaits

**serves 4** | 1 parfait per serving

1 cup sliced hulled strawberries

½ cup blueberries

1 medium kiwifruit, peeled and diced

1 cup high-fiber cereal

1 cup fat-free plain Greek yogurt

1 tablespoon plus 1 teaspoon honey

**per serving**

calories 117
total fat 1.0 g
  saturated fat 0.0 g
  trans fat 0.0 g
  polyunsaturated fat 0.5 g
  monounsaturated fat 0.0 g
cholesterol 0 mg

sodium 75 mg
carbohydrates 29 g
  fiber 9 g
  sugars 14 g
protein 7 g
dietary exchanges
1 fruit, 1 starch,
½ lean meat

In each parfait glass, layer the ingredients as follows: ¼ cup strawberries, 2 tablespoons blueberries, 2 tablespoons kiwifruit, 2 tablespoons cereal, ¼ cup yogurt, 1 teaspoon honey, and 2 tablespoons cereal.

**on-the-go breakfast tip:** Instead of parfait glasses, layer the ingredients in a large plastic cup or thermos for a grab-and-go meal.

Add some vitamin C to your morning with these fruity, nutty parfaits. Pair with a glass of orange juice or fat-free milk and your day will be off to a great start.

# cherry-and-peach parfaits

**serves 4** | 1 parfait per serving

- **2 cups pitted cherries, halved, or frozen unsweetened dark sweet cherries, thawed, halved**
- **1 cup frozen unsweetened peach slices, thawed, diced**
- **1½ tablespoons sugar**
- **½ teaspoon almond extract**
- **1 cup fat-free plain Greek yogurt**
- **¼ cup slivered almonds, dry-roasted**

1. In a medium bowl, stir together the cherries, peaches, sugar, and almond extract.

2. In each parfait glass, layer the ingredients as follows: ⅓ cup cherry mixture, 2 tablespoons yogurt, and 1½ teaspoons almonds. Repeat the layers.

**Go Red brunch tip:** For a more elegant presentation, use stemmed wineglasses.

## per serving

calories 154
**total fat 3.5 g**
  saturated fat 0.5 g
  trans fat 0.0 g
  polyunsaturated fat 1.0 g
  monounsaturated fat 2.0 g
**cholesterol 0 mg**

sodium 21 mg
**carbohydrates 24 g**
  fiber 3 g
  sugars 18 g
**protein 7 g**

**dietary exchanges**
1 fruit, ½ other carbohydrate, 1 lean meat

# drinks and desserts

You'll fall in love with this unique and refreshing beverage! Sweet-tart cranberry juice is infused with the warm flavors of gingerroot and cardamom and topped with a bubbly splash of seltzer.

# sparkling cranberry spritzers

**serves 4** | 1 cup per serving

3 cups 100% cranberry juice

8 slices peeled gingerroot, each about ¼ inch thick

2 tablespoons cardamom pods

1 cup seltzer or low-sodium club soda

**per serving**

calories 105
total fat 0.0 g
   saturated fat 0.0 g
   trans fat 0.0 g
   polyunsaturated fat 0.0 g
   monounsaturated fat 0.0 g
cholesterol 0 mg

sodium 23 mg
carbohydrates 26 g
   fiber 0 g
   sugars 26 g
protein 1 g

dietary exchanges
1½ fruit

1. In a medium saucepan, bring the juice, gingerroot, and cardamom to a simmer over low heat. Remove from the heat and let steep for 30 minutes. Strain into a pitcher, discarding the gingerroot and cardamom pods. Refrigerate for about 3 hours, or until well chilled.

2. At serving time, fill 4 glasses halfway with ice. Pour ³/4 cup juice mixture into each glass. Top each serving with ¼ cup seltzer. Serve immediately.

This festive drink contains no wine, so it's appropriate for all ages. The punch-infused fruit makes a delicious nibble after the drink is gone. *(See photo insert.)*

# sangría-style punch

| serves 8 | 1 cup punch and ¼ cup fruit per serving |
|---|---|

2 small oranges, cut crosswise into 8 slices each, any seeds discarded

2 large lemons, cut crosswise into 8 slices each, any seeds discarded

2 large limes, cut crosswise into 8 slices each, any seeds discarded

½ cup loosely packed fresh mint

¼ cup light brown sugar

2⅔ cups sparkling lime-flavored water, chilled

2⅔ cups 100% white grape juice, chilled

2⅔ cups 100% cranberry-raspberry juice, chilled

2 small Red Delicious apples, diced

⅔ cup frozen pitted cherries, halved

⅔ cup raspberries

8 sprigs of fresh mint

Put half the orange, lemon, and lime slices in a pitcher or punch bowl. Add ½ cup mint and the brown sugar. Using a muddler or a large wooden spoon, mash the orange mixture until the fruit releases about half its juice. Stir in the remaining orange, lemon, and lime slices. Stir in the remaining ingredients except the mint sprigs. Serve over crushed ice. Garnish with the mint sprigs.

**per serving**

calories 162
total fat 0.5 g
   saturated fat 0.0 g
   trans fat 0.0 g
   polyunsaturated fat 0.0 g
   monounsaturated fat 0.0 g
cholesterol 0 mg

sodium 34 mg
carbohydrates 41 g
   fiber 2 g
   sugars 35 g
protein 1 g

**dietary exchanges**
2½ fruit

drinks and desserts

Give yourself a break from your routine and enjoy this luscious tropical beverage. Process all the ingredients in a flash and sip this chilled drink on a hot summer day.

# creamy mango freezers

**serves 4**     ¾ cup per serving

1 medium ripe mango, peeled and chopped into large pieces, or 1½ cups frozen mango cubes, thawed

1 cup fat-free, sugar-free frozen vanilla yogurt or fat-free, sugar-free vanilla ice cream

1 cup ice cubes

¾ cup 100% pineapple juice

3 tablespoons fresh lemon juice

½ teaspoon vanilla extract

2 lemon slices, halved

In a food processor or blender, process all the ingredients except the lemon slices until smooth. Serve in glasses or wine goblets. Garnish each glass with half a lemon slice.

**cook's tip:** You can use 1½ cups of any type or mixture of frozen fruit in this recipe—a great way to use up any partial bags you may have in the freezer. Substitute other fruit juices, such as orange or pomegranate, for the pineapple juice as well.

**per serving**

calories 114
total fat 0.5 g
   saturated fat 0.0 g
   trans fat 0.0 g
   polyunsaturated fat 0.0 g
   monounsaturated fat 0.0 g
cholesterol 0 mg

sodium 36 mg
carbohydrates 28 g
   fiber 1 g
   sugars 19 g
protein 3 g

dietary exchanges
2 fruit

Get the party started with these creamy nonalcoholic shooters served in shot glasses. These sip-size smoothies will be the hit of summertime soirées, when offered with an array of appetizers.

# peach-raspberry shooters

| serves 12 | 2 ounces per serving |
|---|---|

12 ounces frozen unsweetened peach slices, thawed, juice reserved

8 ounces frozen unsweetened raspberries, thawed, juice reserved

⅓ cup water

¼ cup fat-free plain Greek yogurt

3 tablespoons sugar

½ teaspoon almond extract

### per serving

| | |
|---|---|
| calories 40 | sodium 2 mg |
| total fat 0.0 g | carbohydrates 9 g |
|   saturated fat 0.0 g |   fiber 1 g |
|   trans fat 0.0 g |   sugars 6 g |
|   polyunsaturated fat 0.0 g | protein 1 g |
|   monounsaturated fat 0.0 g | dietary exchanges |
| cholesterol 0 mg | ½ fruit |

In a food processor or blender, process all the ingredients until smooth. Pour into shot glasses.

**cook's tip:** Don't want raspberry seeds in your drink? In a food processor or blender, process only the raspberries and water. Place a fine-mesh sieve over a bowl and drain the mixture, pressing down with the back of a spoon to release any liquid. The raspberry seeds will be caught in the sieve. Return the seedless mixture to the food processor or blender, add the remaining ingredients, and process until smooth.

**Go Red party tip:** Don't have enough shot glasses for your guests? No worries. You can order plastic disposable ones online.

The protein in this drink will give you a healthy energy boost as either a breakfast meal or a midafternoon pick-me-up; the chocolate and peanut butter flavors are a classic combination that can't be beat.

# chocolate-peanut butter smoothies

**serves 4**  |  1 cup per serving

2½ **cups fat-free milk**

3 **ounces fat-free vanilla Greek yogurt**

¼ **cup unsweetened Dutch-process cocoa powder**

2½ **tablespoons sugar**

3 **tablespoons low-sodium peanut butter**

1 **teaspoon vanilla extract**

¼ **teaspoon ground cinnamon**

In a food processor or blender, process all the ingredients until smooth.

**on-the-go breakfast tip:** Pour this protein-packed drink into a plastic cup or travel mug on rushed mornings rather than skipping breakfast.

### per serving

calories 193
total fat 6.5 g
   saturated fat 1.5 g
   trans fat 0.0 g
   polyunsaturated fat 1.5 g
   monounsaturated fat 3.0 g
cholesterol 3 mg

sodium 76 mg
carbohydrates 23 g
   fiber 2 g
   sugars 18 g
protein 11 g

dietary exchanges
1 fat-free milk,
½ other carbohydrate,
1 fat

There's nothing like a cup of hot, spiced cider on a cold evening or brisk morning. Ours keeps the warm spices of traditional apple cider, but adds blueberry-pomegranate juice for a drink with a rich burgundy color and deep fruity taste.

# hot blueberry-pomegranate cider

**serves 4** | 1 cup per serving

3 cups 100% blueberry-pomegranate juice

1 cup 100% apple juice

8 whole cloves

2 cinnamon sticks (each about 3 inches long)

1 medium orange, halved crosswise and cut into slices, any seeds discarded

½ teaspoon almond extract

1. In a medium saucepan, stir together the blueberry-pomegranate juice, apple juice, cloves, and cinnamon sticks. Bring to a boil over high heat. Reduce the heat and simmer, covered, for 5 minutes. Remove from the heat. Discard the cloves and cinnamon sticks.

2. Stir in the orange slices and almond extract. Let stand, covered, for 5 minutes.

**per serving**

calories 135
total fat 0.0 g
   saturated fat 0.0 g
   trans fat 0.0 g
   polyunsaturated fat 0.0 g
   monounsaturated fat 0.0 g
cholesterol 0 mg

sodium 36 mg
carbohydrates 33 g
   fiber 0 g
   sugars 24 g
protein 1 g

dietary exchanges
2 fruit

drinks and desserts

This quick and easy cake makes an excellent dessert or snack. Serve it on its own or topped with fresh berries, with a glass of ice-cold fat-free milk.

# applesauce cake

**serves 12** : 3 × 2¼-inch piece per serving

Butter-flavor cooking spray

½ cup sugar

¼ cup light tub margarine

¼ cup canola or corn oil

1 large egg

1 cup unsweetened applesauce

1 cup all-purpose flour

1½ teaspoons ground cinnamon

½ teaspoon baking soda

½ teaspoon ground nutmeg

¼ teaspoon ground cloves

⅛ teaspoon salt

⅓ cup raisins

1. Preheat the oven to 350°F. Lightly spray a 9-inch square baking dish with cooking spray.

2. In a large bowl, using an electric mixer on medium speed, beat the sugar, margarine, and oil until creamy. Add the egg. Beat for 1 minute. Add the applesauce. Beat for 2 minutes, or until combined.

3. In a medium bowl, sift together the remaining ingredients except the raisins. Gradually add to the margarine mixture, beating after each addition. Stir in the raisins. Pour the batter into the pan, gently smoothing the top.

4. Bake for 45 minutes, or until a wooden toothpick inserted in the center comes out clean.

**per serving**

calories 155
total fat 6.5 g
  saturated fat 0.5 g
  trans fat 0.0 g
  polyunsaturated fat 2.0 g
  monounsaturated fat 4.0 g
cholesterol 16 mg

sodium 90 mg
carbohydrates 23 g
  fiber 1 g
  sugars 13 g
protein 2 g

dietary exchanges
1½ other
carbohydrate, 1½ fat

These small treats get big flavor and color from red wine and beets. *(See photo insert.)*

# chocolate and red wine mini cupcakes

**serves 12** : 2 mini cupcakes per serving

Butter-flavor cooking spray

¾ cup white whole-wheat flour

¼ cup unsweetened Dutch-process cocoa powder

¼ cup firmly packed dark brown sugar

½ teaspoon baking soda

¼ teaspoon baking powder

½ teaspoon ground cinnamon

½ cup low-fat buttermilk

½ cup puréed canned no-salt-added beets, with liquid reserved

¼ cup red wine (regular or nonalcoholic)

1 tablespoon canola or corn oil

1 large egg

¼ cup fat-free tub cream cheese

¼ cup fat-free plain Greek yogurt

2 tablespoons plus 1 teaspoon confectioners' sugar, sifted

½ teaspoon reserved beet juice

½ teaspoon cornstarch

1. Preheat the oven to 350°F. Lightly spray a 24-cup mini muffin pan with cooking spray.

2. In a large bowl, stir together the flour, cocoa powder, brown sugar, baking soda, baking powder, and cinnamon until well blended.

3. In a medium bowl, using an electric mixer on medium speed, beat together the buttermilk, beets, wine, oil, and egg. Stir the buttermilk mixture into the flour mixture until the batter is just moistened but no flour is visible. Don't overmix; the batter should be lumpy. Spoon 1 tablespoon of batter into each muffin cup.

4. Bake for 12 to 15 minutes, or until a wooden toothpick inserted into the center of a cupcake comes out clean. Transfer the pan to a cooling rack. Let cool for 10 minutes. Remove the cupcakes from the pan. Transfer to the rack. Let cool completely.

5. Meanwhile, in a small bowl, using an electric mixer on medium speed, beat together the remaining ingredients for 1 minute, or just until smooth (don't overbeat or the frosting will be too thin). Cover and refrigerate for at least 30 minutes. Spread on the cooled cupcakes.

**per serving**

calories 92
total fat 2.0 g
   saturated fat 0.5 g
   trans fat 0.0 g
   polyunsaturated fat 0.5 g
   monounsaturated fat 1.0 g
cholesterol 17 mg

sodium 125 mg
carbohydrates 14 g
   fiber 1 g
   sugars 8 g
protein 4 g

dietary exchanges
½ other carbohydrate, ½ fat

drinks and desserts

245

Two-bite cake pops are a great way to enjoy dessert without overdoing it. Our version tastes decadent, but eliminates the guilt by using heart-healthy ingredients such as cocoa powder and almonds.

# red velvet cake pops

### serves 32 ⋮ 1 cake pop per serving

Butter-flavor cooking spray
1½ cups all-purpose flour
½ cup plus 2 tablespoons sugar
¼ cup unsweetened cocoa powder
1 teaspoon baking soda
1 cup water
1 large egg
2 tablespoons canola or corn oil
2 teaspoons red food coloring
1 teaspoon vanilla extract
1 teaspoon cider vinegar
1 cup confectioners' sugar, sifted
2 ounces fat-free cream cheese
2 teaspoons fat-free milk
½ cup crushed sliced almonds, dry-roasted

**per serving**

calories 75
total fat 2.0 g
  saturated fat 0.0 g
  trans fat 0.0 g
  polyunsaturated fat 0.5 g
  monounsaturated fat 1.0 g
cholesterol 6 mg

sodium 55 mg
carbohydrates 13 g
  fiber 1 g
  sugars 8 g
protein 2 g

dietary exchanges
1 other carbohydrate,
½ fat

1. Preheat the oven to 350°F. Lightly spray an 8-inch cake pan with cooking spray.

2. In a large bowl, stir together the flour, sugar, cocoa powder, and baking soda.

3. In a medium bowl, whisk together the water, egg, oil, food coloring, vanilla, and vinegar. Stir the egg mixture into the flour mixture until the batter is just moistened but no flour is visible. Don't overmix; the batter may be slightly lumpy. Pour the batter into the pan.

4. Bake for 30 minutes, or until a wooden toothpick inserted in the center comes out clean. Transfer the pan to a cooling rack. Let cool for 1½ to 2 hours, or until completely cooled.

5. Meanwhile, in a small bowl, using an electric mixer on medium-low speed, beat the confectioners' sugar, cream cheese, and milk for 2 to 3 minutes, or until combined, scraping the side of the bowl once.

6. Using a spoon, scoop the cake out of the pan. Crumble into the cream cheese mixture. Using an electric mixer on medium speed, beat for 1 to 2 minutes, or until well combined.

7. Using a medium spring-loaded ice cream scoop (1-ounce size), drop 32 scoops of the cake mixture onto a rimmed baking sheet. Roll the scoops into balls.

8. Put the almonds in a shallow dish. Roll the cake balls in the almonds to lightly coat. If serving immediately, transfer the balls to a serving tray. Or, cover and refrigerate for up to five days. Just before serving, insert a lollipop stick into each ball.

cook's tip: Lollipop sticks are usually available in stores that sell craft or baking supplies; if you can't find them, you can use ice pop sticks or wooden toothpicks.

Go Red party tip: For a pretty party presentation, thread a cake ball and a piece of red fruit, such as a fresh strawberry, raspberry, or pitted cherry, on a toothpick.

These golden brown pastries feature dark, sweet cherries in a thickened honey mixture blanketed in layers of crisp phyllo dough. A sprinkle of sliced almonds adds just a hint of crunch.

# cherry phyllo turnovers

**serves 8**  |  1 turnover per serving

16 ounces frozen pitted dark sweet cherries, halved

2 tablespoons honey

1½ tablespoons cornstarch

¼ teaspoon ground nutmeg

Butter-flavor cooking spray

2 tablespoons plus 1 teaspoon sugar

1 teaspoon ground cinnamon

12 14 × 9-inch frozen phyllo sheets, thawed

1 large egg white, lightly beaten

¼ cup sliced almonds

**per serving**

calories 146
total fat 2.0 g
   saturated fat 0.0 g
   trans fat 0.0 g
   polyunsaturated fat 0.5 g
   monounsaturated fat 1.0 g
cholesterol 0 mg

sodium 76 mg
carbohydrates 30 g
   fiber 2 g
   sugars 16 g
protein 3 g

dietary exchanges
2 other carbohydrate, ½ fat

1. In a medium saucepan, bring the cherries, honey, cornstarch, and nutmeg to a simmer over medium-high heat, stirring occasionally. Simmer for 2 to 3 minutes, or until thickened. Remove from the heat. Let cool for 15 to 20 minutes.

2. Meanwhile, preheat the oven to 350°F. Lightly spray a rimmed baking sheet with cooking spray.

3. In a small bowl, stir together the sugar and cinnamon.

4. Keeping the unused phyllo covered with a damp cloth or damp paper towels to prevent drying, place 1 sheet on a work surface. Lightly spray with cooking spray. Working quickly, sprinkle with 1 teaspoon of the sugar mixture. Top with 2 more sheets, lightly spraying each with cooking spray. Using scissors or a sharp knife, cut the stack in half lengthwise.

**5.** Spoon ¼ cup of the cherry filling onto one end of a half stack, leaving 1 inch at the bottom. Fold a corner across the filling and continue folding, corner to corner (the way a flag is folded). The filling expands during cooking, so don't fold the dough too tightly. Tuck the excess dough under the triangle. Transfer to the baking sheet. Repeat with the remaining phyllo, sugar mixture, and filling. Using a sharp knife, cut a few slits in the top of each turnover to help release steam. Brush the turnovers with the egg white. Sprinkle with the almonds.

**6.** Bake for 22 to 25 minutes, or until the turnovers are golden brown. Transfer the turnovers to a cooling rack. Let cool for 15 minutes.

These twice-baked cookies aren't overly sweet, so they are just right for dunking in coffee, tea, or fat-free milk. Chopped dried apricots keep them moist, while pistachios add crunch. Their smaller size allows you to get your chocolate fix without overindulging.

# chocolate-pistachio biscotti with dried apricots

### serves 17 : 2 cookies per serving

Cooking spray

1½ cups all-purpose flour and 2 to 3 tablespoons all-purpose flour, divided use

½ cup white whole-wheat flour or whole-wheat flour

½ cup firmly packed dark brown sugar

½ cup unsweetened Dutch-process cocoa powder

1½ teaspoons baking powder

¼ teaspoon salt

2 large eggs

3 tablespoons canola or corn oil

3 tablespoons unsweetened applesauce

½ cup chopped dried apricot halves

½ cup coarsely chopped unsalted pistachios, dry-roasted

**per serving**

calories 148
total fat 5.0 g
   saturated fat 0.5 g
   trans fat 0.0 g
   polyunsaturated fat 1.5 g
   monounsaturated fat 2.5 g
cholesterol 22 mg

sodium 81 mg
carbohydrates 23 g
   fiber 2 g
   sugars 9 g
protein 4 g

dietary exchanges
1½ other carbohydrate, 1 fat

1. Preheat the oven to 350°F. Lightly spray a baking sheet with cooking spray.

2. In a large bowl, stir together 1½ cups all-purpose flour, the white whole-wheat flour, brown sugar, cocoa powder, baking powder, and salt.

3. In a medium bowl, whisk together the eggs, oil, and applesauce.

4. Stir the apricots and pistachios into the egg mixture. Stir the egg mixture into the flour mixture.

5. Using the remaining 2 to 3 tablespoons flour, lightly flour a flat surface. Turn out the dough. Knead just until blended, 10 to 12 strokes. With slightly moistened hands, form the dough into two 12-inch logs. Transfer the logs to the baking sheet. Slightly flatten to 2 inches wide.

6. Bake for 25 minutes. Transfer the logs to a cooling rack and let cool for 10 minutes. Reduce the oven temperature to 325°F.

7. Transfer the logs to a cutting board. Using a serrated knife, cut the logs crosswise into $1/2$-inch slices to make the biscotti. Place the biscotti with a cut side down on the baking sheet.

8. Bake for 20 minutes, turning once halfway through. Transfer the biscotti to a cooling rack and let cool for 10 minutes.

**cook's tip:** Store any leftover biscotti in an airtight container for up to one week, or put them in an airtight container or resealable plastic freezer bag and freeze for up to one month.

**Go Red party tip:** To add some red to these cookies, use dried cherries or cranberries instead of apricot halves.

Individual ramekins filled with creamy, warmly spiced pumpkin are the perfect lighter substitution for traditional pumpkin pie, with its heavy crust. Whipped egg whites make these soufflés light and airy; a cereal-nut topping adds crunch and a little fiber.

# pumpkin pie soufflés

| serves 4 | 1 soufflé per serving |
|----------|----------------------|

1 teaspoon light tub margarine and 2 teaspoons light tub margarine, melted, divided use

1 cup canned solid-pack pumpkin (not pie filling)

½ cup fat-free sweetened condensed milk

¼ cup fat-free plain Greek yogurt

1 tablespoon whole-wheat flour

½ teaspoon pumpkin pie spice

3 tablespoons barley-wheat cereal nuggets

1½ tablespoons chopped pecans, dry-roasted

½ teaspoon ground cinnamon

2 large egg whites

1. Preheat the oven to 350°F. Lightly grease four 6-ounce ceramic ramekins with 1 teaspoon margarine. Set aside.

2. In a medium bowl, whisk together the pumpkin, condensed milk, yogurt, flour, and pumpkin pie spice until well blended.

3. In a small bowl, stir together the cereal, pecans, cinnamon, and the remaining 2 teaspoons margarine. Set aside. (If you prefer a topping with a smoother texture, process the cereal mixture in a food chopper or small food processor for 20 to 30 seconds, or until smooth.)

4. In a separate chilled small glass or metal bowl, using an electric mixer on high speed, beat the egg whites for 3 minutes, or until stiff peaks form (the peaks don't fall when the beaters are lifted). Working quickly, gently fold the egg whites into the pumpkin mixture.

**per serving**

calories 201
total fat 3.5 g
  saturated fat 0.0 g
  trans fat 0.0 g
  polyunsaturated fat 1.0 g
  monounsaturated fat 1.5 g
cholesterol 5 mg

sodium 131 mg
carbohydrates 36 g
  fiber 4 g
  sugars 28 g
protein 8 g

dietary exchanges
2½ other carbohydrate, 1 lean meat

**5.** Spoon the pumpkin mixture into the ramekins, filling each about three fourths full. Transfer the ramekins to a large roasting pan. Carefully pour in water until it comes about $1/2$ inch up the side of each ramekin to create a water bath. Top each soufflé with the cereal mixture.

**6.** Bake for 30 minutes, or until the soufflés are firm to the touch. The soufflés will rise in the oven, then sink when removed. Transfer the ramekins to a cooling rack. Let cool for 15 minutes. Chill, uncovered, in the refrigerator for 1 hour before serving.

**cook's tip:** Even a single drop of egg yolk will prevent egg whites from forming peaks when beaten, so separate eggs very carefully. Also, before beating the egg whites, make sure they are cold and the bowl and beaters are well chilled. The coldness will improve the stability and volume of the beaten whites.

Along with light cream cheese and fat-free yogurt, a secret ingredient—tofu—gives these cheesecakes a heavenly texture. The oatmeal crust adds a nutty crunch, and a sweet spoonful of strawberry spread tops them. *(See photo insert.)*

# lemon mini cheesecakes

**serves 12** | 1 cheesecake per serving

Cooking spray (optional)

½ cup uncooked quick-cooking oatmeal

¼ cup white whole-wheat flour and 2 tablespoons white whole-wheat flour, divided use

2 tablespoons light brown sugar and ¼ cup firmly packed light brown sugar, divided use

1 tablespoon plus 1 teaspoon canola or corn oil

1 tablespoon fat-free milk

6 ounces light cream cheese

6 ounces light soft tofu, drained and patted dry

½ cup fat-free plain Greek yogurt

1 teaspoon grated lemon zest

¼ cup fresh lemon juice

1 large egg

1 large egg white

2 tablespoons all-fruit strawberry spread (or any berry all-fruit spread)

**per serving**

calories 127
total fat 5.5 g
    saturated fat 2.5 g
    trans fat 0.0 g
    polyunsaturated fat 1.0 g
    monounsaturated fat 2.0 g
cholesterol 26 mg

sodium 90 mg
carbohydrates 15 g
    fiber 1 g
    sugars 9 g
protein 5 g

**dietary exchanges**
1 other carbohydrate,
1 lean meat, ½ fat

1. Preheat the oven to 350°F. Line a standard 12-cup muffin pan with paper bake cups or lightly spray the pan with cooking spray.

2. In a food processor or small food chopper, pulse the oatmeal, ¼ cup flour, 2 tablespoons brown sugar, oil, and milk for 30 seconds, or until the mixture is crumbly. Place 1 tablespoon of the oatmeal mixture in the bottom of each bake cup, pressing down to form a crust. Bake for 4 minutes. Remove from the oven. Reduce the heat to 300°F.

3. Meanwhile, in a large bowl, using an electric mixer on medium speed, beat the cream cheese for 1 minute, or until light and fluffy. Add the tofu, yogurt, lemon zest, lemon juice, egg, egg white, and the remaining ¼ cup brown sugar. Beat for 2 minutes. Stir in the remaining 2 tablespoons flour until incorporated (don't beat). Pour ¼ cup of filling into each bake cup.

4. Bake for 30 minutes, or until the cheesecake tops spring back when touched. Transfer the pan to a cooling rack. Let cool in the pan for 10 minutes. While the cheesecakes are still warm, transfer to a large plate. Spoon the strawberry spread onto each cheesecake. Cover and refrigerate for at least 4 hours, or until firm (can be chilled overnight).

Sweet frozen mango and silky tofu give this mousse its creamy texture, while almonds add a crunchy contrast—and, best of all, this dessert comes together in just minutes.

# almond-mango mousse

**serves 6** ⋮ ½ cup per serving

½ cup whole unsalted almonds, dry-roasted

4 ounces light soft tofu, drained and patted dry

¼ cup water

16 ounces frozen mango cubes

1 teaspoon grated orange zest

¼ cup fresh orange juice

½ teaspoon almond extract

**1.** In a food processor or blender, process the almonds, tofu, and water for 3 minutes, scraping the side as necessary.

**2.** Add the remaining ingredients. Process for 4 minutes, scraping the side as necessary, or until almost smooth (there will still be flecks of almond). Serve immediately while the mousse is still cold or cover and refrigerate until serving time.

**cook's tip:** For a smoother mousse, substitute 1½ tablespoons unsalted almond butter for the almonds.

**Go Red brunch tip:** For an elegant presentation, serve these individually in glass dessert cups or martini glasses. Add some fresh raspberries or a strawberry fan on top of the mousse for a punch of red. To make a strawberry fan, thinly slice the strawberry up to the stem (4 to 6 slices), but *don't* detach the stem. Gently press down with your fingertips to allow the slices to separate slightly to form a fan.

**per serving**

| | |
|---|---|
| calories 130 | sodium 17 mg |
| total fat 6.0 g | carbohydrates 17 g |
|   saturated fat 0.5 g |   fiber 3 g |
|   trans fat 0.0 g |   sugars 13 g |
|   polyunsaturated fat 1.5 g | protein 4 g |
|   monounsaturated fat 4.0 g | **dietary exchanges** |
| cholesterol 0 mg | 1 fruit, 1 fat |

Rice pudding infused with exotic saffron and cardamom is a common Indian treat. Golden raisins lend sweetness to this comforting dish, while a garnish of almonds and pistachios adds crunch and nutty flavor. Serve it warm or chilled.

# saffron-cardamom rice pudding

**serves 4** | ½ cup per serving

3 cups fat-free milk

½ cup uncooked brown rice

4 cardamom pods, seeds removed and ground with a mortar and pestle, or ¼ teaspoon ground cardamom

⅛ teaspoon saffron or ⅛ teaspoon ground turmeric

¼ cup golden raisins

2 tablespoons sugar

1 teaspoon grated lemon zest

1 tablespoon sliced unsalted almonds, dry-roasted (optional)

1 tablespoon chopped unsalted pistachios, dry-roasted (optional)

1. In a medium saucepan, stir together the milk and rice. Bring to a simmer over medium-high heat. Reduce the heat and simmer, covered, for 1 hour, or until the rice is tender but still soupy, stirring occasionally.

2. Stir in the cardamom and saffron. Simmer, covered, for 25 to 30 minutes, or until most of the milk is absorbed, stirring occasionally.

3. Stir in the raisins, sugar, and lemon zest. Just before serving, sprinkle with the almonds and pistachios.

**cook's tip on saffron:** Saffron comes from the flower of the crocus plant, *Crocus sativus,* commonly known as the "saffron crocus." Each flower has three threads, called stigmas, which are dried and sold as a spice. It takes more than 14,000 stigmas to create 1 ounce of saffron, which accounts for its high cost. You can buy saffron in powder form or as threads; the threads are fresher and more flavorful. Crush them just before you use them.

**per serving**

calories 205
total fat 1.0 g
  saturated fat 0.5 g
  trans fat 0.0 g
  polyunsaturated fat 0.5 g
  monounsaturated fat 0.5 g
cholesterol 4 mg

sodium 82 mg
carbohydrates 42 g
  fiber 2 g
  sugars 22 g
protein 9 g

dietary exchanges
1 starch, 1 fruit,
1 fat-free milk

This dessert of under 100 calories is perfect on a hot summer day when you want something light and refreshing. No one will guess how easy it is to make. If you want, save a little of the crushed pineapple for Pineapple Sweet Potatoes (page 222).

# pineapple sorbet

**serves 4** | ½ cup per serving

1 20-ounce can crushed pineapple in its own juice, undrained

1 teaspoon rum extract

1 teaspoon coconut extract

4 sprigs of fresh mint (optional)

**per serving**

calories 91
total fat 0.0 g
  saturated fat 0.0 g
  trans fat 0.0 g
  polyunsaturated fat 0.0 g
  monounsaturated fat 0.0 g
cholesterol 0 mg

sodium 2 mg
carbohydrates 23 g
  fiber 1 g
  sugars 21 g
protein 1 g

dietary exchanges
1½ fruit

1. In a medium bowl, whisk together the pineapple and extracts. Pour into an 8-inch square metal baking pan. Cover with plastic wrap and freeze for at least 8 hours.

2. Using a fork, carefully break up the frozen pineapple mixture. If needed, let the pan stand at room temperature for a few minutes to soften the pineapple mixture.

3. Using a food processor or blender and working quickly, pulse the pineapple mixture in small batches until light and fluffy.

4. Spoon the mixture into chilled dessert dishes. Garnish with the mint. Serve immediately.

**Go Red brunch tip:** For an interesting presentation and additional servings for a gathering, grill or broil 16 pineapple slices and let them cool. Place 1½ teaspoons of sorbet in the center of each. (A melon baller works well for this.) Garnish each with a sprig of mint. Serve immediately.

Fat-free, sugar-free vanilla frozen yogurt takes a sunbath of sorts with a dousing of warm banana-orange sauce. It's an ideal tropical dessert to follow Hawaiian Fried Rice (page 179).

# frozen yogurt with caramelized banana and orange sauce

| serves 4 | ⅓ cup banana mixture and ½ cup frozen yogurt per serving |
|---|---|

1 teaspoon canola or corn oil

2 medium bananas, halved lengthwise, then halved crosswise

2 tablespoons dark brown sugar

½ teaspoon ground cinnamon

½ cup fresh orange juice

1 tablespoon light tub margarine

2 cups frozen fat-free, sugar-free vanilla yogurt

**per serving**

calories 184
total fat 2.5 g
   saturated fat 0.0 g
   trans fat 0.0 g
   polyunsaturated fat 0.5 g
   monounsaturated fat 1.5 g
cholesterol 0 mg

sodium 90 mg
carbohydrates 42 g
   fiber 2 g
   sugars 22 g
protein 5 g

dietary exchanges
1 fruit, 2 other carbohydrate, ½ fat

1. In a large nonstick skillet, heat the oil over medium heat, swirling to coat the bottom. Place the bananas in the skillet. Sprinkle with the brown sugar and cinnamon. Cook for 1½ minutes on each side, or until slightly softened, turning the bananas gently to keep the pieces intact. Transfer to a small bowl. Set aside.

2. Pour the orange juice into the same skillet. Bring to a boil over medium-high heat. Boil for 3 minutes, or until reduced by one-third (to about ⅓ cup), stirring occasionally. Add the margarine, stirring until melted. Pour over the bananas, tossing gently to coat.

3. Spoon the frozen yogurt into dessert bowls. Top with the banana mixture.

The creamy orange-vanilla flavor of these frozen pops is reminiscent of the classic summertime treat. Keep some extra pops in the freezer to pull out for your next backyard barbecue.

# orange-yogurt dream pops

| serves 4 | 1 pop per serving |
| --- | --- |

1¾ cups low-fat plain yogurt

¾ cup 100% pure orange juice concentrate, thawed

2 teaspoons confectioners' sugar

1 teaspoon vanilla extract

**per serving**

calories 160
total fat 2.0 g
   saturated fat 1.0 g
   trans fat 0.0 g
   polyunsaturated fat 0.0 g
   monounsaturated fat 0.5 g
cholesterol 6 mg

sodium 77 mg
carbohydrates 29 g
   fiber 0 g
   sugars 29 g
protein 7 g

dietary exchanges
1½ fruit, ½ fat-free milk

1. In a medium bowl, whisk together all the ingredients until the sugar is dissolved.

2. Pour the yogurt mixture into ice pop molds. Freeze for at least 8 hours.

3. Rinse the outside of the molds with cool water to release the pops. Serve immediately.

**cook's tip:** If you don't have ice pop molds, you can pour the yogurt mixture into 5-ounce paper cups, inserting a wooden ice pop stick when the mixture is partially frozen. When the pops are completely frozen, peel off the cups and enjoy. This recipe doubles or triples easily, and the pops will last three to four weeks in the freezer.

drinks and desserts

# resources

# make healthy lifestyle choices

Some risk factors for heart disease and stroke can't be changed; these include increasing age, family history, and ethnicity. However, many of the most damaging risk factors are things that you *can* control. Making good lifestyle choices now can make a big difference in the likelihood that you'll develop heart disease later.

**Eat well.** To eat well means to focus on the quantity and quality of the food you eat. Consistently taking in too many calories will lead to becoming overweight or obese—a risk factor for heart disease and stroke, as well as other diseases including diabetes. Eating a diet high in unhealthy fats and sodium increases cholesterol and blood pressure levels—both risk factors, too.

**Exercise regularly.** Living an active lifestyle offers many health benefits. Just 30 minutes of moderate physical activity a day can actually help prevent or control high blood pressure, high cholesterol, diabetes, and obesity. Conversely, the risk of living an inactive life seems to be roughly equivalent to that of smoking a pack of cigarettes a day.

**Maintain a healthy weight.** To best manage your weight, you need to eat the right amount of calories for you and engage in regular physical activity that will help you reach and maintain a healthy weight. You have a much higher risk of heart disease and stroke if you're overweight or obese, even if you have no other risk factors. Losing just 10 percent of your body weight will help lower your risk.

**Don't smoke or breathe tobacco smoke.** Smoking is the number one preventable cause of premature death in the United States. Smoking makes blood vessels stiff, greatly increasing your risk of cardiovascular disease and stroke. A smoker's risk of dying from coronary heart disease is two to three times that of a nonsmoker's. The good news is that when you do stop smoking—no matter how long or how much you've smoked—your risk of heart disease and stroke drops rapidly. If you don't smoke, don't start. If you do smoke, stop now!

**Drink alcohol in moderation—or not at all.** Drinking too much alcohol can raise blood pressure, increase risk of heart failure and stroke, produce irregular heartbeats, and contribute to many other diseases. If you drink, do so in moderation, which means no more than one drink per day for a woman and two drinks per day for a man. One drink is equivalent to 12 ounces of beer, 4 ounces of wine, or 1½ ounces of 80-proof spirits. If you don't drink, don't start.

# know your numbers and your risk

Eating well, exercising regularly, maintaining a healthy weight, not smoking, and limiting alcohol can help you reduce your risk of high blood pressure, high cholesterol levels, and diabetes—all major risk factors for heart disease and stroke. Make an appointment with your health care professional for a heart checkup every year to find out your numbers and monitor any changes.

**Blood pressure** High blood pressure (hypertension) is often called the silent killer because it has no symptoms. Have your blood pressure checked at least once every two years—more often if you have a family history of high blood pressure, stroke, or heart attack. Normal blood pressure is less than 120/80 mmHg (millimeters of mercury).

**Cholesterol and triglycerides** High blood levels of LDL (low-density lipoprotein) cholesterol and/or triglycerides and a low level of HDL (high-density lipoprotein) cholesterol increase your risk for heart attack and stroke. Excess cholesterol can form plaque on the inner wall of your arteries, making it harder for your heart to circulate blood. Plaque can break open and cause blood clots. If a clot blocks an artery that feeds the brain, it causes a stroke. If it blocks an artery that feeds the heart, it causes a heart attack. Get a simple blood test to learn your blood levels. Aim for a total cholesterol level of less than 200 mg/dL (milligrams per deciliter); an HDL ("good" cholesterol) level of 50 mg/dL or higher for women and 40 mg/dL or higher for men; an LDL ("bad" cholesterol) level under 100 mg/dL (but check with your healthcare provider for your goal, which may be different); and a triglyceride level of less than 150 mg/dL.

**Diabetes** When you have diabetes, your body doesn't make enough insulin, can't use its own insulin as well as it should, or both. These conditions result in an increase in the level of glucose in your blood. Have your glucose (blood sugar) levels checked regularly, especially if you have a family history of diabetes. Aim for a fasting blood glucose level of less than 100 mg/dL.

**Body mass index (BMI) and waist circumference** Too much body fat—especially at your waist—means that your heart has to work harder and your risk increases for high blood pressure, high cholesterol, and diabetes. Ask your healthcare provider what a healthy BMI and waist measurement are for you. (BMI estimates body fat by comparing height to weight.) A waist circumference of less than 35 inches is usually an appropriate goal for women.

# learn the warning signs of heart attack and stroke

## heart attack warning signs

Some heart attacks are sudden and intense; some may start slowly followed by progressive pain or discomfort. As with men, women's most common heart attack symptom is chest pain or discomfort. But women are somewhat more likely than men to experience some of the other common symptoms, particularly shortness of breath, nausea/vomiting, and back or jaw pain.

Here are some of the signs that can mean a heart attack is happening.

- **CHEST DISCOMFORT.** Most heart attacks involve discomfort in the center of the chest that lasts more than a few minutes, or that goes away and comes back. It can feel like uncomfortable pressure, squeezing, fullness, or pain.

- **DISCOMFORT IN OTHER AREAS OF THE UPPER BODY.** Symptoms can include pain or discomfort in one or both arms, the back, neck, jaw, or stomach.

- **SHORTNESS OF BREATH.** This may occur with or without chest discomfort.

- **OTHER SIGNS.** These may include breaking out in a cold sweat, nausea, or lightheadedness.

## stroke warning signs

Stroke is the fourth-leading cause of death in America and a major cause of severe, long-term disability. Know the signs:

- Sudden numbness or weakness of the face, arm, or leg, especially on one side of the body
- Sudden confusion, or trouble speaking or understanding
- Sudden trouble seeing in one or both eyes
- Sudden trouble walking, dizziness, or loss of balance or coordination
- Sudden, severe headache with no known cause

**F.A.S.T.** is an easy way to remember how to recognize a stroke and what to do. Spot a stroke FAST. **F**ace drooping. **A**rm weakness. **S**peech difficulty. **T**ime to call 9-1-1.

## Dial 9-1-1 Fast!

Heart attack and stroke are life-or-death emergencies—every second counts. If you suspect you or someone you are with has any of the symptoms of stroke or heart attack, immediately call 9-1-1 or your emergency response number so an ambulance can be sent. Don't delay—get help right away! For a stroke, also note the time the first symptom(s) appeared. If given within three hours of the start of symptoms, a clot-busting drug may improve the chances of getting better faster.

# go red menus

The following recipes are ideal dishes for your next Go Red gathering, as well as some to help you incorporate more home cooking throughout your family's day.

# index